Handbook of Metadata, Semantics and Ontologies

HANDBOOK OF METADATA, SEMANTICS AND ONTOLOGIES

Saurabh Pal

ARCLER
PRESS

www.arclerpress.com

Handbook of Metadata, Semantics and Ontologies

Saurabh Pal

Arcler Press
224 Shoreacres Road
Burlington, ON L7L 2H2
Canada
www.arclerpress.com
Email: orders@arclereducation.com

ISBN: 978-1-77469-892-1 (Hardcover)

ABOUT THE AUTHOR

Saurabh Pal received his M.Sc. in Computer Science in 1996 and obtained his Ph.D in 2002. He then joined the Department of Computer Applications, VBS Purvanchal University, Jaunpur as a Lecturer. Currently, he is working as Professor. He has authored more than 100 research papers in SCI/Scopus in international/national conference/ journals as well as authored four books and also guided many research scholars in computer science/applications. He is an active member of CSI, Society of Statistics and Computer Applications and working as editor, member of editorial board for more than 15 international journals. His research interests include bioinformatics, machine learning, data mining, and artificial intelligence.

TABLE OF CONTENTS

LIST OF FIGURES

LIST OF ABBREVIATIONS

AACR2	Anglo-American Cataloging Rules
AI	Artificial Intelligence
API	Application Program Interface
CASE	Computer-Aided Software Engineering
CDIF	Case Definition Interchange Facility
CMS	Content Management Systems
CRM	Customer Relationship Management
CWM	Common Warehouse Metadata Model
DAM	Digital Asset Management
DC	Dublin Core
DCME	Dublin Core Metadata Elements
DCMI	Dublin Core Metadata Initiative
DDC	Dewey Decimal Classification
DPC	Digital Preservation Coalition
DRM	Digital Rights Management
DSOs	Domain Specific Ontologies
EIA	Electronic Industries Alliance
ERP	Enterprise Resource Planning
EXIF	Exchangeable Image File Format
GDPR	General Data Protection Regulation
HIN	Heterogeneous Information Network

ICTs	Information and Communication Technologies
IEEE	Institute of Electrical and Electronics Engineers
IETF	Internet Engineering Task Force
IIM	Information Interchange Model
IO	Integrated Ontology
IPTC	International Press Telecommunications Council
IQ	Information Quality
IRB	Image Resource Block
ISO	International Organization for Standardization
KPIs	Key Performance Indicators
LCMS	Learning Content Management System
LCSH	Library of Congress Subject Headings
LIS	Library and Information Science
LMS	Learning Management Systems
LOD	Linked Open Data
LOM	Learning Object Metadata
LOR	Learning Object Repository
MARC	Machine-Readable Cataloging
MDM	Master Data Management
MeSH	Medical Subject Headings
MODS	Metadata Object Description Schema
NISO	National Information Standards Organization
NSDL	National Science Digital Library
OAI PMH	Open Archives Initiative Protocol for Metadata Harvesting
OCR	Optical Character Recognition
OER	Open Educational Resources
OLAC	Open Language Archives Community

OMG	Object Management Group
OWL	Web Ontology Language
PIM	Product Information Management
QAF	Quality Assurance Framework
RDF	Resource Description Framework
RDFS	Resource Description Framework Schema
SEO	Search Engine Optimization
SQuaRE	Software Quality Requirements and Evaluation
ULR	Universal Land Registry
URIs	Uniform Resource Identifiers
VIAF	Virtual International Authority File
WSMO	Web Service Modeling Ontology
XML	Extensible Markup Language
XMP	Extensible Metadata Platform

ABSTRACT

Metadata research is a new field of study that focuses on providing a variety of digital resources with semantic descriptions, where digital resources are the most common target. These related descriptions form the foundation for more progressive and improved services in a number of applications, such as location and search, customization, and automated information delivery. As a result, metadata research focuses not only on the creation of metadata description languages but also on the practices of creating, disseminating, evaluating, maintaining, and using metadata in a variety of settings and usage contexts. The objective of the Semantic Web is essentially built on Ontology, which has recently emerged as a knowledge symbol infrastructure for the delivery of mutual semantics to metadata. A truly multidisciplinary approach is required because the combination of metadata description methods and ontology engineering creates a new setting for information engineering with certain setbacks and promising applications. The purpose of this volume is to promote interaction among researchers from a variety of disciplines and to provide some fundamental insights into the activity of engineering systems dependent on metadata, semantics, and ontologies.

PREFACE

There are two unique uses of the term "semantic metadata" that are relevant to this discussion. The first involves *data value* meaning, while the second is about what names of things can take on these value meanings. Some values can be used to represent particular ideas in any context where data are present. Associating particular values with specific ideas is one approach to assigning meaning to the data comprised of those qualities. For instance, when seeking to capture the gender orientation of actors, the values of "Male" and "Female" can be used to represent men and women. The semantic terms "male" and "female," "M" and "F," "0," and "1," or "♂" and "♀" can all be used to represent similar ideas by authors.

A mechanism for managing the names of "objects" and the values provided by the metadata registry is managed by a registration authority. This makes it easier to discover and understand "things" in various data sources. An ontology, which is described as an "attempt to develop an exhaustive and rigorous conceptual plan within a particular domain, a commonly hierarchical data structure containing all the relevant factors and their relationships and policies (theorems, regulations) within that dominion," may drive the design of metadata registry for particular purposes. Computer programs could be written to exploit (machine-readable) ontologies to execute a form of data machine understanding defined by those ontologies.

In this volume, semantic metadata is introduced as the definition of value meanings and data component names, at the very least for human reference and probably also for programmatic use. Data's semiotic function implies, among other things, that they are made up rather than self-existing. There is only one way to represent reality in a particular data model for reality representation. Consequently, data are both the objects they represent and those that need to be interpreted. We frequently use language to imply otherwise. Another way to say that data cannot be understood without context is to recognize its representational function, but this goes a little further than that. Data must be acknowledged within the specific context of its foundation (or production) in order to be fully understood.

It is essential to keep in mind that data are developed through a set of choices on how to symbolize reality, even when dealing with relatively straightforward data. These decisions are based on presumptions regarding what covers reality. Formal and contextual data exist. Their meaning is determined not only by what they represent but also by their structure. A person must understand not just what the data is meant to represent, but also the representation conventions they use to convey meaning in order to comprehend the meaning of a piece of data.

Ontology is a formal portrayal of the information sources comprising a number of concepts and their connections and defining a particular domain. A structure for sharing and integrating knowledge is provided by ontology, which seeks to promote knowledge consistency and clarity. Formal ontologies exhibit the common postmodernist trait of seeking to integrate multiple truths and integrate these. They have a dual nature since they are social constructions that reflect different viewpoints or change as the fields develop.

—Author

CHAPTER

1 Typology of Metadata and Metadata Uses

Contents

1.1. INTRODUCTION

Metadata is a data element whose purpose is to store additional information about a file. It can be used in almost any type of file, but it is most frequently used in documents and web pages. Metadata can be used in a variety of ways. Some organizations use it to ensure that they're collecting the right data in the first place—they might not have thought through all of their needs, so they need to make sure they're collecting everything from the beginning. Other organizations use metadata to validate their work—to make sure that they've collected everything that's necessary for a given project.

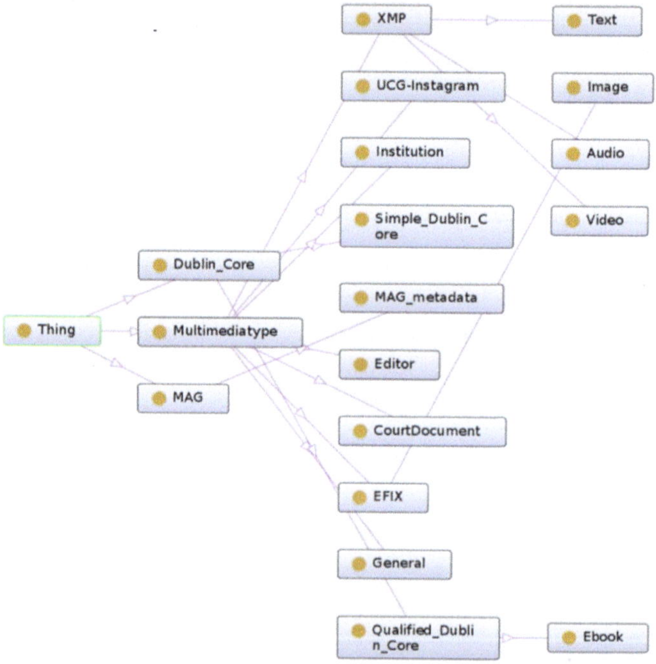

Figure 1.1. *A sample description of the taxonomies of metadata.*

Source: Ibba, & Pani, (2016); Scientific figure on ResearchGate. Available from: https://www.researchgate.net/figure/The-resulting-metadata-taxonomy_fig1_302917738.

And then there are those who use metadata as a way to communicate with users about their data—to make sure everyone involved knows what's happening, when it happens, and why. The types of metadata that are used for different purposes can be broken down into three categories: descriptive, descriptive/additional, and administrative/systematic. Descriptive metadata describes the content of a file and allows users to search for specific pieces of information within it. Descriptive/additional metadata includes things like creator notes or copyright information that are descriptive but not necessary for understanding how to use the file effectively. Administrative/systematic metadata includes things like licensing information or access restrictions that are necessary for making effective use of a file but don't add much value to understanding the meaning behind it (Hooland, 2014) (Figure 1.1).

The typology of metadata and metadata uses is one of the first steps in understanding the techniques used to create metadata. It helps to break down the types of metadata, how they are created, and their uses. When we speak of metadata, we're usually referring to descriptive information about the document itself. For example, if you're looking at a photo online and you see that it was taken by a professional photographer, you might want to know more about who took the photo (name, address) and where it was taken (city).

This sort of descriptive information is useful for searching for similar images or for viewing images in context. Metadata can also be used to describe your own organization's documents or records. You might have an organizational chart that shows who owns what positions within your company and how much they make each year—this type of information would be considered metadata because it describes your organization as opposed to just describing documents within it (Mauney, 2013).

1.2. DESCRIPTIVE METADATA

Descriptive metadata is the first type of metadata. It describes the contents of a document, like its title, authors, and dates. This type of metadata is essential for any piece of text that's going to be used in a search (such as a blog post or an article on Wikipedia). It includes data like the author, the title, and any other information that might be useful for finding or using a file in some way.

For example, if you're looking for a specific document in Adobe Acrobat, you would use descriptive metadata to find it. Descriptive metadata is used to describe content of a document. Descriptive metadata is also known as "metadata about metadata." It allows you to categorize and tag your documents in order to provide more information about the item and its relationships with other documents (Hooland, 2014) (Figure 1.2).

Metadata	Data Type	Description
Title	String	File name (Movie name)
Storage Format	String	Storage format of the movie (Ex- MP4,AVI)
Year	Date	Releasing Year
Director	String	Director of the movie
Actors	String	Actors information
Theme	String	Theme of the movie (Ex- Action, comedy etc)
Language	String	Movie language
Songs	Number	Number of songs in the movie
Fights	Number	Number of fights in the movie
Emotional	Number	Number of emotional scenes in the movie

Figure 1.2. *General descriptive metadata.*

Source: Algur, & Bhat, (2014); Scientific figure on ResearchGate. Available from: https://www.researchgate.net/figure/Construction-of-General-Descriptive-Metadata_tbl2_295431067.

For example, if you're writing up an article about how to use a certain tool, you might include information about how you found the tool in the first place: what kind of search engine you used and what results were returned. You could also include links to any other resources that helped with your research—and even if someone were searching for exactly what you've written about there's no reason they shouldn't be able to read it (Mauney, 2013).

1.2.1. Uses of Descriptive Metadata

Descriptive metadata can be used to help users understand the purpose of an item; for example, if they find an item in the library with descriptive metadata that says "this book teaches children how to read," it may make more sense for them to browse for books about reading than for them to browse for books about math. Descriptive metadata also allows users to search for items by their intended use (for example, if you're looking for a book on how to drive a car), which is useful when there are multiple types of items in your collection (for example, if you have books on how to drive cars) (Figure 1.3).

- **Sentiment Analysis:** In order to perform sentiment analysis on text, it is necessary to first identify the sentiment of the text. The most common way to do this is by using descriptive metadata—information about the content of a piece of text with which users can better understand and interpret its meaning. For example, if you write an article about how much you love your job, you may include metadata in your article that describes what kind of job it is (it could be this really cool new position at [company name]) and how long you've worked there (you've been working there for two years now). This information helps readers understand what your article is about more clearly than if they were just reading a simple sentence like "I love working at [company name]" without any additional context. This type of analysis involves analyzing a user's feedback on an app (or other product) and figuring out how positive or negative their review was based on those analysis results (Hooland, 2014).
- **Personalization and Recommendation Systems:** The role of descriptive metadata in Personalization and Recommendation Systems is to provide the data necessary for the system to build a model of the user. It is indeed a crucial part of input for personalization and recommendation systems. It allows for the system to understand the context in which it is being used so that the right content can be recommended to users. Descriptive metadata also helps the system understand how users interact with content, which in turn helps the system improve its recommendations based on what they have clicked and what they have clicked on previously. Personalization and recommendation systems are used to identify the content that users would like to see, based on their past behavior. This content is then presented to the user, which may include personalized advertising. Descriptive metadata is a key component of these systems because it helps them determine what content users are interested in seeing by incorporating information from other sources, such as previous browsing history.
- **Content Adaptation**: Content adaptation is the process of modifying the content of a website or other digital resource in order to make it more accessible to people with disabilities. Content Adaptation involves taking information from one source,

and adapting it to fit the needs of a different group of readers. The goal of this process is to ensure that the content meets the needs of its user base (Mauney, 2013).

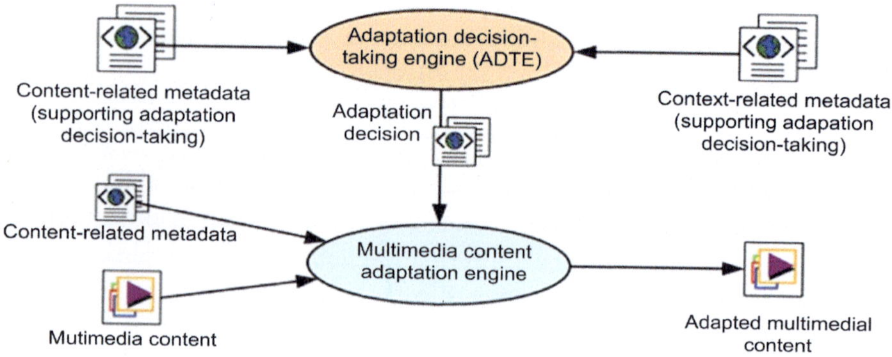

Figure 1.3. *Content adaptation in metadata.*

Source: Furht, (2008); https://doi.org/10.1007/978-0-387-78414-4_45.

- **Contextual Advertising:** Contextual advertising, also known as contextual targeting, is an advertising strategy that uses user data to serve ads based on the content of the resource being advertised. Contextual targeting is a concept that has been around for years but it's only recently that it's been used in a big way. As we become more and more accustomed to targeted ads and personalized experiences online, contextual advertising will continue to grow in popularity. It displays ads based on the user's current context, such as their location or device. Contextual advertising can be used for both contextual marketing (targeting people based on their interests) and contextual advertising (targeting people based on their general location).

1.3. STRUCTURAL METADATA

Structural metadata is a form of metadata that describes the organization and arrangement of resources. It includes information about chapters, sections, tables, figures, and other structural elements within a document or dataset. Structural metadata may also include information about the types of files it contains or how they are organized. Structural metadata is especially useful for cataloging purposes because it allows users to search through files without having to understand their internal structure or format. This makes it easier for users to find exactly the type of information they are looking for.

Structural metadata is divided into two subcategories: subject-based metadata and topic-based metadata.

Subject-based metadata refers to metadata describing the main topic of a document. It can be used in any situation where you want readers to know what your document is about before they start reading it—for example, if you're writing a blog post on how to cook chicken wings, you could add "chicken wings" as a subject-based metadata note (Hooland, 2014).

Topic-based metadata describes specific aspects of your document, such as its content or structure. For example, if your blog post discusses chicken wings in great detail but doesn't do much else, then you might add "chicken wings" as a topic-based note so that people who are looking for information about chicken wings will see it when they scan through your post's content.

1.3.1. Uses

The use of structural metadata is to provide a framework for the organization of data. A structural metadata set will assist in creating a database, as well as providing a basis for searching and sorting data. Structural metadata can be used to organize any type of information, including text, numbers or images. Structural metadata is also used to describe the structure of an information entity (such as a database). The content of structural metadata is specific to each type of entity it describes; for example, the structural metadata associated with an image may be different from that describing a document (Mauney, 2013).

Structural metadata plays an important role in helping people create documents that are easy to read. This can help minimize errors in content creation and make it easier for people to find specific information they want. Structural metadata also helps people understand what they're reading by providing key terms that may be used in the document, as well as how those terms are being used in different parts of the text (for instance, where a term appears). Structural metadata can be used to help readers better understand documents, but it also has the potential to be used for purposes other than comprehension.

For example, if you're looking at a list of countries and you want to know which country is largest in area, you could use structural metadata to help you figure out which one has the most land. To do this, you'd look at the number of countries listed first, then count how many times each country appears in the list. This would give you an idea of which country was most likely to have the most land (or at least be large enough in area). It can also be used to describe the relationships between different pieces of content that are stored in the same database.

For example: if you have a blog post about a recipe for lasagna, you may include structural metadata like "title," "author," "date published," and "tags." The title will be descriptive enough (in this case) so that users can understand what the post is about without having to click around on different pages—they'll know from just reading it's about lasagna. They'll also be able to search within your site or app based on those tags. The author is important because it tells people who wrote this post—that way they know who else has written on similar topics and how they compare with your own writing style. If you write a recipe blog post, then its best if you're known as an expert in cooking/food; maybe even give them some tips on how they can get better at cooking (Mauney, 2013).

1.4. ADMINISTRATIVE METADATA

Administrative metadata is a type of metadata that is used to describe the business processes and internal systems of an organization. It can be used to track changes in these systems and the data that goes into them. Administrative metadata can also be used to track how information is collected, stored, and analyzed. It is used to keep track of organizational structure and policies, as well as other administrative information. This information can include dates and times of meetings, locations where meetings are held, etc.

Administrative metadata is metadata that is used by many different people in an organization to accomplish a common goal, such as managing an event or researching a topic. The goal of this type of metadata is to help an organization use its resources efficiently and effectively. Administrative metadata includes fields such as name, address, and phone number. These fields are often collected by companies for internal use. For example, a company may want to know how many employees it has as well as their names and addresses. This information can be added to a database so that it can be accessed by employees or contractors who need access to specific people's records (Hooland, 2014).

1.4.1. Uses of Administrative Metadata

Administrative metadata is data that is used to maintain and manage information systems. It includes things like data about the users who access the system, the security measures in place to protect user information, and other details about how the system is being used. Metadata can be used for many purposes. For example, administrative metadata can be used to help companies comply with regulations that require specific kinds of information about how a company's systems are being used. Companies may also use metadata to keep track of how many times a particular piece of information has been accessed or shared over time.

The main purpose of administrative metadata is to track how an organization is using its resources, such as employees, funds, or buildings. In order to do this, the administrator must collect and record all the information regarding these resources and their uses. This means that administrative metadata may include things like:

- Employee names and contact information
- Funds allocated to specific projects and programs
- How many people are involved in each project or program?

Administrative metadata can be used for many purposes, such as tracking the usage of resources within an organization so that people can see where their money is going and what needs to be done next (Mauney, 2013).

- **Digital Rights Management (DRM):** Digital Rights Management (DRM) is the process of managing access to digital resources, such as electronic books, video games, and music. It is used to govern the use of these resources by users. Administrative metadata plays a crucial role in managing and enforcing digital rights associated with digital resources; discuss ways in which it can be utilized to manage this process. DRM is an emerging technology that uses encryption to protect content from being copied, redistributed or otherwise transmitted without permission. Metadata associated with a digital resource provides information about the copyright holder, such as the name of the work, its title, author(s), genre, time period it was created/published and so on (Hooland, 2014) (Figure 1.4).

DRM manages access to digital resources, such as software and videos, and can be used to ensure that users have the correct permissions to view or use them. In other words, it controls who can see what and when. Administrative metadata plays a crucial role in managing and enforcing digital rights associated with digital resources. For example, if a video is available for free on YouTube but only for viewing for three days after its release date, then an administrator may need to make sure that the video does not expire before those three days are up. This requires tracking information about how many times each user has viewed the video so that administrators know when they have reached their limit on usage time.

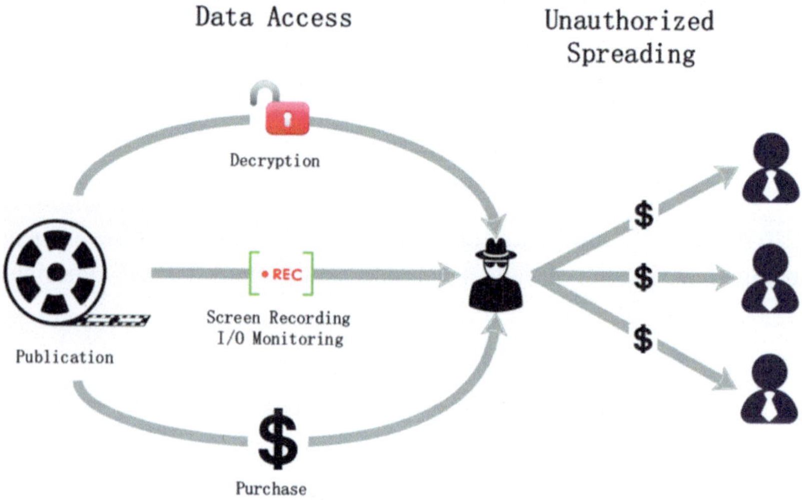

Figure 1.4. *The threat model in digital rights management (DRM).*

Source: Zhao, Fang, Zhang, Ge, Meng, Liu, & Su, (2019); Scientific figure on ResearchGate. Available from: https://www.researchgate.net/figure/The-threat-model-in-digital-rights-management-DRM_fig1_334435715.

There are several types of DRM:

- Content-based: The rights holder controls who can access the content and how they can access it.
- Usage-based: The rights owner controls access to content based on time or usage.
- Media-based: The rights holder controls access to titles by media type such as video game or software title (Mauney, 2013).
- **Versioning and Change Management:** Metadata is a set of data about a resource that describe the resource. Administrative metadata facilitates version control and change management of digital resources. It includes information about the identity of the resource, its properties, and its status. Administrative metadata is also known as a subject area identifier. Metadata helps manage versions of digital resources. This is especially important when you're working with digital assets that need to be tracked over time, like software applications or web pages, which may change over time. Metadata help facilitate change management in

order to track changes made to digital assets as they are being created, modified or updated. This can be particularly useful when managing large amounts of data at scale or in a distributed environment.

In order to facilitate version control, administrators need to create a set of administrative metadata that describes the structure of the digital resources in a document repository. For example, if an organization has multiple versions of its website, each with slight but important differences from one another, then there must be some way to differentiate which version is which. This can be accomplished by using identifiers such as dates or serial numbers. Administrators also need change management tools that allow them to keep track of changes made to digital resources over time or when they are being reviewed by others. Changing one's mind about what should be done with a particular piece of content is difficult enough; making sure that there isn't any confusion about whether something has been changed at all is even harder. Change management helps administrators keep track of who made which changes so that they know who needs to be notified when something changes or needs updating again later on down the line (without having to ask every person involved in changing it) (Hooland, 2014).

- **Long-Term Preservation and Archiving:** Administrative metadata supports the long-term preservation and archiving of digital resources. Administrative metadata includes information related to the creation, maintenance, and use of digital resources. It may include things like who created a resource, when it was created, who used it, where it was used, how it was used, and any other information that would allow for its preservation or archiving. This metadata can be used to describe the structure of a digital resource, provide information about its creation, and indicate how it was intended to be used. Administrative metadata is typically stored in a relational database, although other types of file systems can also be used. Administrative metadata records are usually created by an organization with the goal of documenting the organization's processes.

The long-term preservation and archiving of digital resources is strongly supported by administrative metadata. The primary reason for this is that, although it is often difficult to determine what exactly makes up a digital resource or how it should be preserved, administrative metadata provides the necessary information for these tasks. For example, in order to preserve and archive a digital resource, one must know:

- The format of the original file (i.e., whether it's a PDF or an image file)
- The creator of the original file (i.e., whether it was created by a specific person)
- The creator's name and contact information (i.e., if they are known)

These are just some examples of administrative metadata that can be used to facilitate long-term preservation and archiving (Mauney, 2013).

1.5. PRESERVATION METADATA

Preservation Metadata is metadata that is created to ensure the long-term preservation of the digital objects, and it can be used for a variety of purposes. Preservation Metadata can be used as a way to make sure that an object is kept in its original form, or it can be used to preserve only certain aspects of an object. Preservation Metadata is useful for libraries, archives, museums and other institutions that want to keep certain content accessible to future generations. The term "Preservation Metadata" was coined by the Digital Preservation Coalition (DPC), which is an international non-profit organization that promotes digital preservation and accessibility. It was originally used as a term to describe metadata that is used to preserve digital files in their original formats after they have been converted or migrated to new media formats, such as when their original file format becomes obsolete or no longer compatible with newer technologies (Hooland, 2014) (Figure 1.5).

Name of Sub-Heading	Description	Remark
Element Name	Name of the element	The element name may not be identical to the name of the origin
Sub-element	Indicate existence of sub-elements, labels	
Origin(s)	Source of the element	Mapping to other metadata standards will start soon
Definition	Further explanation for clarification of the purpose of the element.	Further described in "Description" and "Comment" subheadings
Description	A brief statement that defines the concept of the category	
Required	Indicate whether the element value is mandatory or optional	Yes/No
Repeatable	Indicate if the element is repeatable or not repeatable	Yes/No
Example	Local examples	
Comment	Notes to clarify exceptions	

Figure 1.5. *The elements of preservation metadata.*

Source: Alemneh, Hastings, & Hartman, (2002); Scientific figure on ResearchGate. Available from: https://www.researchgate.net/figure/Preservation-Metadata-Elements-Subheadings_tbl1_49518187.

It's important to understand that preservation metadata is not the same thing as preservation processing. Preservation processing is the process by which records are made readable for the first time. Preservation metadata is information about how to preserve or make records readable (e.g., what kind of technology might be needed). Examples of preservation metadata include:

- Technical specifications (e.g., what kind of equipment would be necessary to read and/or decode a particular record)
- User manuals (e.g., how users should interact with an existing piece)
- Training materials (e.g., how users should learn how to use a piece)

Preservation metadata can be used to provide information that is vital to ensuring the long-term preservation of digital records. For example, you may want to know what kind of hardware your file has been stored on or how many times it was modified. There are multiple ways to create preservation metadata:

- You can create a unique ID for each item in order to track its history and make it easier to find an object later on.
- You can use keywords or phrases to find similar items easily without having to scan through the entire database.
- You can have the system automatically create metadata based on specific criteria such as date range, file type, etc., which will allow you to quickly identify specific files without having to manually enter each item's details into a spreadsheet every time you need them (Mauney, 2013).

1.5.1. Uses of Preservation Metadata

Preservation metadata is an extension of the concept of descriptive metadata, which describes how to use and describe items. Both preservation metadata and descriptive metadata are used by institutions to ensure that they meet the preservation requirements of their collections. Preservation metadata is created to allow people to access and use digital objects in a manner that conforms to their original purpose. A digital document may not be useful today; however, it may still be important for future generations. Preservation metadata allows the user to identify what the document was for and how it should be accessed. When applied to a digital object, they can help ensure long-term preservation. The goal of preservation metadata is to preserve the integrity of digital objects, and as such, it should be used as little as possible (Hooland, 2014).

- **Format Migration and Conversion:** When we talk about format migration and conversion, we're talking about the process of moving content to a new format. Preservation metadata supports complex format migration and conversion processes. Format Migration and Conversion: Preservation metadata can be used to support complex format migration and conversion processes. In a preservation metadata project, a number of formats may have to be converted or migrated to another format. This is achieved by using the preservation metadata as a way to store information about the original source document in an accessible and machine-readable form. This allows the source document to be recreated in any other format that can be analyzed by a machine. In addition, it allows metadata about the source document to be created and stored separately from the source document itself. This makes it possible for users with different types of access needs to access information about their original documents without having to use multiple tools or interfaces (Mauney, 2013).

When it comes to moving a format from one application to another, sometimes it's just not practical or possible to simply import the contents of a file into a new application. Instead, you'll have to convert the format from one application to another. Sometimes this is as simple as opening up an existing file in the new format and copying its content over into the new file—but other times, it means going through a process that involves extracting keywords and values from your old file, converting them into a different language, and then replacing those values with their equivalents in the new format. Preservation metadata can help you with these complex processes by providing tools for extracting keywords and values, translating them between languages, and replacing those values with their equivalents in your new file. With preservation metadata at your disposal, you'll be able to quickly move your data from one storage system to another without having to worry about losing valuable information during the process.

In the past, investigating the requirements for a format migration or conversion was an extremely time-consuming process. In many cases, it could take several weeks to investigate a single project and produce a report detailing the findings. Today, however, many organizations are able to conduct their investigations in just a few hours with the help of preservation metadata. This is because preservation metadata provides a detailed analysis of the current state of each document and provides recommendations that can be used to minimize risk during any kind of format migration or conversion process. While this is great news for those who need to make changes to their documents' formats, it also has implications for other departments within an organization. For example, if you are planning on migrating your company's business process from one operating system to another, you will likely need to convert all of your applications as well. With preservation metadata at your disposal, you can avoid costly errors by properly documenting each application's compatibility with the new operating system (Hooland, 2014).

- **Fixity and Integrity Checking:** Fixity and integrity checking is the process of verifying that digital resources remain intact, including their exact location on the Internet, their integrity against unauthorized changes, and their authenticity. Preservation metadata can enable complex fixity and integrity checking processes to ensure the ongoing integrity and authenticity of digital resources. Preservation metadata enables complex fixity and integrity checking processes to ensure the ongoing integrity and authenticity of digital resources. Preservation metadata enables complex fixity and integrity checking processes to ensure the ongoing integrity and authenticity of digital resources. A metadata file can be used for this purpose, because it contains information about the digital resource's content and structure, as well as its creator (Mauney, 2013).

The fixity and integrity checking process is one way that an organization can keep track of digital resources over time, ensuring that they are not altered or removed from their original state. For example, if a company wants to ensure that all of its videos are available on all platforms at all times, it can use preservation metadata to make sure that nothing has been changed or removed from the original files. The preservation process is a vital part of making sure that materials have been prepared for current technologies, such as DVD or VHS, so they can be viewed or heard in the future. If these materials are not prepared properly, they will not play on newer equipment without being altered or damaged in some way. In order to preserve digital materials adequately, it is important to make sure that these materials are fixed—that is, that they can be played back without being altered by either the original creator or someone else who has access to them.

Fixity is the ability to identify a digital object's unique identifier (UUID) or other unique identifier that can be used to identify it with certainty at any time in the future. Fixity is essential for long-term preservation because it ensures that users can access their content without having to re-access it. If a digital resource needs to be changed, then it should be changed only by someone who has access to all of its metadata, such as subscribers or partners who can update the metadata themselves. Integrity is defined as "the property of being whole or unbroken." If there are errors in a digital resource—such as typos or missing characters—then those errors will need to be corrected when they are discovered. If you have an original copy of a document but don't know what changes were made over time, then you don't have an authoritative version of that document anymore; you've lost some crucial information about your work product (Hooland, 2014).

1.6. TECHNICAL METADATA

Technical metadata is information about the technical aspects of a digital file. This can include things like the file's resolution, frame rate, or bitrate. Technical metadata is often used in video processing applications to help make video files more compatible across different platforms and devices. Technical metadata is often useful for archiving, because it is often an indicator of what kind of information will be needed for future reference. For example, if you have collected information about your company's processes for manufacturing and distributing food products, then technical metadata about those processes might include details about the equipment used in production and packing facilities. Technical metadata also has many uses outside of archiving: for example, if you're planning on making a film about a particular topic, then you might use technical metadata to provide details about filming locations or equipment used during production (Mauney, 2013).

For example, if you are writing a piece on "The Best Bluetooth Speaker," you might use technical metadata to describe your research into the different types of Bluetooth speakers available on the market. You might give information about what type of material it is made out of (glass, plastic), how long it lasts before needing recharging, how loud it gets when played at high volumes (not very loud), what frequency range does it cover (all frequencies available). Technical metadata can also be used to track how well a product performs in real life situations. For example, if you are writing about "The Best Smartphone for Your Budget," you could use technical metadata to detail how fast the phone responds when receiving messages or calls while driving or walking around town.

We want people to feel empowered when they interact with our products and services, so we've created a number of tools that allow users to customize their experience. For example, if you create your own avatar in one of our games, you can change its appearance and select from different clothing options. That way, users can express themselves by choosing their own looks and personalities. Another example: If you're creating a video for a product review, you might want to include footage showing how one person uses the product so that viewers can get more context before trying it on themselves. This kind of technical metadata will help people understand what they're getting into so they don't get stuck using something they have no idea how to go about it (Mauney, 2013).

1.6.1. Uses of Technical Metadata

Data Validation and Quality Control

Technical metadata plays a crucial role in data validation and quality control processes. Technical metadata is used to verify the accuracy of data. It helps to identify errors, missing information or other problems that may be present in the data set. Technical metadata is also used to create new records from existing ones. Technical metadata could be found in two main forms:

- Metadata that describes the technical characteristics of a record (e.g., title, creator, creation date etc.)
- Metadata that describes how a record was created (e.g., authoring application) (Hooland, 2014).

Technical metadata is the information provided by the software that describes how it works, including the language it uses, its structure, and any other details. It can also provide information about what features are available and how they function. This information is very important because it helps validate that the software has been properly developed for the task at hand. Technical metadata helps ensure that software is accurate and compliant with regulations such as PCI DSS or HIPAA. It also assists in disaster recovery efforts by allowing users to determine what data has been backed up or restored from backup. For example, a company might use technical metadata to be able to track issues with the quality of the photos that are being used on the website.

Technical metadata can also help to ensure that the information being stored is correct by checking whether or not it matches up with other sources of information stored in the database. For example, if there is an error in the name of a product, it will be easier to find out if this is an ongoing problem or just an isolated incident if there is a record of previous product names which are also incorrect. Technical metadata is used in conjunction with descriptive metadata to help ensure that users have access to the most appropriate information about their data needs. For example, if a user needs to know how many people are living in an area but does not care about their gender or age range, then they would need descriptive metadata as well as technical metadata such as what type of population census it is from and where they can find more information on it online (Mauney, 2013).

- ***Data Extraction and Loading:*** Technical metadata assists in data extraction and loading processes. It includes information about data extraction methods, data sources, data loading procedures, and data transformation requirements. It includes information about data extraction methods, data sources, data loading procedures, and data transformation requirements (Hooland, 2014).
- **Data Extraction:** Technical metadata is essential for ensuring that the right information gets into the right place at the right time. This includes proper configuration of your system to ensure proper access to data sources and loading procedures.
- **Data Loading:** Technical metadata can also be used to ensure that all relevant data is loaded into the system. This may include things like adjusting the format of a file or changing its size or length.
- **Data Transformation:** Technical metadata can also assist you in transforming your data so that it can be used by other systems without any changes or modifications whatsoever required on their part.
- The purpose of technical metadata is to provide information to support the data loading process, so that it can be completed successfully. This can include
- Data source information such as the name of a company or an organization that collected the data or its address.
- Projected use of the data by a user group such as the business department or an end user.
- Processes used in the collection of data such as how it was collected (e.g., online survey) or how it was analyzed (e.g., statistical software).

- The level of detail needed by users who will be using the data for their own internal use or for external audiences such as customers, investors, etc.

The first step in the process of extracting metadata is to decide on the type of metadata to be extracted. This can be based on a variety of factors such as the level of detail required, whether or not it is required for legal purposes, and whether or not it will help improve the usability of the dataset. Once this decision has been made then it is necessary to determine which elements within each category should be extracted. For example if only general information about a dataset is required then it would not be appropriate to extract specific details such as the date on which each record was entered into the system or even what language was used for inputting text into an application. Once this has been decided then there are two options available to extract technical metadata: manual extraction or automated extraction. Manual extraction involves using a human being who manually reads through all records within a dataset looking for specific elements such as dates or names of people involved with a project. Automated extraction involves using software which automatically searches through all records within the system (Mauney, 2013).

1.7. TEMPORAL METADATA

Temporal metadata is the type of metadata that is used to describe the date on which an object was created, modified, or accessed. This is often used when discussing the creation date of a document. This type of metadata can be useful in many ways, including allowing users to search for changes in objects over time, as well as providing information about how long ago certain events occurred. The term "temporal" refers to time as opposed to spatial (or geographic) metadata (Hooland, 2014).

For example, if you have records of customer transactions over the course of several months, you might use temporal metadata to identify when each customer interacted with your company. You could then compare their interactions with each other or with any other relevant metrics to determine which customers are likely to become repeat customers or provide valuable information about the types of products they prefer.

1.7.1. Uses of Temporal Metadata

Temporal metadata can be used for a variety of purposes. For example, if you are creating a report about an event that happened in June and you have data from June 1st through June 5th, then you could include it in your report. This would allow readers to see how events changed throughout the day.

- **Data Versioning and Revision Control:** Temporal metadata supports complex versioning and revision control of data. It allows for the versioning and revision of data over time, which is a vital component to any project that needs to be kept up-to-date and accurate. In order to manage changes to a document over time, temporal metadata allows for the creation of a history of these changes that can be used to determine how the document has changed over time. This is useful for tracking changes in content as well as maintaining history of when a document was last revised or edited. A temporal metadata system is one that allows for easy, granular changes to data. The system can also track all changes to the data, from creation, to modification, and even deletion. Temporal metadata is ideal for tracking changes in a database over time.
- **Temporal Analysis and Trend Detection:** Temporal metadata can be used for a variety of purposes, including temporal analysis and trend detection. Temporal analysis involves examining data over time to identify patterns, trends, and changes. This can be done using various statistical techniques, such as time series analysis, which involves modeling and forecasting data over time. Temporal analysis can be used in a range of fields, such as finance, economics, and environmental science, to identify trends and patterns in data. Trend detection involves identifying changes in data over time, such as increases or decreases in values or the emergence of new patterns. Trend detection can be used to identify emerging trends or to predict future changes in data. For example, in finance, trend detection can be used to identify changes in stock prices or market trends, while in environmental science, trend detection can be used to identify changes in climate patterns or ecosystem health (Hooland, 2014).

Temporal metadata can also be used for data integration and interoperability. By including temporal metadata in datasets, it becomes easier to integrate and compare data from different sources, as the temporal aspects of the data can be aligned and compared. This can be particularly important for data sharing and collaboration, where different datasets may have different temporal resolutions or formats.

- **Event Sequencing and Ordering:** Event sequencing and ordering involves identifying the order in which events occurred and the time intervals between them. This can be important for understanding the cause-and-effect relationships between events and for identifying patterns and trends in the data. For example, in a dataset of stock prices, event sequencing and ordering can help identify the sequence of price changes and the time intervals between them, which can be used to identify trends and patterns in the data. Temporal metadata can include a range of information related to event sequencing and ordering, such as timestamps, dates, intervals, and durations. For example, a dataset of website traffic might include temporal metadata that indicates the time of each visit, the duration of each visit, and the time interval between visits. Similarly, a dataset of social media activity might include temporal metadata that indicates the time of each post or comment, as well as the time interval between posts (Mauney, 2013).

Temporal metadata can be used for a variety of purposes related to event sequencing and ordering, including identifying patterns and trends, detecting anomalies or outliers, and predicting future events. For example, in finance, temporal metadata can be used to identify patterns in stock prices or to predict future market trends. In healthcare, temporal metadata can be used to identify patterns in patient data or to predict future health outcomes (Hooland, 2014).

CHAPTER

2 The Value and Cost of Metadata

Contents

2.1. INTRODUCTION

Data has evolved into the essential resource for many businesses and organizations in the current digital era. Data has multiplied exponentially, and metadata's significance has grown significantly. Metadata, also known as "data about data," gives unstructured data essential context and organization. It includes numerous features that facilitate effective data administration and analysis, including tags, labels, descriptions, and timestamps. The quantity and complexity of information have increased to previously unheard-of heights in today's data-driven world. The amount of data being accumulated, from individual files to organizational databases, is exponentially growing. Metadata stands out as a guiding light in this immense sea of data, showing the way to efficient data administration and utilization. Metadata, also known as "data about data," is very valuable because it gives the information it describes context, organization, and insights. However, because of its importance, there is a need to address the expenses and factors involved in its production and upkeep (Pomerantz, 2015).

2.2. UNDERSTANDING METADATA

At its foundation, metadata acts as the framework for data structure, ensuring that information is understandable and meaningful rather than just a disorganized muddle. It includes a broad range of properties that provide the raw data a descriptive, administrative, and structural context. By capturing specifics like titles, tags, and descriptions, descriptive metadata paints a picture of what the data represents. Technical elements including file format, creation date, and access permissions are the main emphasis of administrative metadata, which sheds light on the data's management and provenance. The links and hierarchies between various data pieces are defined by structural information, which simplifies data integration and navigation. Together, these many types of information create a strong foundation that makes it possible to efficiently search, integrate, analyze, and regulate data.

The best way to think of metadata is as additional context-sensitive information about the data. The basic information or content is represented by the data itself, but metadata completes and enhances this content by providing details about its traits, relationships, and attributes. It serves as a description or set of attributes that make the data easier for consumers to comprehend, interpret, and use. Data organization, discovery, analysis, and governance are just a few of the many functions served by metadata. Users can understand the significance and usefulness of the data since it gives it context and organization. Metadata gives users the ability to search for specific data subsets, combine different data sources, evaluate data quality, and assure compliance with regulatory standards by capturing important information about the data (Clauset, 2017).

Users of data are guided by metadata, making it easier for them to find and understand the data. By giving keywords, tags, or labels that help in finding pertinent material among huge collections, it enables effective search and retrieval. By creating connections between various data items or datasets, it facilitates data integration by promoting easy data interchange and interoperability. By revealing information about the structure, value, and provenance of the data, metadata also aids in data analysis and interpretation, enabling researchers and analysts to come to reliable conclusions and take sensible actions.

In conclusion, metadata acts as the contextual glue that improves the value and usability of data. Users can comprehend the meaning of the data, find relevant subsets, integrate various sources, evaluate quality, and adhere to governance standards by providing more information about the data. By serving as a link between raw data and its practical use, metadata enables both individuals and organizations to fully realize the potential of their data assets (Pomerantz, 2015).

2.3. VALUE OF METADATA

To fully utilize data, metadata provides a wealth of advantages that are essential.

- **Improved Data Searchability and Discovery:** By categorizing and tagging data, metadata offers a strong way to make it searchable and discoverable. Metadata supports effective retrieval of particular data subsets by adding appropriate keywords, labels, and classifications, reducing the time and effort required to find pertinent information.
- **Data Integration and Interoperability:** In the linked world of today, data can be found in a variety of sources, types, and structures. By serving as a bridge, metadata enables the smooth fusion of various data collections. It makes it possible for systems and applications to comprehend and interact with one another, enhancing data exchange, teamwork, and interoperability.

- **Data Integrity and Reliability:** Metadata is essential for assuring the integrity and reliability of data. Organizations may create data standards, spot discrepancies, and confirm the accuracy and completeness of the underlying data by integrating metadata-driven quality evaluations. In order to increase reliability, metadata also helps to establish data provenance by allowing users to track the data's origin and modifications (Clauset, 2017).
- **Data Analysis and Insights are Significantly Improved:** The availability of metadata greatly improves data analysis and insights. Analysts can do more efficient exploratory analysis, determine links between data items, and find hidden patterns and trends by understanding the context, structure, and features of the data through metadata. In order to facilitate deeper understanding and data-driven decision-making, metadata serves as a guide.
- Metadata plays a critical role in maintaining regulatory compliance and efficient data governance at a time when data privacy and security are increasingly the top priorities. Organizations can integrate their data practices with legislative obligations like GDPR or HIPAA by capturing metadata features relating to data sensitivity, access controls, and data usage authorization. Metadata aids in the development of strong data governance frameworks, good data management, and compliance with privacy laws.
- Metadata assists organizations in managing the lifecycle of their data assets in an efficient manner. It offers details on the procedures for creating, modifying, and archiving data. Organizations can maximize resource allocation, streamline data management procedures, and comply with data governance standards by capturing metadata pertaining to data retention policies, access restrictions, and data ownership.
- **Collaboration and Knowledge Sharing:** Within organizations, metadata promotes collaboration and knowledge sharing. Metadata encourages transparency and supports successful team cooperation by supplying details about data authors, contributors, and usage history. Finding subject matter experts, exchanging data insights, and promoting cross-functional cooperation are all made easier.
- **Innovation and Data Monetization:** Metadata promotes innovation and helps monetize data assets. Organizations may

produce new data products, provide personalized services, and establish new revenue streams by contextualizing and supplementing data with metadata. Organizations can use metadata to find chances to monetize their data, gain knowledge that can be put to use, and support their efforts in innovation and digital transformation (Pomerantz, 2015).

2.4. DRAWBACKS OF METADATA

Although metadata has great value, there are some drawbacks and things to keep in mind:

- **Data Collection and Generation:** It can be difficult to capture pertinent metadata during the data generation process. It might be difficult to maintain the scalability and performance while retaining the level of depth and granularity needed for metadata. The design of data gathering procedures that capture the essential metadata attributes without overburdening the data providers requires resources from organizations.
- **Management and Maintenance of Metadata:** Storing and caring for metadata requires specialized resources. Metadata repositories must be created, updated, and synchronized amongst various systems and programs. Versioning, change management, and maintenance methods must be continuously improved in order to ensure the accuracy and integrity of metadata (Clauset, 2017).
- **Privacy and Security Considerations:** Metadata may contain sensitive information that, if revealed, could compromise user privacy. Critical issues include safeguarding private data contained in metadata attributes and preventing unauthorized access to metadata records. Organizations must use robust security measures to stop metadata breaches and maintain data privacy.
- **Metadata Creation and Annotation Overhead:** Manual annotation of metadata can be time- and resource-intensive. Data professionals must put in a lot of work to add metadata features to data sets because doing so can slow down large-scale data projects. This overhead can be reduced and the procedure streamlined by utilizing automated and AI-driven techniques to metadata creation and annotation.

- **Lack of Standards:** Across various systems and domains, metadata frequently lacks standards. Data integration, interoperability, and collaboration can be hampered by inconsistencies in metadata formats, naming conventions, and attribute definitions. Data integration issues can arise when organizations try to mix or communicate data with different metadata structures.
- **Incompleteness or Correctness in Metadata:** Metadata might contain errors, omissions, or out-of-date information. The usability and dependability of the underlying data may be impacted if the associated metadata is insufficient or erroneous. Missing or inaccurate metadata can result in erroneous interpretations, improper analyzes, and poor decision-making. To reduce these risks, consistent quality checks and metadata maintenance procedures are required.
- **Scalability and Complexity of Metadata Management:** Managing metadata for big and varied datasets can be difficult and complicated. The amount of information attributes and relationships can multiply exponentially as data volumes rise, making metadata administration a difficult undertaking. The size and complexity of an organization's data assets require a strong infrastructure and metadata management solutions (Pomerantz, 2015).
- **Overuse of Metadata:** Using metadata excessively without taking the underlying data into account might be harmful. Although the context provided by the metadata is important, it is necessary to remember the actual data and its inherent constraints. Without sufficient data validation or verification, relying entirely on metadata might result in inaccurate assumptions or biased analyzes.
- **User Adoption and Understanding:** Users may have trouble adopting and using metadata if they don't recognize its usefulness or don't know how to do so. Organizations should spend money on user education and training to make sure that people are aware of the goals, advantages, and best practices related to metadata (Clauset, 2017).

Even if metadata has many advantages, it is important to address any potential problems and difficulties. Along with resolving privacy and security threats, organizations should concentrate on standardizing, maintaining correctness, and upkeep of metadata. By overcoming these obstacles, businesses can fully utilize metadata and make sure it is used to create data-driven insights and decision-making.

Metadata becomes a vital asset in this era of data-centricity, revealing the value concealed in the massive amounts of data. Its importance in improving data integration, quality, searchability, analysis, compliance, and governance cannot be overstated. Organizations must recognize the expenses and dangers related to metadata, such as the difficulties in collecting data, the need for upkeep, the privacy threats, and the overhead of annotation. Organizations can maximize the advantages obtained from their data assets by adopting best practices and utilizing automated technologies to create a balance between the value of information and the costs connected with it.

2.5. THE COST OF METADATA

The cost of metadata is influenced by a number of things, including as how resources are allocated, the infrastructure, and maintenance costs. Although metadata improves data management and offers useful contextual information, its generation and maintenance are expensive. Consider the following important factors (Figure 2.1):

- **Data gathering and Annotation:** The gathering and annotation of metadata can be time- and resource-consuming processes. For each data element, it is necessary to allocate human resources for the identification and capturing of pertinent metadata attributes. The time and effort required for metadata collecting may be significant, which has an effect on overall data management expenses, depending on the complexity and size of the data (Pomerantz, 2015).
- **Infrastructure for Metadata:** Building and maintaining an infrastructure for metadata is expensive. This entails making the appropriate technological and tool investments for efficient metadata storage, management, and retrieval. Implementing and maintaining metadata repositories, databases, or systems necessitates infrastructure expenditures and ongoing operational expenses.
- Metadata updates and maintenance are necessary because the data it contains is dynamic and changes over time. Metadata has to be updated and synchronized as data changes or is added. This calls for ongoing maintenance procedures such as data updates,

quality checks, and metadata versioning. To ensure metadata accuracy, consistency, and relevance, organizations must allocate resources, which results in continuing maintenance expenditures.

- To ensure that employees understand the importance of metadata and how to use it effectively, organizations must engage in training and education. This includes educating data authors, data analysts, and other users about metadata standards, best practices, and how metadata affects data management. Programs for knowledge-sharing and training activities raise the overall cost of integrating metadata.
- **Metadata Governance and Compliance:** Metadata governance is crucial for ensuring consistency, accuracy, and compliance with legal requirements. To build metadata governance frameworks and processes, including rules, procedures, and controls, investments in time and expertise are required. Compliance with privacy regulations and data governance rules also raises the cost of maintaining metadata (Clauset, 2017).
- Metadata helps with data integration and interoperability, however establishing seamless integration across various systems and data sources can be difficult and expensive. It takes work to map and align metadata coming from various applications, databases, or sources. Increasing investments in data integration technologies are necessary to ensure interoperability between metadata formats and standards.
- **Metadata Security and Privacy:** Ensuring data privacy and preventing unauthorized access to metadata raises the cost of managing metadata. Investments in cybersecurity technologies and knowledge are necessary to implement security measures including access controls, encryption, and auditing. The possible privacy hazards posed by metadata features that could include delicate or individually identifiable information must be addressed by organizations.
- **Metadata-Intensive Process Overhead:** Processes that require a lot of metadata, such data cataloging, data profiling, or data lineage analysis, can take a lot of time and resources. These procedures rely on metadata to reveal information on the traits, reliability, and history of the data. To carry out these operations effectively, organizations must devote resources and knowledge,

which has an impact on overall operational expenses (Pomerantz, 2015).

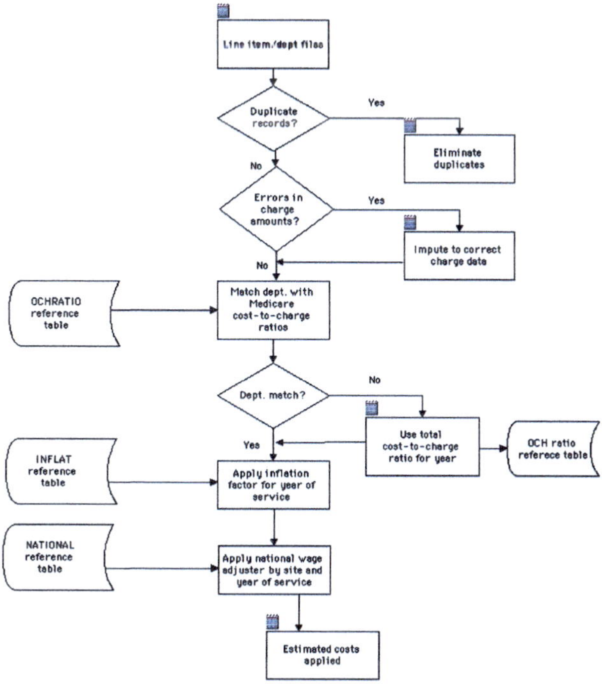

Figure 2.1. *Flow chart for costing business metadata a table of data definitions furnishes the following information.*

Source: Grevenhof, Wagner, Rahman, Naessens, & Evans, (2023); Scientific figure on ResearchGate. Available from: https://www.researchgate.net/figure/Flow-Chart-for-Costing-Business-Metadata-A-table-of-data-definitions-furnishes-the_fig2_242160597.

In conclusion, even while metadata significantly improves data administration and consumption, it has a price. These expenses include allocating resources for metadata annotation and collecting, making infrastructure expenditures, carrying out continuous maintenance tasks, providing training and education, governing metadata, integrating and interoperating, implementing security and privacy controls, and adding overhead to processes that require a lot of metadata. Organizations may maximize the advantages and value received from metadata while maximizing their investments by carefully managing these costs and using effective metadata management procedures.

Based on the characteristics of the data they represent and the function they provide, different types of metadata exist. Here are a few typical forms of metadata:

- **Descriptive Metadata:** Descriptive metadata offers details about the properties and substance of data. It contains information like the title, author, creation date, keywords, abstracts, and subject headings. Users can more effectively search for, retrieve, and discover pertinent information by using descriptive metadata, which enables users to comprehend what the material is about. Information about the features, content, and context of data is provided through descriptive metadata. It seeks to respond to questions about the type, source(s), date(s), accessibility, and intended use of the data. The discovery, searchability, and interpretation of data depend heavily on descriptive information. Important descriptive metadata components include:

    i. Names or titles that only describe the data are frequently included in descriptive information. The content should be briefly and unambiguously summarized in the title. To help readers comprehend the purpose, content, and utility of the data, a thorough explanation or abstract is also provided (Pomerantz, 2015).

    ii. Contributors and Author/Creator: Descriptive metadata records details about the people or organizations who produced or contributed to the data. To provide proper attribution and accountability, this can include information about the authors' names, organizations, contacts, or affiliations.

    iii. Date and Time: When the data was created, edited, or published, metadata keeps track of the date and time. This information aids in tracing the history of data modifications and establishing the provenance of the data. It aids users in locating the most current or pertinent data versions.

    iv. Subject Keywords and Tags: Descriptive metadata includes subject keywords or tags that stand in for the primary subjects or themes covered by the data. These keywords give users the ability to look for and find pertinent information based on particular subject matters or concepts. The efficient use of restricted or standard vocabulary enhances consistency and promotes data interoperability.

    v. Classification and categorization: Descriptive metadata classes or categorizes data according to its kind, genre, or topic matter. In addition to providing a hierarchical or structured framework for data discovery and navigation, this aids in the organization of data sets.

vi. **Language and Format:** Metadata contains details about the language used to write or convey the material. The format of the data is also specified, including whether it is in the form of a text, image, audio, video, or structured data format like CSV or XML. It is imperative to comprehend the language and format in order to process, understand, and provide data compatibility properly

vii. Geographic coordinates, place names, or spatial reference systems are a few examples of descriptive metadata that can be used to describe the spatial range or coverage of the data. The start and finish dates or time intervals that are pertinent to the data, as well as the temporal coverage, can also be included. Citation and Versioning: Descriptive metadata supports version control by storing details about various revisions or versions of the data. To ensure accurate reference and citation of the data, it could contain version numbers, revision dates, or citation information.

viii. **Relationships with Other Datasets, Publications, and References:** Descriptive metadata records details about connections with other datasets, publications, or references that are linked to or supplement the data. It creates connections between several resources, allowing users to examine connected data and context (Clauset, 2017).

ix. **Information on Access and Usage:** Detailed metadata gives specifics on how data can be accessed, utilized, or reused. Information about access limitations, license conditions, usage guidelines, or data usage regulations might be included.

For efficient data discovery, retrieval, and interpretation, descriptive information must be captured and used effectively. It enhances data searchability, gives users the ability to assess the significance of the data, and helps informed decision-making based on insights produced by the information. Data interoperability, collaboration, and the general usefulness of data assets are all improved by properly structured and standardized descriptive metadata (Pomerantz, 2015).

- **Structural Metadata:** Structural metadata describes how data is organized and structured, especially when those formats or hierarchies are complicated. It gives information on how various data items, such tables, fields, or files, are connected and specifies the relationships between them. In file systems, XML-based data formats, and database management systems, structural metadata is frequently employed.

The layout, relationship, and organization of data pieces inside a dataset or information system are all covered by structural metadata. It enables users to comprehend how various components fit together and interact by providing information about the data's structure and schema. Consider the following important ideas while talking about structural metadata:

i. **Data Structure:** Structural metadata specifies how a dataset's data pieces are arranged and organized. It offers details about the data's organizational methods, including whether the data is arranged in tables, files, records, fields, or hierarchical structures. Structural metadata, for instance, describes tables, columns, primary keys, foreign keys, and their relationships in relational databases.
ii. **Schema and Data Model:** The schema or data model, which describes the logical structure and relationships within the data, is included in structural metadata. It establishes the framework for data organization and access by describing the entities, attributes, and their linkages. Relational models, hierarchical models, network models, and object-oriented models are a few types of data models.
iii. **Relationships and Associations:** Structural metadata records the connections and affiliations between various dataset's data pieces. The relationship between the elements is described, including any one-to-one, one-to-many, or many-to-many linkages. For undertaking advanced data analysis or querying, as well as for understanding the linkages and dependencies between data entities, this knowledge is essential.
iv. **Data Constraints:** Structural metadata may contain restrictions and guidelines that control the acceptable ranges of values, data kinds, or data element formats. These limitations uphold business standards or data validation requirements while ensuring data integrity. Unique key constraints, data type restrictions, and referential integrity restrictions

are a few examples of constraints.

v. **Data Hierarchy and Nesting:** Structural information explains how data components are nested and related in hierarchies. It offers details on the parent-child relationships or levels of nesting in data structures. This is especially important for data formats like XML or JSON, where data is arranged in hierarchical or layered structures.

vi. The encoding or serialization format used to represent the data may be specified by structural metadata. When working with data formats like binary, XML, JSON, or protocol buffers, this is extremely crucial. To facilitate accurate interpretation and appropriate data exchange, the metadata specifies the guidelines and standards for encoding and decoding data.

vii. Data interoperability is made possible by structural metadata, which enables seamless data interchange and interpretation between various systems and applications. Structural metadata enables data integration, data sharing, and interoperability across many platforms or data sources by supplying a shared knowledge of the data structure and relationships (Clauset, 2017).

viii. **Data Access and Navigation:** Structural metadata facilitates data access and navigation by describing how to search for and retrieve particular data pieces inside a dataset. It identifies the indexes, pointers, keys, and access pathways that facilitate effective query optimization or data retrieval. Data access can be optimized and data retrieval processes can perform better thanks to structural metadata (Pomerantz, 2015).

ix. Data transformation and integration activities, such as data mapping or data transformation operations across various data models or formats, are aided by structural information. It facilitates data integration and transformation workflows by offering insights into the structure and connections between the source and target data.

x. Structural metadata acts as a documentation tool, assisting users in comprehending the underlying data structure and arrangement. It helps consumers who are not familiar with the data source or data model to better understand the data.

Data usability is improved, collaboration is encouraged, and efficient data integration and analysis are supported by structural metadata documentation.

Structural metadata improves data management, integration, and analysis by supplying details on the structure, schema, relationships, and restrictions of data items. It guarantees data integrity, makes data navigation efficient, and promotes interoperability between various systems and data sources.

- **Administrative Metadata:** The management and administration of data are the main topics of administrative metadata. It contains information about provenance, security levels, versioning, data ownership, access permissions, and data lifecycle management. Administrative metadata supports regulating data access and consumption, guaranteeing regulatory compliance, and upholding data governance (Clauset, 2017) (Figure 2.2).

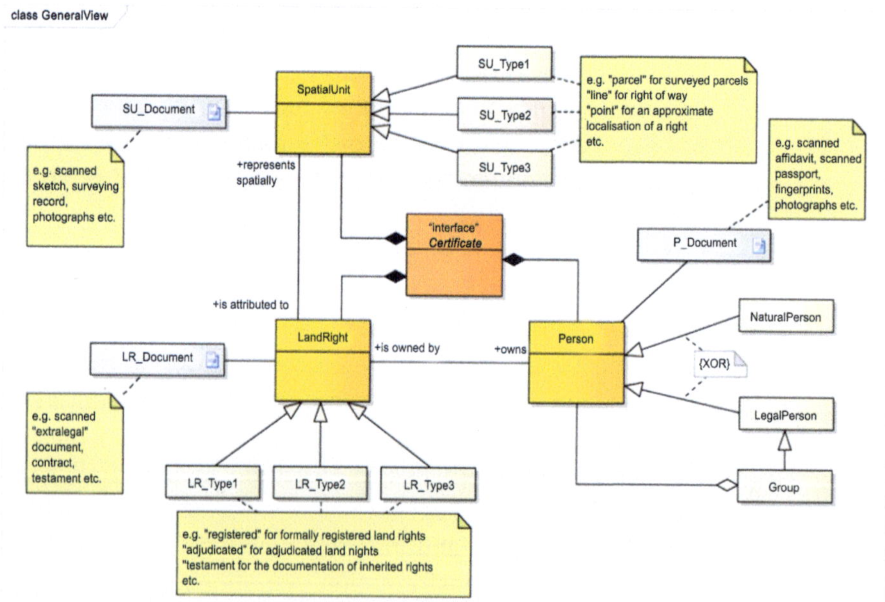

Figure 2.2. *Overview of the data model for the universal land registry (ULR).*

Source: Huber, Mithöfer, Schär, Harvey, & Mukasa, (2008); Scientific figure on ResearchGate. Available from: https://www.researchgate.net/figure/Overview-of-the-data-model-for-the-Universal-Land-Registry-ULR_fig3_271510207.

The information required for managing and administering data throughout its lifecycle is referred to as administrative metadata. Data ownership, access rights, versioning, provenance, preservation, and other administrative details are covered in detail. When talking about administrative metadata, keep the following in mind:

- **Data Ownership:** Administrative metadata keeps track of details on the people, groups, or other entities who are in charge of the data. It contains information like names, affiliations, contacts, and roles. Information about data ownership aids in determining accountability and responsibility for the data (Pomerantz, 2015).
- **Permissions and Access Control:** Administrative metadata records details on who can access and use the data, and under what circumstances. It contains information on user roles, access control policies, permissions, and limitations. Data security and privacy are protected by administrative metadata, which makes sure that access to sensitive or secret data is properly regulated.
- **Versioning and change management:** Over time, administrative metadata keeps track of the many revisions or versions of the data. It contains details such as version numbers, creation dates, modification histories, and justifications for modifications. Versioning metadata helps with data management, data lineage tracking, and good data governance.
- **Data Provenance:** Administrative metadata reveals details about the data's beginnings, sources, and past. It contains specifics like data sources, data creators, data collection techniques, and data processing routines. In research or scientific environments, provenance metadata can be used to establish the authenticity, dependability, and trustworthiness of data.
- Administrative metadata contains details about the various phases of the data lifecycle, including data creation, storage, use, archiving, and disposal. It supports effective data archiving and disposal procedures, the management of data retention regulations, and regulatory compliance.
- Administrative metadata comprises details required for the long-term archiving and preservation of data. It includes specifics like file formats, metadata norms, preservation tactics, and transfer schedules. Data can be maintained and reused in the future with the help of preservation metadata, which helps to assure data integrity, accessibility, and usability across time.
- Information pertaining to data security and privacy safeguards is included in administrative metadata. It contains information about

encryption, access restrictions, data anonymization methods, and adherence to data protection laws. Administrative metadata aids in addressing privacy issues and facilitates the adoption of data security measures.

- Administrative metadata is essential to the procedures involved in data cataloging and discovery. Data sources, data descriptions, and data cataloging standards are all covered. Enhancing data searchability with administrative metadata makes it simpler for users to find and access pertinent data assets (Clauset, 2017).
- **Data Usage Policies and Terms:** Administrative metadata may contain details regarding data usage rules, licensing conditions, or other limitations. It guarantees adherence to contractual and legal requirements for data access, use, and redistribution. Users can better comprehend the conditions of data use with the aid of administrative information.
- Management of administrative metadata serves as documentation that aids in the management and organization of the metadata itself. It contains details on metadata management procedures, metadata standards, metadata schema, and metadata repositories. The effective governance and management of metadata resources are ensured by administrative metadata.

Organizations may efficiently manage data throughout its lifecycle by gathering and exploiting administrative information. Versioning, provenance tracking, data governance, access control, preservation, and regulatory compliance are all supported. Administrative metadata improves data management procedures, encourages data transparency, and makes it easier to manage and make good use of data assets (Pomerantz, 2015).

- **Technological Metadata:** Technical metadata offers details about the data's format, structure, storage, and technological prerequisites for processing or analysis. File format, data size, encoding, data kinds, data schema or data model, and hardware or software dependencies are only a few of its properties. Understanding the technological requirements and limitations involved with using and processing data is made easier by technical metadata.

Metadata referred to as being technological describes the technical specifications and requirements of data. In order to facilitate effective processing, analysis, and interpretation, it gives information about the format, structure, storage, and technical dependencies of data. Take into account the following factors when discussing technological metadata:

- The format in which the data is kept or presented is described by technological metadata. It contains information about things like file formats, compression strategies, encoding plans, or serialization formats. For accurate data interpretation, transformation, and interoperability, it is crucial to comprehend the data format.
- Data Structure and Schema Information on the structure and schema of the data is provided by technological metadata. It contains information about how data elements are arranged, as well as information on data kinds, field lengths, and connections between different data pieces. Understanding the data structure makes it easier to integrate, transform, and interoperate data.
- **Storage Requirements:** Technological metadata records details regarding the data's storage needs. Details like data size, storage capacity, storage location, and storage medium are included. Understanding the storage needs makes it easier to assign enough resources for data management and storage.
- **Dependencies on Hardware and Software:** Technological metadata contains details about the hardware and software requirements needed to process and analyze the data. It includes information needed to interact with the data, such as hardware requirements, software versions, operating systems, or programming languages. Users can set up the proper computer environment for data processing by being aware of the dependencies.
- **Data Integration and Interoperability:** By giving details on data exchange standards, protocols, or interfaces, technological metadata supports data integration and interoperability. It contains information about data integration platforms, APIs, and interoperability frameworks. The seamless flow of data between systems is made possible by technological metadata, which also ensures interoperability across various data sources (Clauset, 2017).
- Technology-enhanced metadata is helpful in the processes of data translation and conversion. It contains details on tools for data conversion, mapping rules, or data transformation. In order to

ensure accurate data representation and the maintenance of data integrity, technological metadata directs the transformation of data from one format or structure to another.

- Information regarding the computational needs for processing or analyzing the data is captured in technological metadata. It contains information about things like memory needs, processing times, or computational techniques. Planning resource allocation and streamlining data processing workflows are made easier by having a clear understanding of the processing requirements.
- **Performance Factors:** Technological metadata gives details on factors that affect data processing performance. It contains specifics like query optimization methods, caching technologies, and indexing algorithms. Technological metadata aids in streamlining data access and retrieval procedures, enhancing system performance as a whole.
- Information about data quality controls, data validation policies, or data cleansing procedures is included in technological metadata. It contains information about the scripts used to validate data, data quality indicators, or data profiling findings. Technology-based metadata helps with data quality evaluation by guaranteeing the data's accuracy, completeness, and consistency.
- **Metadata standards and data documentation:** Technical metadata acts as documentation by outlining the technical details of the data. It contains details on metadata structure, metadata standards, or metadata repositories. Technological metadata documentation facilitates metadata interchange, improves data comprehension, and supports efficient metadata management techniques (Pomerantz, 2015).

Companies can efficiently manage and analyze data by acquiring and using technology metadata. It guarantees the integrity, compatibility, and interoperability of data. Technological metadata improves resource usage, facilitates effective data integration, and improves data processing workflows.

- **Preservation Metadata:** The goal of preservation metadata is to keep data accessible and preserved for the long term. It contains details on data restoration-related metadata, file formats, migration plans, fixity data (such as checksums), and data preservation measures. Metadata for data preservation aids in preserving data accessibility and integrity across time.

The information required for the long-term management and preservation of digital assets is referred to as preservation metadata. It contains information on the procedural and technical steps involved in keeping digital items accessible, real, and used over the long term. When talking about preservation metadata, take into account the following:

- Fixity and Integrity Information concerning the fixity or integrity of digital artifacts is captured through preservation metadata. It contains information like checksums, digital signatures, or hash values that guarantee the data's consistency across time. Fixity information makes it possible to spot data corruption or illegal changes, preserving data integrity.
- **Versioning and file formats:** Metadata for preservation contains details on the file formats used by digital assets. It records information like the format requirements, version numbers, or suggested software for rendering or gaining access to the data. This knowledge aids in managing format obsolescence during preservation and choosing the proper file formats.
- **Migration and Transformation:** Preservation metadata gives details about the techniques used to move or transform digital assets. It contains information on migration strategies, metadata mappings, or data transformation methods. Data compatibility is guaranteed throughout format or platform changes thanks to preservation metadata that aids in tracking the transfer history (Clauset, 2017).
- **File Structure and Dependencies:** The file structure and dependencies of digital artifacts are recorded in preservation metadata. Details regarding internal file structures, file associations, or reliance on outside resources like linked data or online services are all included. Understanding file relationships makes it easier to preserve data and all of its related parts.
- **Technological Environment:** Preservation metadata contains details on the technological setup needed to view and interact with digital artifacts. It records information like hardware requirements, program dependencies, or operating system parameters. The virtualization or emulation of outdated hardware

or software environments for long-term access is supported by technical environment information.

- **Metadata Schema and Standards:** Metadata used for preservation adheres to specified metadata schemas and standards. It contains information on the specific metadata components, controlled vocabularies, or data models that are used to describe preservation-related data. Consistency and interoperability in preservation procedures are ensured by adherence to specified preservation metadata.
- **Preservation Techniques:** Preservation metadata records details about preservation techniques applied to digital items. It contains information about the preservation tactics, migration plans, or preservation standards followed. Digital item preservation procedures are documented in preservation metadata, which makes it easier to repeat those procedures in the future (Pomerantz, 2015).
- **Access Rights and Permissions:** During preservation, preservation metadata records details on the access rights and permissions connected to digital assets. It contains information about embargoes, licensing, and access limitations that apply to the use of saved data. Maintaining access rights and permissions guarantees adherence to legal and moral requirements.
- **Context and origin:** Preservation metadata reveals details about the context and origin of digital items. It records information such as the origin of the digital asset, who created it, or how it was used. The comprehension of the historical context of digital items is supported by provenance information, which also helps interpret them.
- **Events and logs related to preservation:** Metadata related to preservation contains details about the actions taken to preserve digital assets. It records information like preservation procedures, timestamps, or event logs. Information about preservation events aids in tracking the adjustments, actions, and choices taken during the preservation process.

Organizations can guarantee the long-term accessibility and integrity of digital items by collecting and using preservation metadata. Data validity, format sustainability, and effective preservation operations are supported by preservation metadata. It makes it possible to duplicate preservation procedures, makes it simpler to move or modify in the future, and improves the preservation management of all digital assets (Clauset, 2017).

- **Utilization Metadata:** Utilization metadata records details about how data is accessed, used, and consumed. It contains characteristics including user interactions, usage patterns, access logs, and data usage statistics. Data consumption patterns, user behavior, and usage patterns are all revealed by usage metadata, which can be useful for enhancing user experiences or optimizing data services. Utilization metadata is the name for the data that describes how users' access, use, and interact with digital assets. It offers perceptions into the usage patterns, fads, and user habits related to digital resources. When talking about utilization metadata, take into account the following:

i. **Utilization Statistics:** Quantitative information on the use of digital assets is included in utilization metadata. It records information on the assets' interactions, downloads, and views. Utilization data helps evaluate a resource's worth and applicability by revealing its popularity and demand.

ii. **User Engagement:** Metadata on user interaction with digital assets is included in utilization metadata. It records information on things like how long a user had access for, how long they spent on particular pages or parts, or how they interacted with the assets. Data on user involvement offers perceptions into the degree of interest, user preferences, and the efficiency with which the assets satisfy user needs.

iii. Utilization metadata records information on access patterns, such as how frequently, when, and for how long users access digital content. It assists in locating usage patterns, peak times, or recurrent access patterns. Information on access patterns helps with resource planning, infrastructure optimization, and user experience enhancement (Pomerantz, 2015).

iv. Utilization metadata contains information about the search queries that users enter to find or access digital items. It records specifics like the search terms used, the search filters used, or interactions with search results. Data from search queries aids in resource discovery, search functionality improvement, and understanding of user information demands.

v. **User profiles and segmentation:** Metadata relating to usage may contain demographic or user profile data, such as affiliation, age, and gender. This information enables user segmentation and analysis, allowing for personalized suggestions, targeted services, or content that is based on user attributes.

vi. **User Reviews and Ratings:** User reviews, ratings, and comments made for digital items are included in utilization information. It gathers qualitative data on usability, perceived value, and user happiness. User reviews and ratings are useful for evaluating the quality of assets and directing changes to functionality, design, or content.

vii. Utilization metadata also contains information about social interactions with digital goods, such as sharing, bookmarking, and comments on social media platforms. It records information on community contacts, viral reach, and social engagement with regard to the assets. The social impact and influence of digital resources are highlighted through social interaction data.

viii. Utilization metadata collects information on click-through rates, which calculate the proportion of users who click on particular links, adverts, or call-to-action buttons inside digital assets. The success of content placement, advertising campaigns, or user interaction methods can be gleaned from click-through rate data.

ix. Utilization metadata contains information on conversion metrics, such as the number of users who carry out a desired activity or succeed in a particular objective inside the digital assets. It records information like form submissions, purchases, subscriptions, and sign-ups. The effectiveness of assets in producing intended results is assessed using conversion metrics.

x. Analysis of Usage Patterns Over Time is made possible by the use of usage metadata. It aids in the discovery of enduring trends, seasonal variations, or modifications in user behavior. Utilization trends over time support the development of content, resource planning, and strategic decision-making (Clauset, 2017).

Utilization metadata offers important insights into how consumers use, access, and value digital assets. It aids businesses in better understanding user behavior, resource allocation, user experience, and overall digital asset efficacy. Organizations may adjust services to user needs, make data-driven choices, and maximize the use of their digital resources by examining usage metadata (Pomerantz, 2015).

- **Rights Metadata:** Information governing the permissions, limitations, and legal issues pertaining to digital assets is included in rights metadata. It contains information about intellectual property rights, license conditions, usage guidelines, attribution standards, and usage limitations. Rights metadata controls the rights and permissions related to digital materials, allows correct credit, and assures compliance with copyright laws. It details who owns the assets, how they can be used, and when their rights expire. Rights metadata also aids in the understanding and adherence to legal frameworks, such as copyright laws and fair use principles, by organizations and users. Organizations can assure the proper use of digital assets, respect the rights of creators and rights holders, and prevent infringement problems by integrating rights information.
- **Geospatial Metadata:** Information that describes the geographic and spatial properties of data or resources is referred to as geospatial metadata. It contains information about the area, coordinate systems, geographical boundaries, and other geospatial characteristics. Geospatial metadata gives geospatial data useful context and facilitates its discovery, interpretation, and interchange. Geographic coordinates, projection details, geographical resolution, data source, and data quality are frequently included. Users can comprehend the geographic coverage and accuracy of data thanks to geographical information, which also makes it easier to integrate data with other geospatial datasets. It ensures proper use and interpretation of the data as well as efficient search and retrieval of geospatial resources (Pomerantz, 2015) (Figure 2.3).

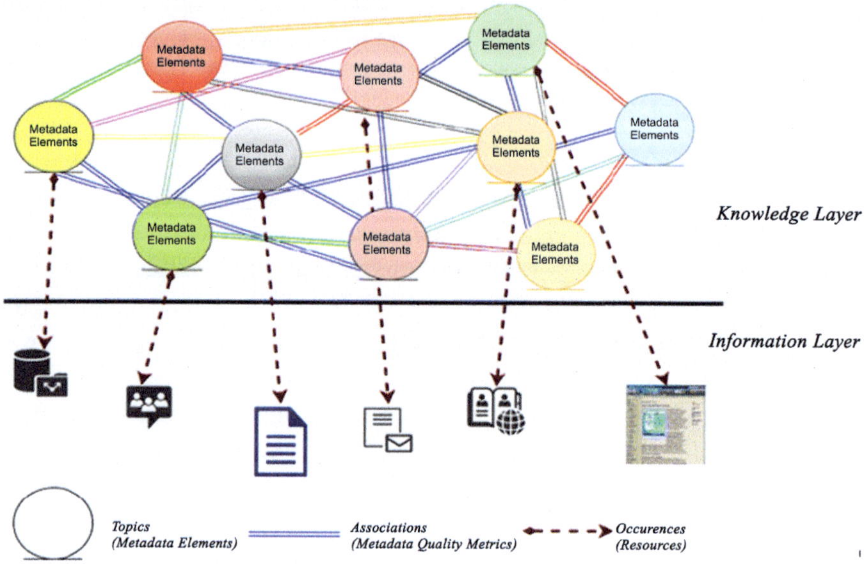

Figure 2.3. *Map representation of geospatial metadata.*

Source: Rajaram, Karnatak, Venkataraman, Varma, Krithivasan, (2018); Scientific figure on ResearchGate. Available from: https://www.researchgate.net/figure/TopicMap-representation-of-geospatial-metadata_fig15_323455846.

2.6. BEST PRACTICES FOR METADATA CREATION AND MANAGEMENT

To effectively organize, use, and access data and digital resources, effective metadata development and maintenance is essential. Follow these best practices to achieve this:

- **Standardize Metadata Schemas:** For consistency and interoperability, use standardized metadata schemas like Dublin Core or MODS.
- Include key details like the title, creator, date, subject, and description to help others find and identify your resources.
- To guarantee correctness and consistency in the generation of metadata, abide by the rules and norms.
- **Include Detailed Descriptions:** Give the resource thorough descriptions to help readers grasp it.
- **Include Rights Information:** For legal and ethical use, record

intellectual property rights, usage authorizations, and licensing information.

- Record Technical Information: For resource interpretation and system compatibility, record technical metadata such as file format, resolution, and encoding.
- Keep track of metadata versions and modifications to ensure correctness and transparency.
- **Implement Metadata Quality Assurance:** Create procedures to check, improve, and certify the accuracy of metadata (Clauset, 2017).
- **Enable Metadata Search and Discovery:** Through indexing, search features, and established protocols, make metadata searchable.
- **Establish Metadata Governance:** To ensure uniform metadata practices, develop policies, guidelines, and governance structures.
- **Documentation and Preservation Metadata:** Record metadata on preservation efforts and plans to ensure long-term usage and accessibility.

The organization, discoverability, and utility of data and digital resources are improved by implementing these best practices. The accessibility, interoperability, and decision-making processes of resources are all improved by well-organized and thorough metadata (Pomerantz, 2015).

In conclusion, in summary, metadata is very important for maximizing the potential of data and digital resources while controlling expenses. It is crucial because it gives context, enhances discoverability, allows for effective search and retrieval, and ensures that resources are used and interpreted correctly. By improving resource structure, usability, and accessibility, metadata promotes better decision-making, more efficient resource utilization, and improved user experiences.

Metadata enables businesses and individuals to successfully use data by capturing crucial information and adhering to agreed schemas. It encourages resource discovery, helps data integration, and streamlines adherence to moral and legal obligations like usage restrictions and rights management. Organizations can use metadata to spur innovation, inform decisions, and maximize resource use by recognizing its worth and implementing effective management practices. In today's linked and data-rich world, metadata is the key to releasing the full potential of data and digital assets (Clauset, 2017).

CHAPTER

3 History of Ontologies

Contents

Ontology is a philosophical area that studies the nature of being as well as other metaphysical notions such as existence and reality. Ontology is concerned with problems such as "Which categories of entities are the most fundamental?" and "How are they formed?" Ontology aims to provide answers to such problems. Ontologists often look for the most basic classifications or sorts and evaluate how diverse items fit into a hierarchy of categories in order to offer a full explanation of everything that occurs. Substances, qualities, linkages, states, and occurrences are some examples of typical category recommendations. These classes include ontologically basic notions like as particularity and universality, abstractness and concreteness, possibility and necessity, and so on. The idea of ontological dependency stands out since it is utilized to establish whether or not things in a certain category exist. The core topic in an ontological dispute is often whether or not anything can be classified and, if so, how it connects to other things and the world around it (Corcho, 2011).

When employed as countable nouns, the words "ontology" and "ontologies" refer to theories within "the science of being," rather than "the science of being" itself. Ontological theories may be divided into a wide range of categories based on the theoretical commitments they make. Polycategorical ontologies give a counterargument to monocategorical ontologies' assumption that there is only one primary category. Hierarchical ontologies demonstrate that some things exist at a more basic level and rely on other objects to operate effectively. A flat ontology, on the other hand, forbids any entities from acquiring privileged status.

Ontologies have deep philosophical roots; nevertheless, its present resuscitation occurred in the second part of the twentieth century within the areas of computer science and information technology. This article gives a quick outline of the evolution of ontologies in the computing sector. Researchers in artificial intelligence (AI) and knowledge representation started experimenting with various techniques to categorize and represent data in a manner intelligible by computers in the 1960s and 1970s. These pioneering attempts made a substantial contribution to the development of ontologies, which owes a great deal to them (Kleinberg, 2017).

Scholars developed the concept of semantic networks, which are graphical representations of knowledge, in the 1970s. Individual ideas are represented by nodes in a semantic network, while the relationships that connect the nodes are represented by edges. Despite the fact that they are not officially ontologies, semantic networks provide the groundwork for future evolution. For the first time, the notion of representing one's knowledge using frame-based systems was pioneered in the 1980s. Frames were utilized to highlight the features of the interactions between distinct products and concepts. The essential ontology ideas of inheritance and hierarchy were initially created by frame-based systems.

The 1980s witnessed the birth of knowledge engineering and expert systems, both of which intended to create robots capable of emulating the talents of human subject matter experts. Knowledge engineers' work in eliciting and organizing information for these systems was a significant input to the development of formal approaches for knowledge representation. In the early 1990s, computer scientist David Gruber is credited with popularizing the word "ontology" to refer to a corpus of knowledge. An ontology, according to his definition, is a formal and explicit portrayal of a notion that serves as a basis for further conceptualizations. This event is seen as the beginning of the modern era of ontologies. A large amount of effort was done in the later part of the 1990s and early 2000s to develop standards for ontology interoperability and sharing. The Resource Description Framework (RDF) and the Web Ontology Language (OWL) are two of the most important frameworks for ontology development on the internet.

The Semantic Web is a development of the standard Web, which was created in the early 2000s. It is a Web extension that allows material to be understood not just by people but also by computers. The Semantic Network makes extensive use of ontologies to accomplish its vision of a network of related data. Ontology Engineering Applications Ontology engineering has recently sparked a lot of attention owing to its broad variety of possible applications. Academics and industry practitioners are both interested in techniques for the building and management of ontologies. Ontologies have a broad range of applications, including information integration, AI, natural language processing (NLP), and data management. Ontology research and clinical practice have experienced a number of notable developments and accomplishments over their history (Corcho, 2011).

3.1. ANCIENT GREEK HISTORY

Parmenides was a founder of the Greek philosophical tradition. He is recognized as being the first to express the ontological essence of existence. On Nature's introductory line, sometimes known as the prologue or proem, provides two opposing views on the cosmos. There is no way to halt the existence of anything since nothing can originate from nothing. This school of thought defines "existence" as the whole of everything that can be conceived of, generated, or gained. As a consequence, ideas like emptiness, a vacuum, and the existence or absence of reality are non-existent. In contrast, the universe as a whole is immobile, infinite, and finite (akin to Parmenides' perfect sphere). As a result, according to Parmenides, the sensation of change in one's daily life is an illusion (Kleinberg, 2017).

Parmenides' monistic Eleatic philosophy stands in stark contrast to the Eleatics' pluralistic perspective of existence. In the fifth century BCE, Anaxagoras and Leucippus provided a more basic and fundamental ontic plurality. They accomplished this by replacing the reality of becoming for the reality of being, which at the time was unique and unchangeable. This issue was advanced in two ways throughout the Hellenistic civilization: the first by Anaxagoras, and the second by Leucippus. These "seeds" were referred to as "homeomeries" by Aristotle in his works. According to the atomism idea, everything began as a vacuum, with individual atoms and atom components that moved independently.

To counteract Leucippus' indeterminism, Democritus (460–370 BC) developed a deterministic materialist atomism. Epicurus, a fourth-century B.C. Greek philosopher, suggested that the original notion of atomism was non-deterministic. Atoms, he claims, are the basic components of all matter. The term atom on originates from the Greek word for "uncuttable." Atoms are infinitesimally small yet immutable. Leucippus was the first to attribute atoms with properties such as "figure," "order," and "position." Atoms are the building blocks of the whole system, and their intrinsic mobility in a vacuum contributes to the system's dynamic and ever-changing condition of existence. Their movement influences the parenklesis, which Lucretius refers to as the clinamen. This impact is mutual. Until the introduction of atomic nature theories in the twentieth century, our understanding of classical physics lagged behind these notions. Plato believed that the only things that exist are eternal and unchanging forms or ideas (forerunners to universals), of which everything that can be experienced by the senses is at best a copy, and of which things are only real to the extent that they duplicate (are "partaken of" the form or concept. Every word, including "beauty," according to Plato, refers to something that already existing, whether it is a perceiving body or an insentient form. Plato, in The Sophist, contends that forms other than being, such as negation and non-being (or difference), must exist. It is unclear if "being" refers to existence, copula, or identity (Corcho, 2011).

Aristotle defined 10 main types of living creatures that might serve as the subject or object of a sentence. Aristotle distinguishes four major ontological dimensions: the several categories or means of addressing a being as such; whether it exists in and of itself or just "comes along"; if it is capable of action or movement; and whether it is totally present. In ancient Greek philosophy, the word "ontology" did not have the same meaning as it has now in computer science and information technology. On the other hand, ontological theory is formed following philosophical discussions and investigation. The ontologies we employ now owe a lot to the Greek philosophical theories outlined below:

Thales, Anaximander, and Heraclitus were only a few examples of pre-Socratic thinkers who strove to understand the underlying essence of the world. They made illogical claims regarding the presence of a primary mover material or principle, which would have been the source from which all else would have flowed. These discussions are about the nature of reality and the purpose of existence, although they are not strictly ontological in nature. Plato, one of the most prominent Greek philosophers, is credited with inventing the notion of Forms, also known as Ideas. Plato claims that the only thing separating our experience of reality from an ideal and infinite universe of Forms is how we perceive it. These Forms are the manifestation of the ultimate truth as well as the whole of reality. Plato's Forms are not ontologies in the contemporary sense of the word; rather, they are abstract representations of the nature of things and their interactions. Aristotle, a Plato student, developed a complete categorizing system and published it in his book "Categories." He established ways for categorizing things and ideas into hierarchies based on their component parts, attributes, interrelationships, and other distinguishing characteristics. Aristotle's categories constitute an early attempt to organize knowledge and get at the heart of things (Kleinberg, 2017).

Aristotle is credited with establishing what is now known as Aristotelian logic, which is based on deduction and reasoning principles. He used categories, definitions, and syllogisms to build his logical framework, all of which are key components of ontological reasoning. Despite the fact that they did not develop ontologies in the contemporary sense, the ancient Greek philosophers lay the conceptual framework for ontological reasoning. Instead of seeking for solutions, they looked into questions like "what is reality made of?" and "how do we classify things?" Modern ontologies, which are constructed on these core ideas, may give more clarity to the areas of computer science and information technology.

The following are some other ancient Greek philosophical notions that provide light on ontologies: Prior to Socrates, the ancient Greek philosopher Parmenides stressed the importance of "being" (which is literally translated from the Greek as "to on"). He asserted that life is infinite, that it cannot be divided, and that it cannot be altered. Parmenides' exploration into the nature of reality, known as the "essence of being," is one of the first instances of what we now call "ontological inquiry."

Heraclitus, a pre-Socratic philosopher, is credited with being the first to introduce the notion of "everything flows," also known as "panta rhei." He highlighted that in a cosmos that is always growing and changing, there is no unchanging essence or existence. Despite seeming to contradict ontological reasoning, his concepts of change and impermanence raise philosophical questions concerning the nature of existence and its representation. These issues are produced by the very essence of life. The Sophists were an ancient Greek philosophical school that emphasized the importance of the individual in the production of their own world and perception of it. They said that the most significant aspects in assessing authenticity and relevance are one's own point of view and societal standards. This point of view calls into question the feasibility of objective ontologies because it emphasizes the need of human interpretation and past experience in the creation of meaning (Corcho, 2011).

Stoicism, a Hellenistic philosophy-based school of thinking, advocated the notion of immutable physical rules or principles. Epictetus and Zeno of Citium, both important philosophers in Stoic philosophy, argued that there was no logical foundation for any part of reality. Even though their conversations did not center on ontology, they did mention universals, indicating that the notion that ontologies may be utilized to include universal ideas and connections is compatible with what they discussed. Today's formal ontologies were created in the context of modern information science and computer technology. Many facets of ontology, however, have been studied in ancient Greek philosophy for years before then. Old philosophers are often credited with establishing the foundation for current ontological theories, and modern ontological systems may want to honor these ancient thinkers.

Further parts of ancient Greek philosophy pertinent to ontological arguments include Aristotle's "Metaphysics" is concerned with the basic problems of what it means to be alive. He analyzes the meaning of concepts like "substance," "essence," and the foundation of "existence." As a consequence of his research of the metaphysical components that comprise reality, Aristotle is able to better appreciate the basic categorizations and qualities of things (Kleinberg, 2017).

Thc notion of participation, or "methexis" in Plato's terminology, was originally established in the Theory of Forms. Material objects are included in Plato's Forms, which symbolize the ultimate reality. Because this statement implies a link between particulars and universals, it raises ontological concerns concerning the nature of the connection and how it should be portrayed. These inquiries address the connection's ontological significance. Neoplatonism flourished as a philosophical and spiritual movement in the late ancient world. It combined Plato's ideas with those of other philosophical traditions. The notion of the One, which may be seen as an ideal center from which all things radiate, is central to Neoplatonist thought. Plotinus is a member of the Neoplatonist school of thought. The One raises ontological problems regarding the interconnectivity of things and the order in which they exist since it seems to imply that there is a unity hidden underneath the world's diversity.

The ancient Greeks were renowned to investigate the link between knowledge and their surroundings. Aristotle's focus on sense experience and reasoned inquiry, and Plato's representation of knowing as remembering (anamnesis) are two examples of epistemological foundations that underpin ontological philosophy. Both of these are instances of how epistemology may help ontological philosophy. The relationship between representation, knowledge, and reality itself has been thoroughly examined throughout these conversations. Although ontologies may be traced back to ancient Greek philosophy, they were not effectively stated and used within the framework of computer technology until much later. The origins of ontological theory may be traced back to ancient Greece. These philosophical preoccupations from the past have had an ongoing impact on present ontology research.

3.2. HINDU PHILOSOPHY

Hindus of the Samkhya school have maintained ontological ideas from the first century BCE. Purua, which refers to pure, formless awareness, and prakti, which refers to matter, are the two basic components of the cosmos in Samkhya theory. The dualism that occurs between purua and prakti is analogous to, but separate from, the dualism that exists between the mind and the body. Since Descartes' writings, this dualism has been at the core of several philosophical debates in the West. Prakriti, the more delicate element, relates to the mind, according to Samkhya. This energy center is made up of three parts: the ego (ahakra), the intellect (buddhi), and the senses (manas). These abilities are useful for a number of purposes, but they cannot develop awareness on their own. Because awareness is an ontologically unique category, only Purua can generate it. When it comes to purua and prakti, both the Yoga and Samkhya schools agree that these ideas are dualistic at their foundation. Unlike Samkhya atheism, it does not deny the notion of a "personal, yet essentially inactive, deity" or a "personal god" (Ishvara). Both of these schools oppose Advaita Vedanta, which argues for non-duality by proving that the apparent diversity of things is an illusion (Maya) that hides the essential oneness of reality (Brahman) (Corcho, 2011).

Hindu philosophy involves a broad range of perspectives on themes such as existence, awareness, and reality. Some of the most essential notions that constitute Hindu ontology are as follows: Advaita Vedanta, founded by Adi Shankara, may be called the governing philosophy of atheism. It claims that everything we perceive to be real around us is an illusion known as maya, and that the only thing that is genuine is Brahman, which is the ultimate truth. Advaita Vedanta teaching emphasizes the oneness of all living things as well as Brahman. This emphasizes the ontological component of a hidden unity that exists underneath the appearance of variety.

Samkhya is one of Hinduism's oldest schools of thought, and it offers a dualistic view of the cosmos. Purusha, which means "consciousness," and Prakriti, which means "matter" or "nature," are two separate and constant principles. Purusha is Sanskrit for "consciousness," whereas Prakriti is Sanskrit for "matter" or "nature." In Samkhya philosophy, these two major concepts interact with one another to offer insight into the nature of reality, giving an ontological viewpoint. The logic and epistemology school known as Nyaya separates many types of occurrences in order to establish an ontological framework. There are six distinct components: content, quality, action, generalizability, specificity, and intrinsic character. The Nyaya philosophical system emphasizes precise definitions and logical analysis in order to aid ontological research into the nature of things and the properties they contain. Other Vedantic traditions, such as Vishishtadvaita Vedanta and Dvaita Vedanta, provide ontological interpretations of Advaita Vedanta. One of these systems of thought is Advaita Vedanta. Ramanuja's Vishishtadvaita Vedanta is capable of producing a qualified version of nondualism due to its stress on the cosmos' inclusion of both Brahman and individual souls. Because Madhva's Dvaita Vedanta is a dualistic school of philosophy, it allows for the ultimate existence of both Brahman and individual souls

(Kleinberg, 2017).

Patanjali's Yoga Sutras give an outline of the intellectual foundations of yoga as a way for obtaining self-realization and moksha. Despite its focus on the practical components of spiritual practice, yoga philosophy has ontological implications for the relationship between individual consciousness (purusha) and the phenomenal reality. A major field of study in Hindu philosophy is the idea of atman, which is often known as a person's personality or spirit. Various ideologies see the nature of the Atman and its connection to the Brahman, which is characterized as the ultimate truth, in a number of ways. There is a chance that these lectures will provide the answers to ontological issues regarding the nature and existence of individual things. It is critical to recognize that Hindu philosophy contains a wide range of opinions on ontological questions. Even in current times, investigations and knowledge of numerous Hindu philosophical systems and conceptions may aid conversations on ontological thinking.

The following are some examples of ontological theory found in Hindu philosophy: Advaita Vedanta, a philosophical school, is sometimes connected with the term "Maya" since it views the phenomenal world as an illusion. In other words, Brahman is a cosmic drama, also known as a Lila, and all we perceive is an illusion generated by Brahman. This ontological viewpoint questions the premise that there is a separate material reality by emphasizing the cosmos' inherent oneness and the illusory nature of its existence.

Kashmir the Shaivism school of thought, which originated in Hinduism, employs the tattva principle to get to the bottom of things. The Tattvas are the primary categories that comprise reality. There are various levels of manifestation, including Shiva, who represents pure awareness, and Shakti, who represents boundless creation. The study of tattvas, when seen from an ontological standpoint, reveals the fundamental order of reality as well as the link between consciousness and the perceptual world. The concept of karma, which has deep ontological foundations, appears in many incarnations across Hindu philosophical traditions. This school of thinking holds that an individual's perspective on the universe is determined by the choices they make in the present. It is thought that karma is the driving force behind the never-ending cycle of reincarnation known as samsara. The actions of the person, the individual's notion of self, and the evolution of reality, according to this ontological approach, are all intertwined and mutually constitutive (Corcho, 2011).

The Puranas are a collection of cosmic stories, each of which provides an ontological insight into the nature of the universe. The Puranas are a collection of Hindu scriptures dating back to ancient times. Cycles are often used in these works to represent the processes of creation, maintenance, and, eventually, obliteration. They provide an ontological viewpoint on the Big Bang, heavenly spheres, and godly actions in the earth. The Vedic hymns, the oldest form of Hindu literature, include cosmagogical compositions that probe the origins and nature of the universe. These hymns provide metaphorical and mythical explanations of the creation process as well as the divine's presence in the cosmos. Despite the fact that they are not ontological in the contemporary sense, they help us make sense of the ancient Indian worldview and its ontological implications. It is important to remember that Hindu philosophy encompasses a broad variety of ontological notions and frameworks, as well as influence from many other traditions and sources. These basic ontological ideas in Hindu thinking are still open to investigation and interpretation (Kleinberg, 2017).

In Hindu philosophical philosophy, there is a vast range of ontology-related ideas. The Upanishads, considered the pillars of the Vedanta intellectual tradition, delve into the essence of Brahman, also known as the ultimate truth. Brahman, which may be seen as either an ultimate awareness or a pervasive substance, is the source of everything that exists. The Upanishads are an ancient text collection that delves into the ontological nature of Brahman as well as its connections to the phenomenal realm and the human soul (Atman). Both Samkhya and Yoga believe in three basic characteristics, or gunas: rajas (energy), tamas (laziness), and sattva (purity, balance). The phenomenal cosmos is supposed to be built from these gunas, which act as building blocks. The study of gunas provides an ontological lens through which to explore the many forms and aspects that reality might take.

Hindu philosophical thought often reflects the cyclical nature of both time and existence. By using the yugas as an example, we may describe cosmic epoch cycles with variable proportions of good and evil. Because time flows in cycles, it is ontologically possible to imagine reality as having cyclical patterns and occurrences that repeat themselves. This is due to the fact that time itself flows in cycles. Avatars are celestial incarnations of gods or other higher beings, and the great majority of Hindus believe they are true. Avatars from higher realms may take the form of people or something altogether else. This hypothesis has ontological implications since it raises questions about the interaction between the spiritual and material worlds, as well as the formation of a varied spectrum of superior species.

The Bhagavad Gita and the Brahma Sutras, both sacred writings that function as ontological texts, provide philosophical insights into the essence of life and reality. Both of these works of literature are regarded to be Hindu in nature. Ontological issues such as one's place in the universe, what it means to be human, and one's connection to God are thoroughly examined in these volumes. They are in favor of an ontology based on Hindu philosophical conceptions. It is important to remember that Hindu thought is fairly broad and may be interpreted in a multitude of ways. Hindu philosophy's ontological components weave a complicated web of philosophical investigation into concerns concerning the nature of reality, existence, and awareness (Corcho, 2011).

3.3. MEDIEVAL

Aristotle's views had a considerable effect on the ontology that emerged throughout the Middle Ages. In addition to substance and form, philosophers of this age often relied on Aristotelian ideas such as essence, act, and potency. Some of the most well-known medieval ontologists were Avicenna, Thomas Aquinas, Duns Scotus, and William of Ockham.

Being may be essential, contingent qua conceivable, or impossible, according to Avicenna's grasp of Greek Aristotelian and Platonic ontological ideas. According to Avicenna's medieval philosophical viewpoint. It is said that something is "required to exist" when its absence would result in a contradiction. Anything has the potential to be, and nothing should be taken for granted. It came into existence as a consequence of procedures unrelated to its essential qualities or ontological position. In contrast to the core life, which can sustain itself and cannot be leased out, this life is dependent on others to live. Making the case for the impossible is a paradox in and of itself (Kleinberg, 2017).

Thomas Aquinas' ontology is based on the idea that essence is different from existence. It is widely assumed that the combination of essence and existence underpins all life. The essence of something, or what anything is all about, is what defines that object. God is the only being in the cosmos whose essential essence and existence are coterminous, making Him genuinely unique. For everything else that is restricted in scope, however, there is a clear distinction between essence and existence. This difference presents itself, for example, when we may understand the essence of something while being fully unaware of its existence. Being, according to Aquinas, is an act that puts the power supplied by essence into action. The interconnected condition of being is constrained by a variety of constraints imposed by a large number of diverse essences. Both cats and trees have the essence, existence, and composition of material forms. Aquinas accepts Aristotle's difference between matter and form, claiming that the essence of material objects, as opposed to immaterial creatures like as angels, is the combination of their substance and form. This is in contrast to Aristotle's belief that the essence of immaterial objects is just their nature. For example, the material composition of a marble statue, as well as the sculptural form it adopts, contribute to its look. This example highlights the notion of form universality since it shows that things made of various materials may have the same shape. It is conceivable that the forms of a material be either trivial or critical to its function. When matter experiences massive metamorphoses, it is entirely altered and cannot live in any other form.

Significant advances in ontology occurred within the setting of Christian philosophy and scholasticism during the entire Middle Ages, from the fifth to the fifteenth centuries. The following are key features of ontologies that evolved throughout the medieval period: There was a growing interest in the teachings of ancient philosophers throughout the early Middle Ages, notably Plato and the Neoplatonists who followed in his footsteps. The introduction of neoplatonic principles into Christian thought has contributed significantly to the success of current philosophical ontological frameworks. Boethius's Presentation of the Concept of God Thinking Boethius, a sixth-century philosopher, is credited with being the first to articulate the Neoplatonic concept of heavenly ideas. It is often assumed that God knows everything and that thoughts from heaven served as models for the construction of the material cosmos. The domain of the skies is related with the cosmos' planning, according to this ontological worldview (Corcho, 2011).

Scholasticism, the most significant intellectual movement of the middle Ages, was concerned with creating a systematic approach to understanding and reconciling religion and reason. Thomas Aquinas, a major scholastic philosopher, recognized Aristotle as one of the key influences for the philosophical framework that he developed. Thomas Aquinas' metaphysics provided an ontological framework for the exploration of the nature of reality and its connection to God. It was founded on philosophical concepts such as "substance," "essence," and "existence," which served as its foundation. Universals, which may be described as abstract conceptions or forms that exist independently of specific things, were a hotly debated issue among medieval philosophers. During ontological discussions about the nature of abstract concepts, realist philosophers Peter Abelard and John Duns

Scotus argued for the reality and objective existence of universals. These discussions focused on the nature of universals.

The fundamental point of starting for the nominalist philosophical movement was realism's ontological standpoint. William of Ockham and other nominalists, like him, were hostile to the notion of universals, emphasizing the importance of particulars. Ockham's razor, often known as the principle of parsimony, argued that there should not be more than one explanation for each entity in an ontology. The Mereological Method for Solving the Universals Problem The issue of universals, often known as the dilemma of the one and the many, was a major ontological topic explored throughout the Middle Ages. Philosophers studied the link that exists between particulars and the traits that they share with other things in order to understand the existence of universals and how they are connected to particulars. The study of parts and wholes, also known as mereology, was one technique for solving this challenge and comprehending the ontological structure of existence. By offering a framework for such inquiry, the development of scholasticism and medieval philosophy lay the basis for later ontological investigation. Despite the fact that following philosophical debates on the nature of existence and reality were nonetheless affected by religious concerns and the framework of Christian philosophy, substantial ontological advances occurred throughout the Middle Ages. These findings sparked subsequent philosophical debates on the nature of life and reality (Kleinberg, 2017).

3.4. MODERN

Ontology is gaining momentum as a credible area within the greater study of philosophy in today's society. The intellectuals Baruch Spinoza and Christian Wolff are two noteworthy examples of people who hold this viewpoint. They saw ontology as a logical field of philosophy that starts with a small number of assumptions. Immanuel Kant strongly disagreed with the rationalist notions prevalent in metaphysics and ontology. He claimed that many rationalist statements must be rejected because they go beyond what experience can sustain.

The separation of the mind and the body suggested by René Descartes in his ontology is regarded as one of the most basic components of his philosophical system. His view of the human body is that of a stretched object, but the brain is seen as a distinct entity capable of autonomous cognition. Both intellectual development and population growth may occur in their own unique ways. We're talking about things like opinions, uncertainties, choices, volitions, sentiments, and emotions when we speak about modalities of cognition. When we discuss modalities of extension, we are referring to the forms that physical things may adopt. Modes are not as real as other types of phenomena since they can only function when paired with an external material. Compounds, on the other hand, may exist independently of one another. According to Descartes' substance dualism, each finite substance may be classified as either a thinking substance or an extending substance. Because doing so would contradict what the great majority of people consider to be common sense, this theory does not suggest that our physical bodies and mental states are entirely separate things. It offers the sense that our minds and bodies are two independent entities that, in principle, may be separated. For a long time, substance dualism has failed to give an adequate account for the causal interactions that occur between the brain and the rest of the body. These interactions include scenarios in which a desire drives a limb's movement or in which light affects the retina to provide an aesthetic experience (Corcho, 2011).

The notion of substance monism, which claims that all physical things may be reduced to a single component, is attributed to Baruch Spinoza. The fact that he refers to this entity as "God or Nature" demonstrates both his pantheism and naturalism. He claims that this substance has an endless number of properties, which he defines as "what the intellect perceives of substance as constituting its essence." He feels that this substance has these features. The human mind can only access two of these characteristics, namely knowledge and growth. Modes are material-generated features that can only be discovered in a derivative form. Spinoza opposes Aristotle's and Cartesian philosophy's substance-mode dualism, believing that all things, including people, rocks, and animals, may be regarded as modes. Modes are the fundamental building blocks of deterministic systems, and the dynamics of their interactions determine the results. Each deterministic system is associated with a particular quality, which may be defined in numerous ways such as "extensibility," "cognitivity," "intelligence," and so on. Causal relationships between systems can exist only when those systems operate independently of one another and do not interact with one another. Natura naturata (Latin for "nature natured") refers to the features that Spinoza thinks to be the genesis of modes, whilst Natura naturans (Latin for "nature naturing") refers to the mode system. Spinoza did not believe in dependent components since he considered that everything was essential. Because the mode system is dependent on characteristics, this is the correct interpretation (Kleinberg, 2017). Christian Wolff defines ontology as "the science of everything that is." In addition to cosmology, psychology, and natural theology, he classified this topic as metaphysics. It is a branch of deductive reasoning based on two axioms, according to Wolff: the law of non-contradiction (which states that "it cannot happen that the same thing is and is not") and the law of sufficient reason (which states that "nothing exists without a sufficient reason for why it exists rather than why it does not exist"). The predicates that identify a certain entity are unarguable truths that cannot be disputed in any manner. The three distinct subcategories that may be used to categorize determinants are essentials, traits, and modes. Essential features are those that are basic to an object's identity and hence necessary for the object's survival. In contrast to modes, characteristics are formed from essentialia via the conclusion drafting process. According to Wolff, existence is only one of many options that an item may choose not to pursue since there are so many others. The concept of "being" as opposed to "existence" is central to ontology. It is possible to give persuasive evidence in favor of anything's existence. In the absence of any objective truth, the justification for anything is the sum of all the deductions that constitute its basic components. When Wolff claims that anything justifies its existence, he is referring to a "reason of being," rather than a "reason of becoming," as the explanation for the thing's existence.

Metaphysical voluntarisms such as Arthur Schopenhauer see free will as the ultimate reality. Kant links the idea of the thing-in-itself with the presence of just one volition. Will, like Kant's idea of the thing-in-itself, is immutable and exists beyond of time and space. However, unlike Kant's thing-in-itself, the will is predicated on prior experiences. It appears as a want, a yearning, a feeling, and so on. Trees, trucks, and a variety of other everyday items are simply surface characteristics; there is no substantial substance underneath them. Schopenhauer refers to them as "objectivities of the will." Each of these objectivations may be seen as a sequence of different "steps" that correspond to platonic forms. Every aim is motivated by a desire to satisfy something. This tethering is controlled by the principium individuation, which allows for the connection of numerous independent items situated in different times and locations to a single purpose (Corcho, 2011).

3.5. 20TH CENTURY

During the twentieth century, the three most prominent schools of thought in the subject of ontology were phenomenology, linguistic analysis, and naturalism. Thinkers like Martin Heidegger and Edmund Husserl are from the phenomenological ontology school of thought, which is inspired by descriptions of real lived experiences. The thesis of Rudolf Carnap that the truth value of existence-claims is dependent on the linguistic context in which they are developed exemplifies the relevance of language in ontology since it illustrates how existence-claims are generated. When it comes to naturalism, the natural sciences are significantly weighted in the study and assessment of ontological arguments. Quine's ontology method, which explores the ontological commitments of scientific theories, is an excellent illustration of this notion.

In his works, Edmund Husserl describes ontology as the study of essences. The distinction between factual and essence sciences is that factual sciences may be understood ahead of time and serve as a basis for essence sciences, but essence sciences can only be learnt after the fact. Ontology is more concerned with essences than real facts since it is the study of essences, and this is true whether or not essences have concrete examples. Husserl distinguished two types of ontology: formal ontology, which explores universal objectivity, and regional ontology, which investigates the essences that all things associated with a region share. Both types of ontology look at the connection between universal objectivity and localized essences. Nature, individual awareness, and collective spirit are allegorically represented by the regions, which are allegorically indicative of the three highest categories of physical creatures. Husserl used eidetic variation as a systematic instrument in his studies into ontology and other basic subjects. It requires inventive thinking since you must picture and then change the qualities of the object being examined. If the item's original functionality is retained after modification, the updated feature is not necessary for this kind of item. A triangle, for example, may exist even if one of its sides is stretched, but if a fourth side is added, the triangle can no longer exist. In the subject of regional ontology, this method is used to extract the core properties of species belonging to higher taxonomic groupings (Kleinberg, 2017).

The idea of ontological difference, sometimes known as the contradiction between "being as such" and "actual realities," is central to Martin Heidegger's philosophizing. He claims that the philosophical tradition has forgotten this difference, leading people to think of existence in terms of a metaphysical principle or force, such as "idea, energeia, substance, monad, or will to power." Heidegger's "fundamental ontology" is an effort to discover a solution to this problem by emphasizing the centrality of "being," a job analogous to modern meta-ontology. One way is to look at the inner workings of the human person, which Heidegger calls the Dasein. This is because our pre-ontological understanding of reality influences how we see the world. Phenomenology may be able to aid in the elucidation of this knowledge; nevertheless, it must be supported with hermeneutics in order to prevent mistakes caused by being amnesia. Later in his philosophical career, Heidegger sought to recreate the "history of being" in order to explain how different conceptions of "being" predominated at different eras in the evolution of philosophical thought. He attempts to resurrect the sense of presence that existed in early Greek philosophy before it was buried by subsequent thinkers. This sensation of presence was lost as a result of future philosophers' influence (Corcho, 2011).

Nicolai Hartmann was a 20th-century philosopher who made significant contributions to the continental school. In his opinion, ontology is the study of the nature of things and categories, as well as their interrelationships. The academic study of what really happens in the world. Hartmann believes the three most inclusive categories to be "moments of being" (being and essence), "modes of being" (reality and ideality), and "modalities of being" (possibility, actuality, and necessity). Each and every item exists and is at the same moment. Ideality and realism, on the other hand, are diametrically opposed ideas; things can only be classified as either actual or ideal. Real entities are unique individuals who can be withdrawn from existence, but ideal entities are present everywhere, may be recovered, and never vanish. Mathematics' objects and the values connected with them are both perfect creatures in their own right. Actuality and non-actuality are instances of relative modalities, while possibility, impossibility, and necessity are examples of absolute modalities. Reality and non-actuality are examples of absolute modalities. The basic reason for the need of absolute modalities is that anything that is feasible, impossible, or necessary is dependent on the validity of some other notion. According to Hartmann, reality is made up of four distinct worlds: inanimate, living, psychological, and spiritual realms (Kleinberg, 2017).

The truth value of ontological statements concerning the existence of things, according to Rudolf Carnap, is dependent on the language context in which the claims are made. As a result, they are often worthless since the only thing that counts is adhering to the norms and standards defined by the framework. Mathematics, for example, establishes the rules and concepts that allow numbers to be deemed significant in an analytical setting. The problem with traditional ontologists, according to Carnap, is that they seek to make assumptions about what is happening that are not based on any particular theoretical framework. This is the issue with traditional ontologists. According to Carnap, such assertions are either pragmatic enquiries into the suitable framework to use or absolutely useless in and of themselves. For example, truth assertions concerning idealism and realism are affected by their surroundings. It is more productive for philosophers to focus on "conceptual engineering" rather than attempting to explain the universe. This process includes both the creation of persuasive frames and the investigation of the potential consequences of such frames. Because there is no universal reality notion, pragmatic concerns such as effectiveness and efficiency must guide the selection of the suitable framework (Corcho, 2011).

Willard Quine and Van Orman, two famous philosophers who have made substantial contributions to the field of ontology, both lay a strong emphasis in their separate bodies of work on the idea of ontological commitment. If a theory cannot be established in the absence of a given thing, we say it is ontologically linked to that entity. According to Quine's reasoning, the underlying theory may be turned into first-order predicate logic, which allows for easy identification. Existential quantifiers, which are logical constants whose meaning corresponds to statements like "there exists." or "for some.," are important in translating this phrase. They are necessary in determining the values of any variables that follow a quantifier in an expression. Variables that are constrained by existing quantifiers indicate the theory's ontology-focused perspective. Quine's saying that "[t]o be is to be the value of a variable" perfectly describes this strategy. This approach is unsuitable for ontology since ontological commitments need the use of a theory. Quine believes that the best scientific conceptions must be included into the building of an ontology. Others followed Quine's lead, expanding his ideas to include a far broader range of themes, such as "everyday conceptions expressed in natural language."

CHAPTER

4 Brief History of Metadata

Contents

4.1. INTRODUCTION

As per the definition provided by the National Information Standards Organization (NISO) in 2004, metadata refers to organized data that elucidates, describes, locates, or simplifies the process of retrieving, utilizing, or administering an information resource. Metadata is a term commonly used to describe information that pertains to data, or information that describes other information. The presence of metadata in nearly all systems enables expedient and uninterrupted retrieval of information resources. Metadata plays a crucial role in organizing the world, facilitating interoperability among various systems, and identifying key information elements (Cooke, 2014).

Two instances that exemplify this are tax codebooks and drive-through menus. Metadata can serve a dual purpose of being both structural and descriptive, commonly known as "descriptive metadata." Its function is to provide characteristics of entities that aid in their identification and location. There exist discrete standards for organizing and describing data. Prominent standards organizations, namely NISO, Dublin Core, and the Internet Engineering Task Force (IETF) are dedicated to the advancement and improvement of metadata systems for diverse undertakings, encompassing open-source code endeavors, union library catalogs, and packet headers. As per Jane Greenberg's findings, contemporary metadata initiatives have expanded their scope beyond the conventional library setting to cater to the rapid growth of the Internet. Within the field of library and information science (LIS), metadata has conventionally been linked to the ability to access information sources, including books and union catalogs. However, the advent of the Internet has significantly transformed the documentation and information access landscape. Despite the continued development and maintenance of information registries, there is a dearth of research analyzing the social process of metadata evolution. It is acknowledged that the development of schema design and metadata creation involves both objective and subjective elements. According to several scholars, metadata exhibits context-dependency, as it is subject to the influence of the systems, individuals, and customs of its surrounding environment. Bowker and Star contend that the operation of infrastructure is reliant on classification and standards, which they describe as being "standards down" (Huettmann, 2018).

The process of stabilizing and preserving metadata can sometimes obscure their origins, including the methods of their production and their connection to infrastructures. The assessment of metadata is focused on the demonstration of expertise and dependability. Sociohistorical analyzes of metadata typically focus on the establishment of a structured standards organization, examining the processes by which its legitimacy is established, developed, nurtured, and internalized within communities of practitioners. The aforementioned phenomenon is observable in the contemporary chronicles of standards, digital formats, and the proliferation of telecommunication, as opposed to the origination or building of metadata. The development and dissemination of metadata schemes by standards organizations like Dublin Core, NISO, and IETF are crucial. However, the process of designing these schemas is often lengthy and fails to account for their stability or historical ontology.

4.2. HISTORY OF METADATA

The development of standards and standardization, such as metadata creation and maintenance, are cultural practices that shape and determine the communication and cultural production of our society. Over the last ten years, there has been a notable shift in the correlation between individuals and metadata. Owing to the fixed configuration of the computing infrastructure during the year 1970, users were able to seamlessly transition across different computers. However, the production of user-generated content was restricted due to the constraints imposed by the Arpanet nodes. Wireless data networks have become widely accessible to users, resulting in the continuous generation of metadata as a result of mobile device connectivity to the network over the past four decades. Scholars from various fields, including forensic science, privacy research, and computer science, have conducted studies that suggest that the generation of metadata by users through mobile devices and Internet-connected mobile networks offers limited possibilities for anonymity or obfuscation. The integration of mobile and wireless data networks with networked ICTS introduces novel forms of subjectivity by producing vast quantities of user metadata. As per the historians of technology and information specialists, the structure of ICT standards has a significant impact on human experiences. It is believed that these standards not only influence the physical world but also shape our social lives and even our identities. As previously mentioned, the development and establishment of infrastructure, including technology, standards, physical objects, and modes of collective communication, are interconnected with the historical ontology of metadata as an object (Cooke, 2014) (Figure 4.1).

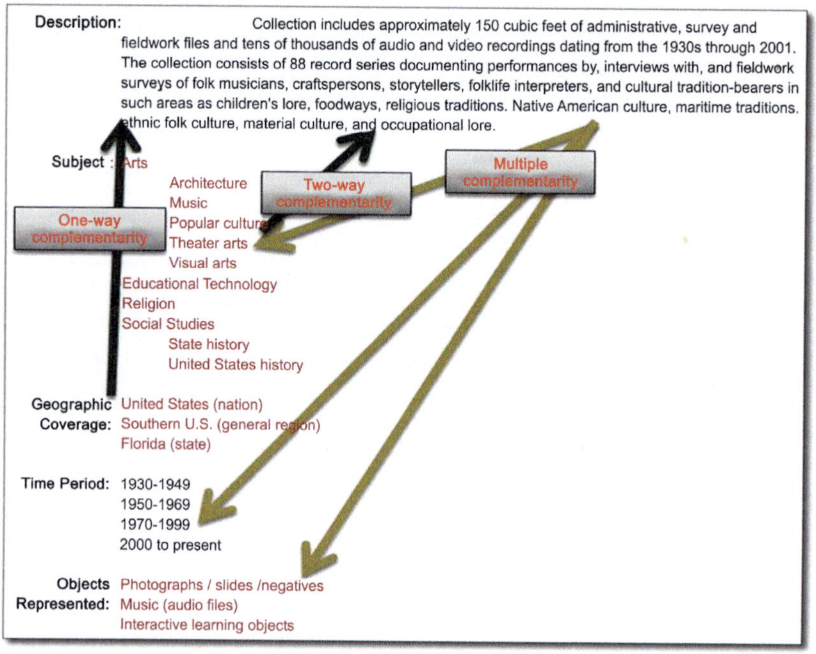

Figure 4.1. *An example collection-level metadata record.*

Source: Zavalina, (2013); Scientific figure on ResearchGate. Available from: https://www.researchgate.net/figure/An-Example-Collection-Level-Metadata-Record-Three-Kinds-of-Complementarity-This-Figure_fig4_271993479.

The field of infrastructure studies has gained significant attention in various academic disciplines such as science and technology studies, information science, and the history of technology in recent times. The term "infrastructure" refers to a collection of devices, technical standards, network components, and architectural frameworks that facilitate the functioning of information and communication technologies (ICTs). The aforementioned pertains to global information and communication technologies that facilitate the transmission of data across regional and international borders. The comprehension of the development, framework, and societal possibilities of ICTs enriches research in the field of information science under the impact of norms and metadata on our perception of these technologies. The field of infrastructure studies endeavors to attain this objective by making a valuable contribution toward a holistic comprehension of the evolution of information infrastructure, encompassing the establishment of norms and regulations. The examination of extensive information and communication technology (ICT) systems encompasses various areas such as privacy and surveillance scenarios, the proliferation of the Internet, and scholarly communication utilizing cyberinfrastructure. Scholars specializing in the areas of the history of technology, science and technology studies, and information science have shown interest in diverse illustrative instances of extensive infrastructure and communities. The examination of infrastructure provides an avenue to explore the historical convergence of networking. The aforementioned accounts of networking infrastructures offer valuable perspectives on the interplay between technological advancement, governmental oversight, global cooperation, and standardization, as well as the dynamic between expansive networks and the communities that utilize and engage with them (Cooke, 2014).

4.2.1. Between 1965 – 1985

The worldwide Press Telecommunications Council (IPTC) was established in 1965 to protect the telecommunications interests of the global press. Since the 1970s, the organization has prioritized the creation and distribution of industry standards for the exchange of news data. Since 1979, the worldwide Press Telecommunications Council has been used by photographers to create a set of metadata components that are appended to photographs. The company has maintained a significant role in metadata production. Newspapers and other news organizations received images via an early facsimile machine for a long time. Along with the caption and other information, the image was placed on a rotating disk and transmitted over telephone lines (Huettmann, 2018).

In 1965, news organizations collaborated to establish a standard for the transmission of data from source to recipient. This eventually evolved into the International Press Telecommunications Council (IPTC) or NAA standard for photography, which ensured that when images were shared as digital objects, the caption, byline (author), headline, source, credit, and date of creation were also sent as part of the file. This information was present in the file, at the specified location in the file header. When image manipulation applications such as Photoshop were first introduced, they also adopted IPTC as the standard for sending metadata. This is the File Info panel in Photoshop. Like any other entity, organizations soon adapted their version of the standard. The Associated Press decided that the title would be the "line of heads" or the last name of every individual depicted, a practice that continues to this day. This reminds me of the oft-quoted aphorism by Andrew S. Tanenbaum: "The great thing about standards is that there are so many to choose from. "Adobe introduced Extensible Metadata Platform

(XMP), an XML-based platform, to replace IPTC's "image resource block (IRB)" technology in the mid-1990s when a more extensible metadata system was required. This necessitated that digital asset management (DAM) systems, such as ours, recognize both IPTC and XMP. Any system worth its salt would be capable of organizing and prioritizing this data so that users could determine if it was current and accurate. Depending on how the data was processed before being added to a DAM collection, IPTC and XMP data did not always match. As the market adopted XML and Adobe's XMP flavor, MerlinOne developed a flexible approach that facilitates the correct mapping of IPTC, XMP, and XML into Picture Desk and its archiving application. Various industries, including digital audio files, the Internet, and museum collections, employ numerous metadata standards. Information about a programming language, the tools utilized in its construction, and supplementary resources can be found on a website. By way of comparison, a collection housed in a museum would encompass metadata that specifies the artistic style, the identity of the artist, and the year of origination.

The IPTC, an acronym for the IPTC, formulated a set of standards in 1979 that delineated the specifications for the data and attributes that are permissible to be appended to images. During the latter part of the 1980s, the IPTC initiated the creation of the Information Interchange Model (IIM). This model is comprised of a file structure that encompasses information elements that are relevant to various media types, including images and text. The conclusion of the early 1990s facilitated the expeditious exchange of news among local, national, and international newspapers. The initial standard of IPTC, namely IPTC 7901, facilitated a connection between teleprinters and computers (Cooke, 2014).

4.2.2. Between 1987–1999

1987 marked the beginning of CDIF development by the Electronic Industries Alliance (EIA) in response to the demand for CASE tool integration. CDIF utilized object-oriented entity relationship modeling to construct meta-models for specific CASE tool topic areas to resolve the issue. The CASE tool industry recognized the CDIF standards far too late. In the 1980s, many companies, including IBM, introduced metadata repository management systems based on mainframes. These were the earliest attempts at metadata, although they largely ignored business metadata in favor of technical metadata. The preponderance of these early metadata repositories consisted primarily of advanced data dictionaries for DBAs and data modelers. In addition, the companies that created these repositories did little to educate customers about the advantages of this technology. Consequently, few businesses viewed these early repository applications as advantageous (Huettmann, 2018).

Until the 1990s, when new technology expanded the scope of data handling to include business metadata, some corporate executives did not recognize the value of metadata repositories. During this period, the industry gained an understanding of the prospective advantages of business metadata, which include the following:

- Construct a semantic layer between the operational and business intelligence systems of an organization and its users.
- Decreased training costs
- Highlight the significance of strategic data, which enables analysts to make recommendations that increase profits (e.g., data warehousing, CRM, SCM, etc.).
- Produce knowledge that can be applied;
- Reduce erroneous judgments.

In contrast to the traditional mainframe platform, client-server computing was utilized in the metadata repositories of the 1990s. Before the development of decision support systems requiring access to metadata, the market for repository services was stagnant. Rochade, RELTECH Group, and BrownStone Solutions were among the first to enter the market with innovative novel repository products. Numerous larger and more established computer companies attempted to enter the industry by acquiring these creative repository providers, with varying degrees of success, after recognizing the market's potential. Computer Associates acquired Platinum Technologies in 1999, following acquisitions of RELTECH, BrownStone, and LogicWorks.

In the mid-to late-1990s, the World Wide Web, the Year 2000 (Y2K) deadline, and data warehousing all rose to prominence, increasing the importance of metadata for businesses that labored to comprehend their information resources. Initiatives have been undertaken to standardize business application communication and metadata definition. 1995 saw the establishment of the Dublin Core Metadata Elements (DCME) by the Dublin Core Metadata Initiative (DCMI) in Dublin, Ohio, and the CASE Definition Interchange Facility (CDIF) by the Electronics Industries Alliance (EIA). The first elements of the ISO 11179 standard for defining and standardizing data components became accessible between 1994 and

1999. Microsoft and Oracle argued during this period over the development of a metadata standard. In 1998, Oracle and Object Management Group (OMG) developed the Common Warehouse Metadata Model (CWM). In 1995, Microsoft supported the MDC's Open Information Model, but by 2000, the two standards had merged into CWM. The CWM standard has been extensively adopted by repositories of metadata (Cooke, 2014).

Several products received CWM capabilities at the turn of the century, along with modifications to existing metadata repositories for online deployment. Several data integration providers began to emphasize metadata as an additional product offering around this time. Numerous products from the early 2000s can now be found in the product portfolios of larger corporations, such as Informica's ownership of Superglue and IBM's ownership of Ascential.

Few companies, however, have invested in or constructed metadata repositories, let alone created a controlled metadata environment that is utilized throughout the organization by "Universal Metadata Models." This is due to the difficulty of creating and integrating metadata, the scarcity of people with practical knowledge of metadata, and the less-than-stellar success of some initial efforts at businesses that did not plan with enterprise data management best practices in mind (lack of enterprise data governance, enterprise data architecture, etc.).

Since the late 1990s, when demand began to increase, the market for tools has remained stable for the most part. Few individuals are aware of the economic benefits of metadata management. Numerous specialists have placed greater emphasis on technical data and obsolete programs than on commercial information and use. Businesses are beginning to perceive the utility of metadata in light of the emphasis on analytics and the need to evaluate data for decision-making. The significance of unstructured data and other non-traditionally structured metadata sources is growing. These elements have contributed to the resurgence of interest in metadata management:

- There are a variety of new and established software vendors on the market; some specialize in metadata administration, whereas others incorporate metadata into their existing product lines.
- The development of enterprise-wide initiatives such as information governance, compliance, enterprise architecture, and automated software reuse; the difficulties faced by many businesses attempting to comply with legal and privacy regulations utilizing

fundamental technology (Huettmann, 2018).

Some of the most sophisticated businesses and organizations have acknowledged at the highest levels that information is an asset that must be managed effectively. Additionally, the existing metadata standards have been enhanced. The information about the year 280 BC. The words "alpha" and "beta" are often used in a variety of academic disciplines, such as computer science, finance, and statistics (Cooke, 2014).

According to historical records, the Great Library of Alexandria is where metadata was first used. The library staff added a little label to the end of each parchment under the guidance of Zenodotus, a Greek grammarian and literary critic. The scrolls were created in a way that made categorizing and retrieving information simple. This was accomplished by placing important information about each book on the scroll, such as its author, title, and subject. As a result, the process of returning scrolls to their allocated category was made simpler because customers were not required to unroll each scroll to determine its contents. In medieval manuscripts, the illuminations that were placed at the beginning of each chapter had two purposes. They served as a visual anchor for the audience of the time, who could not read, in the first place. In addition, they acted as the author's signature. The modern use of metadata is a byproduct of the development of photography. In the early days of photography, particularly in 1839 with the invention of the daguerreotype, photographers resorted to scratching names, dates, and places onto the frames of these photographic plates to identify the content of photos. An early example of the use of metadata is the Dewey Decimal Classification (DDC) system, a widely used system for classifying library holdings. Melville Dewey developed the DDC in 1876. The 1960s: The MARC standards are a group of digital formats used to represent the information in library catalogs. A system was created by Henriette Avram at the US Library of Congress to make it easier for libraries to share digitized papers and make them viewable on computers. The television program "Meet the Press" offers conversations with well-known figures in journalism, politics, and other professions.

The IPTC was founded to protect the press's telecommunications needs and establish rules for the distribution of news. An essential set of information elements for photographs has been produced by the IPTC. The topic at hand is the Hardy-developed software (Huettmann, 2018).

Several firms started developing software to make managing paper-based documentation easier in the 1980s. The aforementioned methods made use of tangible records including printed and published items, paper documents, photographic prints, and duplicates. The first versions of document management systems were complicated and lacked several metadata management-related features. To make the administration of digital picture resources easier, the IPTC has unveiled a unique standard known as the "IIM." This specification relates to data that is encoded as binary within the file. Martijn Koster's ALIWEB is regarded as the first search engine to make use of metadata. The formal debut of MetaCrawler, a metasearch engine, has occurred. The most recent versions of search engines include the best results from well-known platforms like Google, Yahoo!, Live Search, Ask, About.com, MIVA, and others. As the year 2000 shown, a knowledge of metadata is necessary for the widespread application of digital information systems. Enterprise content management systems (CMS) are a result of the growth of metadata collections for recordkeeping and preservation purposes. After carefully examining the metadata related to the watching habits of its 44 million users worldwide, the world's largest streaming video company, Netflix, has recognized its support for the popular TV program "House of Cards."

Information science fields including infrastructure studies, science and technology studies, and the history of technology have made infrastructure and metadata major issues. Recent years have seen a substantial increase in interest in these topics. In evaluations of infrastructure and information and communication technology (ICT), the provenance and permanence of metadata are frequently disregarded. In contrast to other methods, the process of creating standards through expert consensus and the ensuing development of metadata are explored in several historical accounts. Contrary to common narratives, the histories of metadata frequently place a higher priority on the operations of important standards bodies and the development of their institutional structures, highlighting the political and cultural dynamics of expert communities that influence these standards. This method frequently ignores the important part that metadata plays in forming infrastructures before they are formalized and standardized. It is thought vital to examine network technologies like the Internet and mobile telephony with infrastructure and metadata. The distinction between infrastructure and metadata research signifies that a certain area of study has already reached its conclusion. The rationale for this is that the operation of network infrastructure, including its underlying protocols, is intrinsically related to the adoption of certain metadata standards, which will afterward control the operational parameters of this infrastructure. Furthermore, as demonstrated in our analysis, the creation of substantial metadata standards during the development of network infrastructure, frequently in the form of protocol, might have unintended consequences. A predetermined quantity of metadata that is essential to the operation of such infrastructure has been produced as a result of the creation of metadata standards and their assigned responsibilities in network infrastructure. A key component of network infrastructure is infra data, a type of data generated as a result of regular network activities. This solution stands out for its primary objective of providing network infrastructure with the necessary metadata. The study of infradata concentrates on the purposeful design decisions that result in some types of infra-data in network architecture while ignoring others. In addition, allied subjects including economics, professional conduct, ethics, and values are covered in this field of study. Any network architecture must include infrastructure, and it is believed that this infrastructure will always be present (Cooke, 2014) (Figure 4.2).

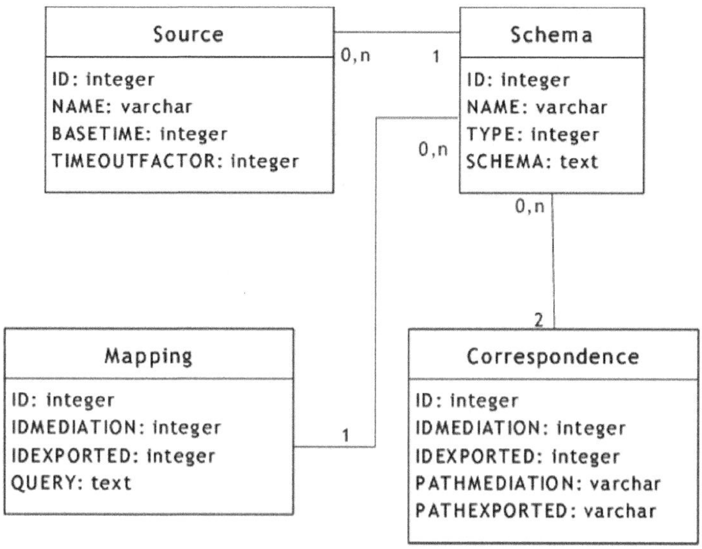

Figure 4.2. *UML diagram of the meta data-base.*

Source: Zechinelli, José, Vargas-Solar & Cuevas-Vicenttín, (2006); Scientific figure on ResearchGate. Available from: https://www.researchgate.net/figure/UML-diagram-of-the-meta-database-schema-A-schema-is-identified-by-its-id-a-name-and-its_fig7_280751071.

In 1988, Leaf, Inc. created the Leaf Desk, designed by Bob Caspe. The Leaf Desk was one of the earliest devices created to transmit field images. It featured a digitizing stage for a 35 mm film strip with three images, a captioned keyboard, a modem, and a small computer screen. Due to the Leaf Desk's lack of a digital memory device, the scanning, captioning, and transmission processes had to be repeated whenever the same image was transported to a different location. Some of the earliest discussions on metadata as we know it today occurred just before the introduction of the Leaf Desk. At a National Press Photographers Association digital exhibition in San Francisco, Associated Press photo editor Stephen Hart, Senior AP Photo Editor Grant Lamos, and AP Photo Editor. The Spooler, an external hard drive that enabled photographers to capture and save images before transmission, was introduced not long after the Leaf Desk. Photographers may submit a collection of photographs by digitizing a few of them. In 1990, IPTC created the IIM. IMM provides the metadata field standard. Adobe adopted the standard in 1995 when it chose 20 picture information fields from the IIM to include in Photoshop, although it was never intended specifically for use with images. In 1999, the IMM schema was modified. In 1997, Adobe Systems, Inc. standardized the IRB information storage technology, which adds multiple forms of image data, including metadata, to a digital image. Adobe's publication of the specifications for incorporating the data in a digital IRB, also known as IPTC headers, marked a conceptual stride forward for photo metadata. Adobe chose 20 categories for Photoshop 95. The ability to incorporate data into JPEG and TIFF images serves as the foundation of the current image management system, albeit with some limitations imposed by current standards (Huettmann, 2018).

In 1994, Adobe created a technology that facilitated the integration of metadata into digital photo files through the use of IPTC headings. This development significantly enhanced metadata features and standards. Despite not fully incorporating the entire IIM structure, Adobe acknowledges and accepts the metadata definitions established by IPTC. It has been observed that images that possess IPTC headers are typically in the format of either TIFF or JPEG files. There exists a plethora of metadata standards and methodologies, alongside specialized and extensively employed models for the categorization of metadata types. Bretherton and Singley (1994) classified metadata into two categories: guide metadata and structural/control metadata, as explicated in their publication titled "Metadata: A User's View." The provision of guide information, commonly in the form of Meta tags containing keywords expressed in simple language, facilitates the process of identifying particular entities for academic researchers. Structural metadata pertains to the identification and classification of various components within a database, such as tables, columns, keys, and indexes (Cooke, 2014).

4.2.3. Between 2000–2008

In 2001, Adobe introduced the XMP to supplant IRBs. XMP employs Extensible Markup Language (XML) and Resource Description Framework (RDF), a condensed general-purpose digital language for characterizing information, to represent the same type of metadata as IPTC. Adobe states, "With an XMP-enabled application, information about a project can be captured during the content-creation process and embedded within the file and into a content management system. This information can include meaningful descriptions and titles, searchable keywords, and current author and copyright information." In the 2000s, as more and more data and information were preserved digitally, metadata standards were used to define this digital data. The first description of "metadata" for computer systems was made in 1967, according to David Griffel and Stuart McIntosh of the MIT Center for International Studies. "In conclusion, we have statements in an object language describing data subject descriptions and token codes, statements in a meta-language describing data relationships and transformations, and ought/is relations between norm and data," they said.

Metadata standards can be found on websites, digital audio files, museum collections, and so on. By defining the content and context of data or data files, their value is increased. A web page, for instance, may contain metadata describing the programming language it was written in (such as HTML), the tools used to create it, the topics it covers, and where to find additional information about those topics. Artists, vocalists, and composers whose work is featured on a CD may be listed in the CD's metadata. This metadata can enhance the reader's experience and facilitate online viewing of the web page. In numerous nations, government agencies routinely collect records of emails, phone calls, websites, video traffic, IP connections, and mobile phone locations (Huettmann, 2018).

With the introduction of XML in 2001, Adobe drastically enhanced its information monitoring. Even in the present day, XMP enables publishing platforms and applications to identify digital content with the required metadata during the creation process. Because it was open-source and supported the metadata standards of other parties, the technology for embedding metadata in digital files gained popularity rapidly. It's an ISO standard now. The Exchangeable Image File Format (EXIF) is utilized by the vast majority of consumer-grade digital cameras, but it is just one of several additional data formats. These and other developments in metadata monitoring prompted the creation of metadata standards, such as Dublin Core, which make it easier to locate online information. AltaVista pioneered the concept of searching the Internet using "descriptions" and "keywords" that can be added to the head sections of web pages using the HTML Meta element. Search engines make extensive use of HTML title elements, which appear in the title bars of most Web browsers and users' bookmarks. Metadata has consequently become an essential component of SEO for the vast majority of website developers.

The use of metadata has given rise to legal issues as a result of its growing significance and volume. In 2005, a US magistrate court ruled in Williams v. Sprint/United Mgmt. Co. that any data provided during the discovery phase of a trial must include relevant metadata. In 2010, the Arizona Supreme Court ruled that metadata associated with public records is itself a public record. The 2013 revelation by Edward Snowden that intelligence agencies were gathering extensive information from millions of civilian phone conversations provoked widespread outrage. The 2015 USA Freedom Act prohibits the extensive collection of phone data. The practice was deemed unlawful and presumably unconstitutional by the 9th Circuit Court of Appeals of the United States in 2020 (Huettmann, 2018).

Metadata is a small quantity of data used to provide context for other data. The Great Library of Alexandria, for example, attached a small marking to the end of each papyrus around 280 B.C. Without unrolling each scroll individually, library patrons could deduce the title, subject, and author from the markings and return the scrolls to their proper location. Although the information on the identifiers was not referred to at the time as "metadata," it is one of the earliest known examples of metadata. The use of card catalogs in libraries a few decades ago was inspired by this type of metadata. Stuart McIntosh and David Griffel of MIT investigated the need for a digital "meta language" in 1967 when they discussed the need for a digital "meta language."

One of the primary purposes of metadata is to help academicians find pertinent information and resources. Metadata is also used to organize electronic resources, provide digital identification, and enable the preservation and archival of data. "Meta tags" refer to the keywords incorporated in descriptions. Metadata facilitates the discovery of resources by identifying pertinent criteria and supplying geographical information. In digital marketing, metadata may be used to exhibit and organize content, thereby enhancing marketing efforts. Metadata increases brand visibility and facilitates "findability. "All legible data associated with a digital file is considered metadata. In addition to numerous words in prose, a word processing document also includes the creation and modification dates. It could have also contained information such as the author's byline. Metadata consists of data used to characterize a file. Define and describe the data's structure, including any pertinent information, so that it can be utilized in the future with greater ease. In other words, metadata makes it easy to locate your possessions, and superior metadata makes it even easier! Metadata with intent (Huettmann, 2018).

In 2001, National Information Standards Organization (NISO), an entity that focuses on establishing industry standards for the information sector, including publishers, libraries, and software developers, published Metadata Made Simpler: A Guide for Libraries. As per the manual, a multitude of metadata classifications exist, encompassing descriptive, administrative, and structural categories. Metadata serves the purpose of describing a resource for identification and discovery. A scholarly article typically comprises a title, abstract, authorship, and keywords. The administrative metadata of a resource provides information to the management regarding its date and mode of origination, technical parameters such as file type, and accessibility details. Rights management metadata refers to a category of administrative metadata that pertains specifically to the management of intellectual property rights. The concept of structural information pertains to the organization of composite entities, exemplified by the configuration of pages within chapters (Cooke, 2014).

In 2001, Adobe introduced the XMP. The XMP format is capable of transmitting metadata categories that are equivalent to those of IPTC. It utilizes two distinct technologies, namely the XML which utilizes encoded instructions to exhibit text, and the Resource Description Framework (RDF), which is a basic, versatile digital language that is utilized to express information. By utilizing an XMP-enabled software, it is possible to gather metadata and a content management system during the content creation process, which can subsequently be incorporated into the file. The aforementioned elements, namely the title, authorship, searchable keywords, and copyright details, have been explicitly delineated with precision. The category of technical metadata, specifically about structural and control aspects, encompasses the data that is retained within the source of your data. The current schema encompasses all tables, columns, and associated data. This category of data is commonly utilized in the creation of a data dictionary. A gap analysis can be conducted to identify any deficient or absent data by comparing the metadata repository and the data dictionary. Business metadata pertains to the information contained within a data warehouse, encompassing the data that is present, its origin, and the interconnections between the data. The process metadata delineates the functional outcomes of the data warehouse's operations. The metadata associated with a process encompasses details of the traceability, provenance, and auditability of metrics that are collected during the functioning of a given system (Huettmann, 2018).

In 2003, Priscilla Caplan, who held the position of Assistant Director for Digital Library Services at the Florida Center for Library Automation, opted to advance the generation of metadata. The author employs a classification system for metadata schemas based on their predominant functional constituents, including but not limited to the descriptive elements of discovery, identification, and selection. Descriptive information may also contain instances of collocation and acquisition. Structural metadata pertains to the internal arrangement and organization of a given entity. In the digital realm, logical resources are commonly comprised of several physical components. The function of administrative metadata is to furnish details of the management of a resource, whereas structural metadata serves to establish connections between abstract entities and concrete files. The aforementioned comprises the particulars about an item's inception, the agent accountable for restricting its availability, and any measures taken to manage or regulate it.

The phrase "rights management metadata" pertains to the ownership of intellectual property. The primary aim of preservation metadata is to facilitate effective management. To ensure the legal distribution of content and appropriate compensation for rights holders, systems must assess rights management vis-à-vis user profiles, which have been verified using correct identity authentication. The acquisition of this information is imperative for conserving and documenting content. The primary objective of the methodology referred to as "digital preservation" is to guarantee the perpetual accessibility of a given resource. Technical metadata systems are commonly utilized in the field of information technology and for computer-to-computer communications and are known for their extensive nature. Technical metadata pertains to details regarding technology, encompassing aspects such as database ownership, physical attributes, optimization of performance, and so on. The technical metadata pertains to the hardware and software necessary for the reproduction of digital recordings, encompassing video formats such as MPEG and PDF (Cooke, 2014).

The functionality of Google's search engine was modified in the year 2007. In its early days, Google's search results consisted of a compilation of pertinent links, including both organic and sponsored options. The search engine giant, Google, has recently incorporated news, images, and video functionalities into its search engine platform. As a result, the incorporation of fresh data would enhance the relevance and discoverability of websites and their content, thereby optimizing them for SEO objectives. The utilization of metadata has become a crucial tool for contemporary online and digital marketing practices. The utilization of metadata on a website can facilitate its accessibility and retrieval by its intended audience. The utilization of metadata can enhance the discoverability of a website's content and potentially augment its traffic, provided that it is implemented effectively. The utilization of online metadata organization enables marketers to optimize the dissemination of their content. For a website to be discovered, it must comprise precise and systematically arranged metadata (Huettmann, 2018).

The influence of metadata on SEO is noteworthy as it constitutes a constituent of Google's search algorithm and is visible on the Search Engine Results Page (SERP). By optimizing metadata to be keyword-rich and conversion-focused, it is possible to increase traffic. Automating metadata is the process of using software or other technological tools to automatically generate or manage metadata associated with digital content. Octopai offers machine learning technology that employs a unified searchable interface to automatically map and govern metadata obtained from multiple information systems within an enterprise. The manual tracking of the data stream to locate particular information was a time-intensive process for the trio of co-founders. A considerable amount of time would pass, and the results were often imprecise. Amnon Drori, Gal Ziton, and Itai Kahalani employed these challenges to construct an automated platform that facilitates the expeditious identification of shared data by BI scholars. The program implemented resulted in a noteworthy reduction in time-to-market, a notable increase in productivity, and a reduction in the potential risks that may arise due to inaccurate data.

With the 2005 release of Adobe's Creative Suite 2, the revised IPTC Core was included. IPTC core was established through a collaboration with Adobe. The majority of IIM parameters that Adobe previously utilized are now included and specified. New field additions included subject, scene, and intellectual genre identifiers. As a result of two geographic information enhancements, photographers are now able to photograph regions outside of municipalities, smaller than city-sized locations, and country codes.

Although the IPTC Core panels required manual installation, they were backward compatible and could be utilized in Photoshop CS (Huettmann, 2018).

In 2008, both the worldwide Press Telecommunications Council Core and the worldwide Press Telecommunications Council Extension schemas were revised. The IPTC Extension 1.0 Schema augments the IPTC Core metadata properties with new fields that are shared with the PLUS schema, such as model and property release information, more precise location data, and many others. Every digital camera currently includes Exchangeable Picture File Format (Exif) metadata regarding the creation of an image. The Exif data consists of the camera's manufacturer, model, serial number, date and time of capture, shutter speed, ISO, and the lens used. Exif was founded in 1985 by the Japanese Camera Industry Association, the predecessor of the Camera & Imaging Products Association. Exif is supported by certain image processors. RAW camera processing software can utilize Exif data to render photographs accurately. Exif Print is a new printing technology that combines photographic data with printing processes to enhance results. Exif is now governed by the Japan Electronics and Information Technology Industries Association.

Metadata is a small quantity of data used to provide context for other data. The Great Library of Alexandria, for example, attached a small marking to the end of each papyrus around 280 B.C. Without unrolling each scroll individually, library patrons could deduce the title, subject, and author from the markings and return the scrolls to their proper location. Although the information on the identifiers was not referred to at the time as "metadata," it is one of the earliest known examples of metadata. The use of card catalogs in libraries a few decades ago was inspired by this type of metadata. Stuart McIntosh and David Griffel of MIT introduced the concept of metadata for computer systems in 1967 (Cooke, 2014). Metadata serves numerous purposes. With its assistance, users can gain access to pertinent resources and data. Additionally, it can assist with resource archiving and preservation, digital identification, and resource categorization. Metadata enables users to access resources by "allowing resources to be found by relevant criteria, identifying resources, bringing similar resources together, distinguishing dissimilar resources, and providing location information" (Huettmann, 2018). Multiple national government agencies collect metadata regarding telecommunications activities, such as Internet traffic. This information is also used for traffic analysis in addition to bulk monitoring (Huettmann, 2018).

4.2.4. 2018

On May 25, 2018, the General Data Protection Regulation (GDPR) was implemented. In compliance with the latest GDPR, any identifiable customer data within the EU must undergo anonymization or be completely eradicated. The utilization of data for Big Data research is still feasible, albeit precluding its application for individual surveillance. To adhere to regulatory requirements, enterprises must possess an unparalleled degree of understanding regarding data to achieve a comprehensive understanding of a company's data, it is imperative to have access to the corresponding data. The implementation of metadata management enables the discernment of data provenance, its placement across various systems, and its intended purpose. The implementation of metadata is deemed necessary as a data control mechanism to ensure compliance with the GDPR. Metadata is data that specifies the significance of other data. For example, the date and time of a text message are metadata, but the message itself is not. Combining the terms data and meta- (in the epistemological sense of "about") produces metadata. Metadata facilitates data discovery, management, and use. It may pertain to any advantageous aspect of the data, such as its origin, context, structure, or quality. It admits any variety of data, including information discovered on ancient papyri and information from contemporary websites. Metadata may be documented and referenced in any format, but due to its origins in computer science, it is most commonly associated with computers. The word's popularity has increased as a result of the expanding use of technology in a variety of industries. Even those who dealt with large amounts of information before computers, such as librarians and publishers, now use metadata in academic and professional settings (Cooke, 2014).

For metadata to be it must be organized to reiterate the principal elements of the data it represents. For instance, the author, title, subject, and call number of each work are typically included in the digital record of a library. As more academic and business disciplines learned to digitally monitor their data, each adopted or developed its metadata standard, which describes the structure of the data. Only the International Organization for Standardization (ISO) is responsible for protecting and enhancing these standards. Other regulatory organizations, such as the European Broadcasting Union, also regulate standards as part of their broader responsibilities. The IPTC has had a major impact on the systematization of metadata. In 1979, the IPTC was one of the first organizations to develop a metadata standard by identifying and categorizing the various categories of data that may be used in images. In the 1990s, as a continuation of this previous work, the IPTC developed the IIM, a file structure for information about text, images, and other media. Adobe Systems made it feasible to embed data within a computer file rather than another file beginning in 1994. Adobe developed these "headers" using IPTC information standards (Huettmann, 2018).

Computer-aided software engineering (CASE) software was one of the earliest commercially available technologies that provided metadata services. In the 1970s, CASE technology first appeared. CASE technology facilitates the development of databases and software applications by storing information (called "metadata") about the data they manage. Developers of various CASE systems were shortly approached by users requesting interfaces for merging data from multiple CASE applications. These companies were hesitant to provide such APIs because they believed the repository would include the functionality in its product. This made sense, given that they desired to prevent firms from rapidly switching to a competitor's solution. Although some interfaces were developed using vendor-supplied or proprietary interface tools.

In conclusion, with each organization implementing metadata standards, the significance of metadata in administering an organization's information assets, and the need to optimize that value systematically and consistently, the history of metadata management and controlled metadata environments continues to expand (Cooke, 2014).

CHAPTER

5 Metadata Quality

Contents

5.1. INTRODUCTION

Metadata quality is difficult to define. We recognize it when we see it, but expressing the entire set of assumptions and experiences that allow us to recognize it is a different matter. Because of this and other factors, few outside authors have written about defining metadata quality. Even less attention has been paid to the issue of enforcing quality in ways that do not require excessive amounts of human effort (Quarati, 2021).

Work is currently being done to set the stage. According to a 2002 study by Jewel Ward on the usage of elements by 82 OAI data providers, eight Dublin Core (DC) elements were used on average per record. Five of the eight elements were involved 71% of the time. According to Ward's study, the majority of metadata providers only use a small portion of the DC element set, but she does not attempt to assess the accuracy or value of the data contained in those few elements. Another paper, published in 2003 by Naomi Dushay and Diane Hillmann of Cornell University, discussed methods for evaluating metadata. It also detailed some common mistakes and quality issues found in harvested metadata, as well as a method for evaluating metadata using a commercially available visual graphical analysis tool. Although neither of these efforts makes it explicit, it is clear that both have some kind of definition of quality in mind (Motta, 2019).

The quality of the data contained within the objects themselves and the quality of the associated metadata are the two components of data quality. Quality is a multifaceted concept. There are many different kinds of metadata errors, but all of them prevent access to resources.

The quality of the metadata has a significant impact on the quality of services that can be provided to users. The value of a resource can be increased if the metadata is based on sound resource analysis. Even when users are unsure of their own needs, high-quality metadata can help them find what they need. To fully comprehend what a good metadata record is, both a micro- and macro-mindset are required. On a smaller scale, the mechanics of creating high-quality metadata are of interest. At the macro level, metadata is integrated into the larger context of an information retrieval system.

The characteristics of metadata quality are determined by several factors. To determine the quality of metadata records, several metadata researchers assessed their accuracy, provenance, consistency, logical coherence, timeliness, accessibility, subject term specificity, and exhaustivity. The majority of people agree that the appropriateness of any metadata element should be determined by weighing the cost of creating the descriptions against the specificity of the knowledge that can be represented in it and queried from it. All mentioned the importance of metadata quality and how, despite the lack of agreement on conceptual and operational definitions, the quality of the metadata record that describes a digital object can influence its discovery, access, and use.

Various institutions have developed numerous metadata procedures, tools, and quality assurance mechanisms. As shown in Figure 5.1, various metadata analysis tools enable staff to assess overall metadata quality in terms of how well existing (automatically and/or manually generated) metadata represents existing digital resources in general (Motta, 2019).

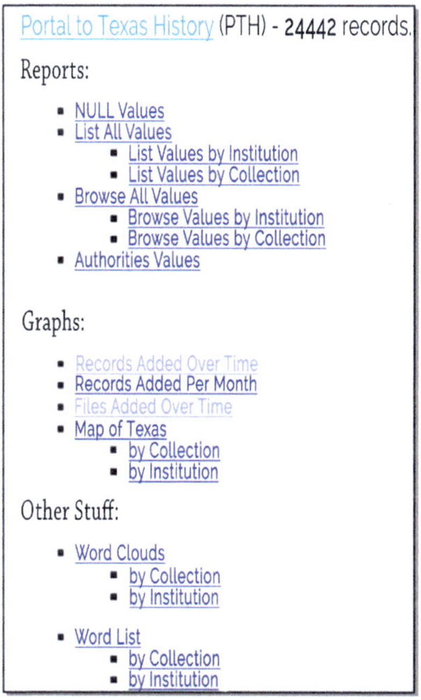

Figure 5.1. *University of Texas (UNT) libraries metadata analysis tool.*

Source: Alemneh, (2009); Scientific figure on ResearchGate. Available from: https://www.researchgate.net/figure/Figure-2-UNT-Libraries-Metadata-Analysis-Tool_fig5_227720842.

Figure 5.1 depicts some of the metadata analysis tools available through UNT Libraries. These tools enable users to view data in visually appealing formats such as geographic mapping functions and word clouds highlight usage and trends, and identify errors and redundancies. The metadata analysis tools generate reports and statistics based on data gleaned from digital object metadata. The tools enable the digital projects team to quickly notify contributors of metadata quality control issues (Quarati, 2021).

5.2. CHALLENGES IN APPROACHING QUALITY QUESTIONS

New metadata standards are being developed at a rapid pace, and their adoption by new communities has sparked debate about their quality. Because of the early adoption of metadata as a cure-all for information overload and the all-too-rapid realization that quality investments are required for even modest gains, this process has moved more quickly in some communities than others. Furthermore, as communities of all kinds attempt to aggregate metadata (and eventually services) via harvesting protocols such as the Open Archives Initiative Protocol for Metadata Harvesting (OAI PMH), quality standards and measures are severely lacking.

Practitioners and implementers in these communities come from a variety of backgrounds, with little to no background in information technology or library procedures. The documentation and examples available to them may appear overly "generalized," and any research from ongoing projects that may be useful is hidden away in areas unrelated to their field. The notion that there might be general strategies available to them that could inform their work and allow their metadata to interoperate is frequently resisted by specialist communities, which tend to regard their data as unique. Isolation and a proclivity to produce specialized solutions for issues that are generic impede coordinated quality thinking.

Resource constraints, particularly those that arise as projects scale up, work against common perceptions of quality. By ignoring characteristics that might make their data more useful to hazily imagined and thus easily dismissed groups of outsiders, specialists frequently ignore those that are important to them. The potential cost of establishing interoperability is frequently cited as a justification for ignoring external influences. Budgets for projects rarely include enough funds to effectively plan and implement metadata components, and projects are quick to forego investments that benefit anyone other than the most immediate target audiences. Altruism that benefits others is regarded as too costly.

Even now, members of project or grant review panels who are knowledgeable about metadata standards are rare. Planners' assessments of information technology needs frequently focus solely on the design and construction of websites or databases, without considering how their information might function when exposed to aggregators or reused in other settings or by other services. Because of how quickly standards and technologies evolve, even the most cautious planners and managers find it difficult to determine when they comply with current standards. Indeed, cautious efforts are more likely to be surpassed because a painstaking approach implies significant time spent in consensus building and review (Motta, 2019).

Legacy data presents unique challenges for many communities because it rarely converts seamlessly to new metadata formats. It was common practice to heavily compress data when storage was expensive; however, most of this data was created specifically for specialized applications rather than for general use. Despite these obstacles, some topics for productive debate are emerging. In 1997, the IFLA Study Group on the Functional Requirements for Bibliographic Records issued its final report. As part of that effort, the group identified four generic user tasks that could be completed with the help of bibliographic records:

- To find entities in a file or database that match the user's specified search criteria (i.e., to find a single entity or a group of entities by utilizing an entity's attribute or relationship).
- To differentiate between two or more entities that have similar characteristics, or to confirm that the entity described matches the entity sought (Quarati, 2021).
- To select an entity that is appropriate for the user's needs (i.e., an entity that meets the user's needs in terms of content, physical format, and so on), or to reject an entity as inappropriate for the user's needs.
- To buy or gain access to the described entity (via a loan, purchase, etc.) or to access it electronically via a web connection to a distant computer.

Despite their difficulty in quantifying, these tasks provide a useful foundation for evaluating the effects of metadata quality (or lack thereof) on potential users. Furthermore, they broaden the debate over metadata quality to include support for broader functionality that is more applicable to a broad definition of digital libraries. It is important to note that the "user" in question is not the metadata aggregator, who is also a user but at a "wholesale" rather than "retail" level, but rather someone searching for materials on a website. Quality always trickles down from the creator to the aggregator to the user.

The majority of the quality definitions discussed in this chapter have an impact on the aggregator first, and then on the website user, who relies on the fact that someone, somewhere has been paying attention.

5.3. QUALITY METRICS AND MEASUREMENTS

This section attempts to define the broad characteristics of good metadata. Because of the high demand for domain-independent qualities, characteristics must be abstract. Rather than using checklists or quantitative systems with clear applications, these qualities could be considered as areas to look for quality in collection-specific schemas and implementations. Because the majority of metadata projects face severe resource constraints, the approach is managerial and pragmatic rather than idealistic. Implementers are all too often caught in the bipolar thinking trap, pitting the perfect against the good. Realistic approaches balance the functionality of the metadata against the relevant constraints to maximize the value of the valuable assets: the data itself, the willingness of data providers to provide it, and the time and money budgeted for the organization, creation, and review of the metadata.

Statistics Canada's (STC) Quality Assurance Framework (QAF) for statistical data, later applied to metadata assessment by Paul Johanis, provided some guidance for the categorization of quality measures used here. Relevance, timeliness, precision, and interpretability the six dimensions of information quality (IQ) listed in the original STC QAF were accessibility, coherence, and consistency. We rethought these in a way that is more appropriate for the growing number of large-scale projects that combine metadata from multiple source providers into a single metadata resource. However, the points listed below are applicable in any situation where metadata is shared. Seven of the most widely recognized qualities of high-quality metadata are completeness, accuracy, provenance, conformance to expectations, logical consistency and coherence, timeliness, and accessibility (Motta, 2019).

5.3.1. Completeness

Metadata must be comprehensive in two ways. First, the element set used should describe the target objects as completely as is economically possible. Although it is almost always possible to describe something in greater detail, it is not always possible to prepare and maintain such information. It is pointless to prescribe a specific element set if the majority of the elements are never used or cannot be relied on across the entire collection. Second, the element set should be applied as completely as possible to the target object population.

5.3.2. Accuracy

The description of objects in metadata should be accurate. At the very least, the values information must be accurate and factual. The next level of accuracy is simply excellent editing, which includes removing typographical errors, standardizing the expression of people's and place names, using accepted abbreviations, and so on. In large or heterogeneous collections, accuracy may not be directly verifiable; sampling techniques, statistical profiles, or other alternatives to time-consuming inspection may be required (Quarati, 2021).

5.3.3. Provenance

The provenance of metadata is frequently used as a foundation for quality assessments. Knowing who created the metadata, how experienced they may be, how good their judgment is, or having some idea of their level of knowledge regarding the relevant field and metadata standards, in general, is sometimes required. Another option for ensuring dependability and quality is to rely on well-established or certified methodologies. Scientists and statisticians are very comfortable evaluating data quality based on the procedures used to collect and handle it. This is especially true when specific items cannot be directly verified. The Anglo-American Cataloging Rules (AACR2) are just one of many content standards and best-practices manuals available. However, the use of creation and handling methodology as a quality assurance measure is not limited to the sciences. The creation information is all that exists at the start of provenance. Furthermore, one should be aware of any transformations made to the data since its creation. When dealing with metadata that is second or third-hand, it is useful to know whether a value has been added or subtracted since its creation, in addition to who created it, how it was created, and where it has been.

5.3.4. Regard for Expectations

The metadata provider guarantees the user certain standard metadata element sets and application profiles. They also bring with them the community's expectations of what these promises entail, how realistic they are, and how they should be fulfilled. In general, element sets and application profiles should contain elements that the general public would expect to see. False promises should be avoided, as should components that are unnecessary, irrelevant, or impossible to implement. The target audience's needs should guide the selection of controlled vocabularies, which should then be communicated to users further downstream. Expectation compliance issues can occasionally be misinterpreted. According to Moen et al. (1998), problems with omitted metadata arise frequently because users perceive the specific element to be irrelevant or unnecessary. As a result, what appears to be a problem with completeness is a problem with conformance to expectations.

Finally, metadata decisions must take into account what the community considers to be acceptable implementation compromises. Most of the time, the metadata provider cannot afford to make a project untouchable by making it exhaustive. It is rare for a metadata project to include everything that anyone could want. As a result, community expectations must be gathered, considered, and realistically managed. Rather than attempting to be all things to all people, it is preferable to reach an agreement on a well-documented and carried-out compromise (Quarati, 2021).

5.3.5. The Logic's Coherence and Consistency

Consistency and coherence are typically regarded as issues only for single collections presented in a series of "releases" over time, or for heterogeneous, federated collections. Even at their inception, however, very few collections exist in isolation. Almost always, elements must be designed and presented to users in ways that are consistent with accepted definitions and concepts in the field or other relevant domains.

The use of standard mechanisms such as application profiles and common crosswalks improves downstream users' ability to judge the intended level of coherence. Standard mechanisms build up a history of intent over time, allowing metadata implementers to easily compare instantiations (Motta, 2019).

The attribute "searchability" is a good example of the value of consistency. Users expect to be able to search collections of related objects using related criteria, and they have grown accustomed to expecting search results and indicative indexes to look and function in the same way. This consistent, dependable user experience is critically dependent on the presentation of coherent, consistent metadata across collections.

Barton et al.'s 2005 paper describes an intriguing and dysfunctional variation on the concept of "over-coherence" or "false coherence." The real issue is one of precision. The same metadata records are inappropriately applied to various parts of an object or objects in this case, as if by habit. The same study that Barton used to back up his claim discovered problems with relying too heavily on software-provided presets for some elements.

5.3.6. Timeliness

We use two different terms to describe two different aspects of metadata timeliness: "currency" and "lag." "Currency" issues arise when the target object changes but the metadata does not. "Lag" issues arise when the target object is distributed before some or all metadata is known or available.

- **Currency:** Stale Uniform Resource Identifiers (URIs) are the archetype for metadata currency issues, but almost any element or value can drift away from its intended use or target over time. Information objects move around, whether on bookshelves, websites, or conceptual maps of an intellectual discipline. When metadata is out of sync with these movements, its quality deteriorates over time. Synchronization must recently be examined and verified, in addition to being aware that the metadata is in sync with its target object. This highlights an important finding from our analysis: high-quality practices not only accurately describe the target objects but also increase user confidence in the description.
- **Lag:** The dissemination of the metadata does not always coincide with the dissemination of the object to which the metadata applies. Defining, categorizing, and cataloging new objects takes time, especially when human judgment is required. The problems that arise as a result of this are exacerbated if the thing being described must be distributed immediately while the metadata takes some time (Quarati, 2021).

The official citation of judicial opinions provides an instructive, if horrifying, illustration. Official citations are frequently derived from printed volume page numbers and must therefore be used after the volume has been published. From the time the original opinion is delivered in the case of the federal appellate courts in the United States, this can take up to eighteen months. Many publicly accessible Internet archives never return to the subject, leaving opinions available but unofficially uncited (Motta, 2019).

- **Timeliness as an Area of Cultural Differences:** The aging of metadata presents obvious issues in the form of potentially broken URIs, drifting controlled vocabularies, and evolving, occasionally

> divergent, conceptual maps of the underlying corpus. These are straightforward issues, but given the cultural differences between collection developers and maintainers, they may be difficult to resolve. The computing and library communities' deeply ingrained and disparate expectations about audiences, the durability or persistence of metadata design decisions, and the dependability of technology all contribute to subtle difficulties. Printed material is typically cataloged under the assumption that metadata will only need to be created once. Only when there is a compelling economic or political incentive are library catalog records revisited and new metadata perspectives developed. Consider the strategies developed by libraries to avoid costly updates to authority records, such as personal name headings, when renowned authors die, as an example. To avoid having to update existing catalog records with a new heading containing a death date, it is now standard practice to add the death date and the information source to the body of the name authority record rather than the heading (even if a birth date already exists).

Computer scientists, on the other hand, come from a world where methods are constantly evolving and improving. This encourages a more exploratory, iterative approach to tasks like metadata extraction. Furthermore, audience customization appears to be more feasible as a result of the more flexible view of metadata provided by searchable and dynamic databases. Unfortunately, it has taken this group some time to understand and implement useful and effective updating techniques. For example, the OAI Protocol for Metadata Harvesting initially proposed a definition of a metadata record "update" that required harvesters to replace records in their systems that only affected the administrative portions of the metadata record.

It is not always preferable to use computers or libraries. The main takeaway is that different members of the project team will approach data aging issues from different angles. Some people may prefer a "do-it-once-right-and-forget-about-it" strategy, believing that iterative strategies are ineffective. Others, on the other hand, will only use iterative methods, dismissing front-loaded tactics as unnecessary and time-consuming. Then, it may be useful to consider not only what provides the greatest utility for the user, but also what provides the greatest utility for the user in the shortest amount of time and the long run. We must strike a balance between these opposing concerns (Quarati, 2021).

5.3.7. Accessibility

Dimension	Measure	AssociatedData	Desc.	Author	Date	...
Vertical incompleteness	30%	references to a table and a column	...		04/05/2008	...
Horizontal incompleteness, batch unavailability	20%	data source, batch identifier, missing time window	...		03/05/2008	...
Confidence	90%	references to a table, a column and a cell	...		05/05/2008	...
Consistency	95%	select Diagnosis from Diagnoses where Doctor="John Smith" and Date < 1-1-2008	...	Peter	10/07/2008	...
Confidence, entity resolution	80%	references to a pair of tuples candidates for merging	...	John	11/05/2008	...
...	...	...	...	...	...	...

Figure 5.2. *Example quality metadata to be stored in the data warehouse.*

Source: Daniel, Casati, Palpanas, Chayka, & Cappiello, (2008); Scientific figure on ResearchGate. Available from: https://www.researchgate.net/figure/Example-quality-metadata-to-be-stored-in-the-data-warehouse_fig3_220918786.

Metadata is useless because users cannot read or understand it. The difficulties could be either mental or physical. There are numerous ways to restrict access. Metadata may not be easily linked to the target objects because it may be physically separate from the target objects, originate from a different source, or be incorrectly keyed or linked to the object being described. It may also be unreadable due to a variety of technical reasons, such as the use of obsolete, unusual, or proprietary file formats that require specialized hardware or software to read. Metadata is sometimes regarded as "premium" information that users must pay to access or proprietary information that is never made public. This is frequently the case because the creator or publisher wishes to maintain the competitive advantage represented by the metadata. In other words, rather than being technical or organizational, economic or trade barriers may exist (Figure 5.2).

It is difficult to reduce or eliminate intellectual access barriers in a world where both objects and metadata are used by various audiences and the extent of dissemination is unpredictable. Controlled vocabularies are particularly difficult in this regard. While classification systems for legal materials, such as the West key-number system, provide excellent fine-grained organization for experts, they are of little use to those with different perspectives, such as hospital administrators interested in public benefits law. To meet the needs and expectations of various audiences, different views or arrangements of metadata must be provided (Motta, 2019). Even though metadata providers are powerless to make users understand any specific element or set of elements, some intellectual barriers can be reduced by carefully considering the needs of potentially diverse audiences when designing and documenting metadata implementations. Above all, it is critical to reject the notion that formal, succinct expressions of metadata structure are sufficient documentation. Extensible Markup Language (XML) schemas do not express thought or intention. For proper intellectual access, practice manuals and other similarly comprehensive forms of documentation are required.

It's natural to wonder which of the seven previously discussed dimensions is the most important or is required right away for a given project. How and where should we begin to promote quality? The nature of the objects to be described, whether the implementer is a source provider or an aggregator, and—perhaps most importantly—how the metadata is to be created or derived all influence how these various criteria are prioritized. Three well-known examples demonstrate the variety of options for creating metadata: a collection that heavily relies on author self-submission to gather both data and metadata; a project that heavily relies on human judgment to create classificatory metadata; and a project that extracts metadata from a text corpus using automated text-extraction methods.

Each of these techniques can be used to produce high-quality results in a variety of ways. In contrast to a churning pool of student employees assigned to a markup project, assuming a relatively stable corpus (a sometimes dangerous but reasonable assumption), a computer program that extracts metadata will produce consistent results over an indefinite time. A project that relies on voluntary submissions cannot make the same assumptions about coherence and accuracy that one person does. The accuracy of topical classification is less important in a project that only uses it to create rough boundaries for full-text search or a current-awareness service than it is in one that aims to produce a fine-grained taxonomic survey of a large body of literature (Quarati, 2021).

5.4. DEFINING THE METADATA LEVELS OF QUALITY

Any definition of quality must consider the semantic structure (also known as the "format" or "element set"), the syntactic structure (including the administrative wrapper, which is typically expressed via a "schema"), and the actual data values. All of these can be validated automatically to some extent. In this chapter, "element set" will be used to refer to metadata semantics instead of "format" or "schema," while "schema" will refer to syntax and syntactic binding. Although the term "schema" is frequently used to refer to both areas, doing so in this context would cause unnecessary confusion.

To begin, automated metadata validation or evaluation is typically less expensive than human validation because it is more practical. The use of automated methods could free up human resources for more complex assessments. The "least one can do" to ensure metadata quality is to use low-cost machine-learning techniques, with potentially more expensive human techniques coming later.

- The ability to validate the schema, which denotes the existence of a defined schema that can be checked for validity using programming techniques, whether it is an XML or another syntax, is one definition of a "first tier" of quality indicators.
- using the appropriate namespace declarations; each data element must be defined within a specific namespace, which may or may not be machine-readable.
- the presence of an administrative "wrapper" with the bare minimum of provenance (metadata identifier, source, and date)—each record of metadata described in this manner should have a unique identifier. The metadata's creation or modification date, as well as its source, should be disclosed.

Beyond these fundamentals, one could argue that the following characteristics (keeping in mind that "presence" is frequently verified by automated means) improve metadata quality:

- controlled vocabularies expressed through distinct tokens linked to publicly accessible sources of terms, such as Internet Mime Types (Motta, 2019).
- components listed in a publicly accessible application profile that a specific community has designated as necessary for locating that community's resources.
- a complete set of generic components important for general discovery, unrelated to any specific community, and free of assumptions about the metadata's intended audience. Ward's five universal components most likely define an efficient minimum for mostly textual objects.
- more specific provenance data, such as the methodology used to

create the metadata, in addition to the source, date, and identifier.

- After this point, it is less likely that quality assessments can be made automatically. Nonetheless, the following quality indicators are useful:
- a statement of metadata intentions based on an explicit, documented application profile that has been approved by a specialized community and is registered under a general metadata standard.
- a trustworthy data source with a track record of regularly updating metadata, such as controlled vocabularies. This includes explicit adherence to current norms and schemas.
- full provenance data, including nested data, as original metadata is collected, enhanced, and re-exposed. It should refer to practice documentation that details the augmentation and upgrade procedures used by specific aggregators, even if it does not document changes at the element level (Quarati, 2021).

5.5. IMPROVING THE QUALITY OF METADATA CURRENTLY AND IN THE FUTURE

Better documentation at various levels has long been at the top of metadata practitioners' wish lists. The first and most fundamental is the application of standards. Basic standards documents should include examples and best practice recommendations. Volunteer documentarians are still in short supply, although such documentation is frequently recommended and described. The vast majority of projects do not budget for internal documentation, let alone volunteer staff time to create such services for the general public. Many people also do not make their internal procedures and materials public. This assistance will never be as readily available as everyone agrees it should be until it is made available and recognized as valuable (possibly compensated) work.

Better documentation and exposure of local vocabularies in metadata would significantly increase implementers' willingness to use them. Support should include making a vocabulary available in a variety of ways, such as through a web interface or harvestable files. It is also necessary to support a community-based updating and maintenance process. Fear of revenue loss has undoubtedly been fueled by the shrinking market for printed goods and a lack of viable business models for web-accessible vocabularies, limiting the availability of machine-readable vocabulary files for quality assurance purposes.

Application profiles are only now beginning to emerge as the preferred mode of communication between specialized communities and the larger metadata world. Because application profiles are, by definition, models created by community consensus, they necessitate a level of documentation of practice that is unusual for individual projects or implementers to attempt. Because they combine general and specific metadata elements, they also provide an alternative to the proliferation of metadata standards that reuse the same general concepts with definitions that are sufficiently different to impair interoperability (Motta, 2019).

Documentation is important for improving overall quality, but cultural shifts maybe even more important. We must encourage the development of an implementer and aggregator culture that prioritizes training, tools, methodologies, and the dissemination of research findings, as well as better documentation practices. The Library of Congress has sparked initiatives in the world of libraries in this area, but no single organization can take on this leadership role for the vast array of specialized communities that could benefit from it. Leadership in non-library metadata communities is most likely distributed, just like data. It is difficult to persuade these organizations and their members to donate time, server space, technical know-how, and training materials for the benefit of everyone rather than just one group. The Dublin Core Metadata Initiative (DCMI), OAI, and other metadata and technical standards communities offer numerous volunteer opportunities as well as technical infrastructure for the dissemination of tools, ideas, and research. This type of effort can already be directed through some established channels (Quarati, 2021).

More in-depth research on the use of practical metadata and the impact of quality on that use is needed. One ongoing project with a lot of potentials to provide answers is the National Science Digital Library (NSDL) MetaTest Project, led by Elizabeth Liddy at the Syracuse University School of Information Studies. The goal of this project is to determine whether automatically generated metadata is as useful to users as manually generated metadata and whether metadata can assist users in locating resources. This research has the potential to assist the digital library community in moving beyond the untested, sometimes dogmatic assumptions that underpin current discussions of metadata and toward a more thorough understanding of the role of metadata in upcoming implementations.

Another way metadata quality resembles pornography is that it is a theater of types rather than individuals, as Susan Sontag once observed. It is difficult to compile a list of specific quality-assurance techniques that can be used in a variety of domains, media types, and funding levels. For this reason, we may not have attempted it here. Project managers, on the other hand, can benefit from a playbill that lists the various types. It advises aggregators on where to look for problems in legacy data and data from multiple sources. It can serve as a jumping-off point for communities and implementers as they develop standards and documentation, two quality indicators that are frequently lacking in practice. The prevalence of quality issues is one indicator that the metadata community is maturing. The next step is to build the ability to use broad generalizations across community boundaries as a starting point for practical solutions (Motta, 2019).

5.6. QUALITY ASSESSMENT FRAMEWORKS

Digital libraries and other information centers are dedicated to managing various data typologies and the associated metadata, which can come from a variety of sources. Researchers have been investigating how to evaluate the quality of the metadata in such settings since the early 2000s when networked repositories first became popular. Barton and Hey (2003) note in their analysis of the Learning Objects and e-Prints communities of practice that quality assurance for metadata is a much more difficult problem in an environment where each metadata repository or archive is part of a larger system aiming for interoperability. Stvilia and Cole (2004) agree that one of the most difficult problems in IQ theory is how to account for the context-sensitive nature of IQ and value. As most authors have pointed out, metadata can be of high quality when used in its original context but of low quality when used in an aggregated environment. This is common because quality parameters appropriate in the original context may differ from those used in the aggregated environment, where metadata will most likely be used for a purpose other than the one for which it was created. Controlled vocabularies used in metadata fields are an example of information that may not be explicitly specified in the original context because it is assumed knowledge; however, in the aggregated environment, this unspecified information degrades quality by preventing accurate data interpretation. As a result, as digital repositories grow in size, number, and diversity, and become more prevalent in aggregated environments, the issue of ensuring a sufficient overall level of quality becomes critical (Quarati, 2021).

5.6.1. Bruce and Hillmann Framework

One of the first attempts to provide a general definition of metadata quality dimensions was made by Bruce and Hillmann (2004). They define high-quality metadata as having seven general characteristics: timeliness, accessibility, logical consistency and coherence, provenance, completeness, accuracy, and conformance to expectations. These seven dimensions are intended to be domain-agnostic, so rather than being checkboxes or quantitative systems that can be used right away, "one might think of these characteristics as places to look for quality in collection-specific schemas and implementations."

The authors introduce each dimension and its characteristics while also describing them, but no formal definitions or metrics are provided. In addition to the seven dimensions, they define several levels of metadata quality, including the element set or metadata scheme level, the syntactic level, and the actual data values. Indeed, they argue that any definition of quality should take into account metadata's characteristics on such a wide range of scales.

The authors emphasize that determining which of the seven dimensions they describe is most critical or urgently required for a given application is impossible because the significance of each quality criterion is directly influenced by the nature of the resource that needs to be described as well as the context in which the metadata is to be created or derived. There is a lot of emphasis on the idea that context alone determines how quality is perceived (Motta, 2019).

As an application of the seven quality dimensions that comprise their framework, the authors propose a "what to ask for and where to look" compliance checklist. In practice, they propose a set of queries that could be used to determine whether the metadata being evaluated meets the established standards, as well as a set of quality compliance indicators that could be used to provide the answers. The presence of controlled vocabularies, provenance information at various levels of detail, and advanced documentation as an expression of metadata intentions are just a few examples of compliance indicators that can be automated, human, or both. The checklist questions suggest a subjective assessment and provide no means of quantifying the quality criteria.

Concerning the aforementioned framework, Hillmann and Phipps (2007) state that "[a]lthough the criteria] provide opportunities to converse about quality, [they] remain frustratingly beyond reach without ways to measure that quality." They recommend considering a viewpoint in which Application Profiles are viewed as a "template for expectation" and metadata under assessment can be compared to that template to obtain quantitative measurements of the quality parameters. Hillmann and Phipps envision the following dimensions being evaluated in particular:

(i) completeness, which can be easily determined by relying on the profile's "obligation" and (ii) conformance to expectations, which can be determined using descriptions of the conditions that should occur when a value is present. (iii) accuracy, where the percentage of incorrect vocabulary terms can be calculated, for example, when a vocabulary encoding is used. These authors acknowledge that using application profiles to express expectations may be too difficult, if not impossible, to evaluate the other dimensions (Quarati, 2021).

Several studies have suggested that the Bruce and Hillmann Framework be expanded to include additional shareability-related dimensions. Based on their experiences in cultural heritage institutions, Shreeves et al. (2005) observed that while metadata may be of high quality within a local database, this quality may be lost when metadata are combined in a federated environment. As a result, "understanding of the criteria for high quality, 'shareable' metadata is crucial to the next step in the development of federated Digital Libraries" (unquote). As a result, Shreeves proposes shareability as an additional metadata quality dimension. According to the authors, shareable metadata is metadata that aggregators can understand and use outside of their local environment to provide more sophisticated services. To put it another way, given the resource described, shareable metadata should be valuable and usable for services outside of its immediate context. To accomplish this, they recommend the following characteristics, in addition to those of high-quality metadata created specifically to evaluate shareability:

(i) The content is intended to be shared; (ii) consistent practices are reflected in the metadata of shared collections; (iii) coherent metadata;(iv) context; (v) direct or indirect communication between the metadata provider and aggregators;(vi) metadata and sharing tools that adhere to industry standards.

It is important to note that, as the demand for descriptive metadata to be made publicly accessible has grown, the concept of "shareability" has become fundamental in the cultural heritage community. The significance of this concept and the closely related concept of "interoperability" has become clear in the context of digital library infrastructures as one of their primary problems (Motta, 2019).

5.6.2. Ochoa and Duval Framework

The Bruce and Hillmann framework is directly related to the Ochoa and Duval (2009) framework. The work of Ochoa and Duval aims to propose a framework that includes meaningful quality parameters, or quality parameters that human reviewers might use, linked to automatically calculable quality measures. Bruce and Hillman created their framework to assist human reviewers. They specifically supplement the Bruce and Hillmann framework by recommending automated measurement techniques for each of its seven parameters. For each quality parameter, one or more metrics are suggested, along with a justification, calculation formulas, and some guidelines.

The proposed metrics, the authors note, should be viewed as "a first step for the automatic evaluation of metadata quality" rather than a complete or final set. In reality, the following characteristics and constraints are observed:

Although the initialization parameters are context-dependent, (i) they are simple to implement in real environments and can be used for a variety of digital repositories, (ii) they are standard- and community-of-practice-agnostic, and (iii) they are primarily designed to work over text and numeric metadata. New approaches are required for metadata containing information that is not alphanumeric; they are primarily designed for metadata instances that adhere to a relatively stable metadata schema; metric normalization may not always be possible; and the mix of quality parameters determines the overall quality of the metadata instance. However, no suggestions are made as to how to combine the quality parameters because the characteristics may have multiple tradeoffs (Quarati, 2021).

Ochoa and Duval (2009) conducted three validation studies to evaluate the proposed metrics' performance as automatic low-quality filters and their correlation with human-made quality assessment, key property discrimination, and various metadata sets. The following results were obtained:

- While some metrics appear to be unrelated to human reviewers, others appear to be. The Qtinfo metric, which measures the information content of text fields, appears to be a particularly good approximation of perceived quality.
- The metrics are effective at distinguishing manually generated

metadata from automatically generated metadata (which is expected to be of high quality). As a result, human reviewers tend to evaluate metadata as content, assigning a higher score to longer and more specialized text than to shorter text. The metrics show that human experts choose a more diverse set of categorical values and fill in more fields than the automated approach.

- Some of the metrics, as well as the mean of all suggested metrics, are effective methods for developing automatic quality filters.
- Although some quality parameters, such as categorical value variability, are difficult for humans to evaluate, the metrics were able to do so (Motta, 2019).

5.6.3. Stvilia et al. Framework

Stvilia et al. (2007) proposed their idea in response to the need to define a general framework and an efficient measurement model, both of which are required for IQ. They discover that most previously established IQ assessment frameworks in the data management field are "ad hoc, intuitive, and incomplete, and may not produce robust and systematic measurement models" after revising them. As a result, in contrast to context-specific quality assessment models that rely on variables determined by local needs, these authors focus on understanding the causes of quality changes and present a framework comprised of typologies of IQ problems, related activities, and a systematically organized taxonomy of IQ dimensions. An IQ issue occurs when an information entity's IQ falls short of the requirements of activity on one or more IQ dimensions, according to this framework. Any attribute that describes the IQ concept is defined as an IQ dimension. In any case, the authors expressly acknowledge the contextual nature of IQ and assert that their framework could serve as "a knowledge resource and guide for developing IQ measurement models for many different settings." Mapping, information entity changes, underlying entity or condition changes, and context changes are the four main contributors to IQ issues (Quarati, 2021) (Figure 5.3).

The authors examine these sources and develop a taxonomy of 22 IQ dimensions that are classified into three categories:

(i) intrinsic, or characteristics that can be measured by comparing informational elements to a reference standard (such as spelling errors);

(ii) relational dimensions, or those that assess the connections between information and specific aspects of how it is used (such as accuracy); and

(iii) reputational, or IQ traits that assess an information entity's standing within a specific structure (such as authority).

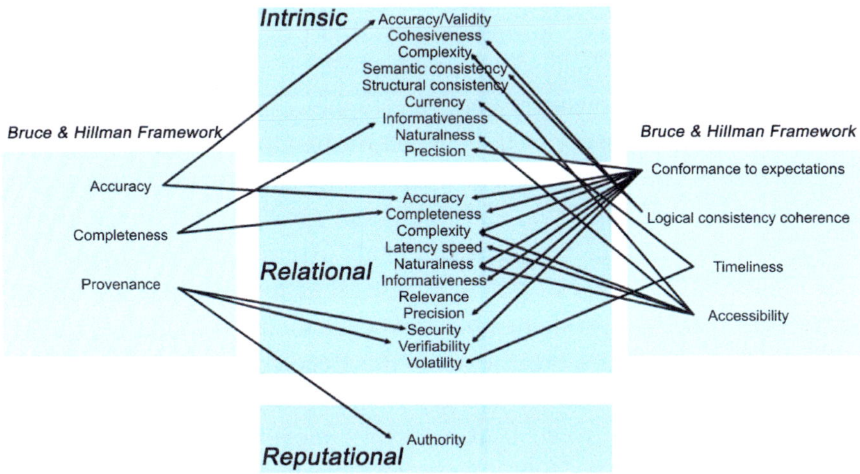

Figure 5.3. *Mapping between the Bruce & Hillman framework and the Stvilia framework.*

Source: Shreeves, Knutson, Stvilia, Palmer, Twidale, & Cole, (2010); Scientific figure on ResearchGate. Available from: https://www.researchgate.net/figure/Mapping-between-the-Bruce-Hillman-framework-and-the-Gasser-Stvilia-framework-Note_fig1_32954881.

In addition to the taxonomy, a set of 41 general metric functions, 30 of which are object- or collection-based and 11 of which are process-based, is proposed. The authors also provide a Java implementation of these functions.

Based on their analysis of the sources of such issues, the authors also propose grouping the information activities that are impacted by IQ issues:

- activities that rely on how accurately an entity or condition is represented by information.
- de-contextualization, or the use of information in contexts other than those for which it was created.

Stability-dependent activities are those that are dependent on how stable the information is, whereas provenance-dependent activities are those that are dependent on how reliable the provenance of the information is. A framework like this can be used to analyze a specific context and develop an appropriate IQ measurement model. System activities are analyzed to determine which system activities are likely to have quality issues and to select the appropriate IQ dimensions and metrics (Motta, 2019).

5.6.4. Other Quality Assessment Approaches

The frameworks presented in this section depart from the methodology of Bruce and Hillmann. Hughes' (2004) framework for assessing metadata quality, in particular, considers context. Hughes discusses the problem of evaluating metadata quality in the context of the Open Language Archives Community (OLAC). According to him, any measure of metadata quality "benefits from both contextual and referential assessment – metadata on a per record and collection basis is legitimately assessed against the baseline of the broader community of practice, as well as for compliance with any external standard" As a result, he proposes seven metrics (Archive Diversity, Metadata Quality Score, Core Elements Per Record, Core Element Usage, Code Usage, Code and Element Usage, "Star Rating") and an algorithm that assigns a score between 0 and 10 to a metadata record to indicate how closely it adheres to Dublin Core best practices and domain-specific controlled vocabularies.

Martin and Sumner (2009) present an alternative approach to the automatic characterization of resource quality in the context of educational digital libraries to aid in the identification of resources to use for learning objectives. The most foretelling quality indicators are prestigious sponsor, age-appropriate content, sponsor, identification of learning goals, presence of instructions, and organization of learning goals. These indicators are "Boolean," which means they can all be present or absent when assessing a specific resource. Furthermore, the authors propose a method for detecting the presence of such indicators that employs machine learning models (Quarati, 2021).

In conclusion, the use of critical resources for our information society is effectively influenced by metadata quality, a significant but difficult issue. Although no definitional agreement has yet been reached, it is widely acknowledged that metadata quality is a subjective, multidimensional, and context-dependent concept. When dealing with "big data" scenarios in which metadata (a) comes from numerous and heterogeneous sources, (b) is collected using various techniques, and (c) is expected to be used in contexts other than their original ones, all of the issues that define it in a given community of practice are amplified (Motta, 2019).

CHAPTER

6 Ontologies in System Theory

Contents

6.1. INTRODUCTION

Ontologies are a form of system theory that describe the structure and relationships of systems. They can be used to describe any system, including biological ones. In system theory, an ontology is a set of terms that describe how things work. These terms are typically used to describe relationships between entities in the system, their properties and characteristics, and connections between them. Ontologies are especially important in system theory because they have been shown to be useful for classification and understanding. Ontologies are helpful in explaining the behavior of systems, as well as predicting their behavior. In addition, they help us understand how certain concepts relate to each other. Ontologies do describe things like data, procedures, and relationships between things. They can be used to help people understand a system or process more clearly. Systems theorists use ontologies to make sure the information in their systems is accurate and can be accessed by anyone who needs it (Bunge, 2012) (Figure 6.1).

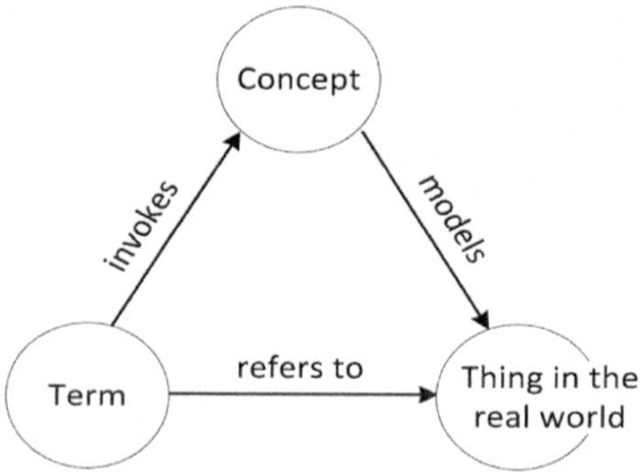

Figure 6.1. *A systems approach to building ontologies and concept maps.*

Source: Rousseau, Billingham, & Calvo-Amodio, (2018); http://dx.doi.org/10.3390/systems6030032.

Ontologies also represent a system's shared understanding of the world. For instance, when you look at a map, you're using ontologies provided by the geography professor in your university, who has spent years studying and thinking about where certain places are located on land. Ontologies can be used in many different ways to help people understand the world around them. They can be used for navigation purposes, for example, to help people find their way around in an unfamiliar area. They can also be used for scientific research purposes-for example, to help map out the relationship between different species or genetic structures of organisms. Ontologies can also be used as part of storytelling; for example, if a writer wants to share their own experience with readers who may not have been there themselves but would like to know more about what they experienced firsthand (Smith, 2012).

6.2. CONCEPTUAL FOUNDATIONS OF ONTOLOGIES IN SYSTEM THEORY

The conceptual foundations of ontologies in system theory are the tools that are used to create an ontology. The tools include:

- Theory of types
- Theory of sets
- Theory of relations
- Theory of functions

System theorists believe that every system must have an ontology-a set of terms and their relationships-and that these ontologies are the foundation for all other aspects of a system. System theory is based on the idea that systems are comprised of multiple levels, each with its own particular characteristics. In order to understand how these levels interact, it is necessary to create different kinds of models for each level. These models include definitions for each term in the ontology as well as rules governing how the terms relate to one another. In order for a system to function properly, it must have a correct structure and its parts must be interconnected in such a way that they produce an outcome that is beneficial to all members of the system. For example, if you wanted to build a car you would need to know what materials are needed (such as steel), how much material you need (how many cars), what kind of engine should be used (an internal combustion engine), when it was built (in 1973), where it will be used (on the road).

In order for an ontology to be useful, it must be able to describe all possible states that any given entity may be in. When studying human behavior patterns, for example, we would want to know what attributes might be associated with different states such as sleeping, working etc… In order for this information to be useful, it must also include all possible states that any given entity may take on during its lifetime. This includes things like going through puberty or changing jobs throughout life etc (Bunge, 2012).

6.2.1. Introducing the Theory of Types

In system theory, a type is a set of objects that share some common characteristics. Types are used to classify information and can be used to create additional information about the data by comparing it with existing data. Types are also known as classifications. Types are often used to represent different categories of objects or events for which the same general properties apply. Types in ontology systems are used to classify different concepts and concepts have different properties, attributes and relations with other concepts. There are several types of ontologies such as: basic ontologies, domain ontologies, domain specific ontologies (DSOs), integrated ontology (IO) etc. The theory of types is a means by which to create an ontology for a system. The first step in creating an ontology is to choose and label a type of system under study. Once this has been done, the next steps involve constructing and labeling other types according to their similarities and differences. This process is known as classification. The final step involves determining how each type can or cannot be broken down into smaller parts or subtypes (Smith, 2012) (Figure 6.2).

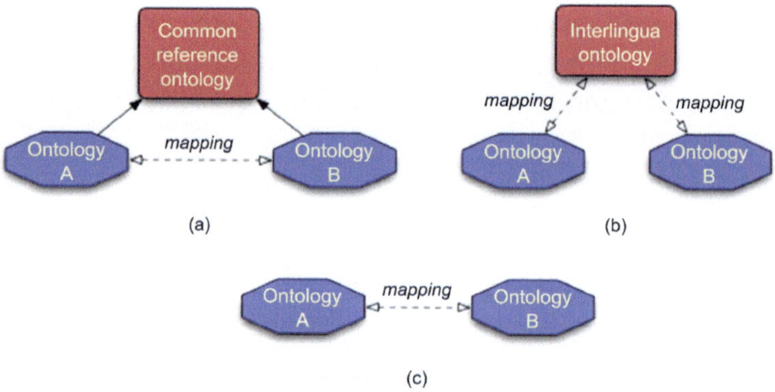

Figure 6.2. *Different types of ontology mappings.*

Source: Freitas, Stuckenschmidt, & Noy, (2005); Scientific figure on ResearchGate. Available from: https://www.researchgate.net/figure/Different-types-of-ontology-mappings_fig4_262447807.

Ontologies are important in system theory because they provide a conceptual foundation for the whole system. They give the user a way to understand what each part of the system is, what it does, and why it's important. Ontologies also help us determine which goals we should be pursuing as a whole. It attempts to explain how systems can be classified and classified properly. The theory of types has been used to classify systems into categories, and it is still used today. The theory of types originated in the 1960s with the work of Charles S. Peirce (1839–1914), who was a philosopher, logician, mathematician, and scientist who studied the relationship between ideas and reality. He coined the term "ontology" as a combination of "onto" (meaning: on) and "logy" (meaning: study or knowledge). This is because ontology means "study of being," which is what we call philosophy or theology today. Peirce proposed that every concept has an associated type or kind (e.g., redness, sweetness), which a general category that describes objects is falling under that concept. For example, redness can be described by its color (red), shape (round), size (small), etc., but not by its taste or smell—which would be characteristics associated with different kinds within that type instead (Smith, 2012).

6.2.2. Introducing the Theory of Sets

The theory of sets is a foundational concept in system theory. It is the basis for other concepts, such as the building blocks of systems and the relationships between sets. The theory of sets is a foundational concept in system theory. It is the basis for other concepts, such as the building blocks of systems and the relationships between sets.

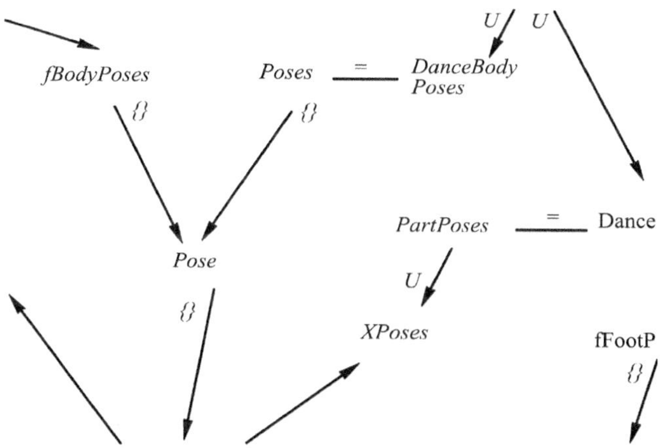

Figure 6.3. *Sample fragment of graph of set-theory relations for the General Terms module of the dance ontology.*

Source: Kleshchev, & Shalfeeva, (2008); Scientific figure on ResearchGate. Available from: https://www.researchgate.net/figure/The-fragment-of-graph-of-set-theory-relations-for-the-General-Terms-module-of-the-dance_fig3_226917092.

Set theory was first developed by Georg Cantor, who introduced it to explain set-theoretical paradoxes that had arisen in mathematics at the time; it provides a foundation for many other branches of mathematics and has been used extensively to model natural phenomena as well as computer science applications (Bunge, 2012) (Figure 6.3).

In system theory, ontologies are concerned with describing the structure of an object or system. Ontologies are often used to describe complex systems like social networks or biological organisms, which have multiple parts that are interconnected. For example, one part might be a person who lives in New York City, another part might be their favorite restaurant in the city, and yet another part might be the type of coffee they like to drink. Ontology describes how these different parts relate to each other and work together to form a complete entity. It's important because ontologies can help us understand how different parts fit together into larger wholes—and this is especially true when it comes to understanding an ecosystem like a human body or an ecosystem like the Earth's atmosphere.

The theory of sets is one of the most important concepts in ontology. It describes the way a system can be represented and conceptualized, and it allows for the division of information into discrete categories. The theory of sets explains how we can use terms like "red" or "dog" to refer to a given thing, and it also explains that these terms can be used to describe different things at different times-for example, if someone says "this is red," they might mean that it has a certain color or that it's made up of certain components. A system's ontology refers to all the ways in which individuals within that system may be described (and therefore referred to). For example, if we were describing animals, we might describe their behavior with terms like "sluggish," "aggressive," or "scared." These terms would then be used by another individual within our system when describing that animal's behavior (Smith, 2012).

6.2.3. Introducing the Theory of Relations

Typically, system theory aims at understanding the relationship between the components of a system. A system has a number of interdependent parts that work together to produce some effect. These parts can be human, animal, machine or any other type of object. In order to understand how these parts work together, we must first look at each of their individual characteristics and then see how these characteristics together create something new that is greater than the sum of its parts. This is where ontologies come into play; they are intentional systems with defined sets of rules that govern the relationships between things. Ontologies are used to categorize information and make it easy to find relevant information based on specific criteria such as classification or tags applied to them by users within an application program interface (API).

This is done using the concept of ontology, which is defined as "the study of being, or reality." The central concept in relation theory is ontology, which means "the study of being or reality." Ontology can be thought of as the study of what things are; it's the study of what exists. It's also the study of how things exist, and it involves looking at relationships between things. Ontology is a big part of system theory because it's an important part of understanding how systems relate to one another. If you want to understand how a system works, you have to understand not just what it does but how it does it—and that has everything to do with its relationship to other systems. The theory of relations is also based on the idea that any two concepts can be related to each other through a series of relations. These relations can be defined as either positive or negative (Bunge, 2012).

A positive relation between two concepts would mean that one concept is dependent on another for its existence. For example, if I am studying for a test and I have to write an essay about what I've learned about chemistry, then this essay must be written before I start studying for the test because without it, I wouldn't know what to study. A negative relation means that one concept is independent from another—that they can exist independently of each other. This might be something like when someone drives home from work at night without turning on their headlights because they're not using their car right now (the headlights are not needed). In both these examples, there is still some kind of relationship between them but it isn't necessarily a strong one: they aren't mutually dependent on each other like they could be if they were related by some stronger type of relationship such as causation or mutual exclusion.

6.2.4. Introducing the Theory of Functions

System theory also uses the concept of functions, which can be defined as relationships between different variables. A function, which has many possible values, describes how one variable changes when another variable changes. For example, if we want to know what happens to temperature when volume increases, we would use a function to find out the value for temperature at various volume levels. We can either calculate the average temperature for each level or find out how many times larger or smaller the volume level is than another level, and then use those numbers as keys into our database to look up what our new key values were at each level. The theory of functions explains that an ontology is a set of objects and their properties. These properties are ordered by categories and are used to classify different types of objects (Smith, 2012) (Figure 6.4).

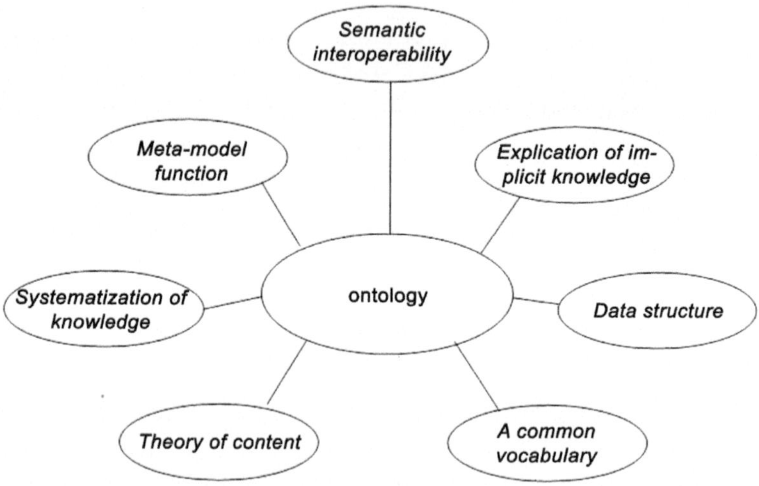

Figure 6.4. *Roles of ontologies.*

Source: Pundt, (2023); Scientific figure on ResearchGate. Available from: https://www.researchgate.net/figure/Roles-of-ontologies_fig1_228724410.

In this way, an ontology can be thought of as a kind of classification system for concepts. The main difference between an ontology and other classification systems is that it uses terms rather than numbers or colors to classify things. An example of an ontology could be the word "tree" or "bird." It could also be "fruit," "plants," or even "animals." Ontologies are useful because they allow us to organize our knowledge about the world around us in such a way that we can better understand it and make sense of it.

6.3. TYPES OF ONTOLOGIES USED IN SYSTEM THEORY

The goal of system theory is to study the structure and processes of an entire field or community of inquiry, including its history and current state. System theorists typically divide ontologies into two main categories: those that describe objects (e.g., classes) and those that describe relationships between objects (e.g., properties). An ontology can also include both types of concepts at once; for example, a class may have both a name and a description in the same ontology. Systems can be either physical or non-physical. Physical systems are those that have parts that interact with each other, while non-physical systems are those that do not have parts and therefore cannot interact with each other (Smith, 2012).

Systems can be classified into two types based on the way they relate to their components: monolithic and modular. A monolithic system has a single component that is connected to all other components; a modular system has multiple components that are connected only to each other. Ontologies provide an organized structure for storing knowledge about specific topics, such as information technology or biology, which makes it easier for researchers and designers working on these topics to navigate large amounts of data without getting lost in it. Here are some common types of ontologies in system theory;

6.3.1. Domain Ontologies

Domain ontologies are the most common type of ontology used in system theory. They capture the knowledge and concepts specific to a particular domain or subject area within system theory. Domain ontologies are used to describe and explain complex concepts that cannot be represented by a single term, e.g., the domain of "organizational structure." A domain ontology may be created for each system theory, but it may also be shared across multiple systems. Domain ontologies are used to define, describe and communicate the domain itself. They provide the foundation for all other ontologies within the domain. This type generally depends on dependencies i.e. (Bunge, 2012).

This type of relation between two ontologies is defined by their shared definitions and axioms. There are two types of relations between an ontology A and B: shared definitions and shared axioms allow two ontologies A and B to refer to each other using the same names but with different meanings. A shared definition is not necessary for this relationship because it only defines shared axioms that allow one ontology A referring to another one B without having any differences regarding their meanings. They describe the classes of entities that exist in specific domains; they are used to provide a conceptual foundation for representing knowledge about these domains. For example, if you want to represent academic information about science, you would use an academic domain ontology instead of just using your own domain knowledge about science itself.

6.3.2. Application Ontologies

The ontologies used in system theory are application ontologies. These ontologies are designed to map the relationships between concepts and objects, and they are often used to create systems that can be applied to real-world problems. An application ontology is different from a domain-specific language, which is a language used for describing specific problems or situations. An application ontology describes all components within an application or service, including their inter-relationships. An application ontology may be used to describe the structure and behavior of software applications, databases or other computer programs. For example, an application might have an ontology of people who have purchased a particular product, which is stored in a knowledge representation ontology. In this case, the application is using the data stored in the knowledge representation ontology to make decisions about users who have purchased certain products.

Knowledge representation ontologies are used to describe how things are related to each other within a particular domain. For example, one could use knowledge representation ontologies to describe how different types of people relate to each other (e.g., employees vs. contractors), or how different pieces of equipment relate to each other (e.g., computer hardware vs. software). if you needed to develop an application for your phone that would help people navigate through their day-to-day lives, you would use a high-level ontology (such as OBO Foundry's OBO-WISDOM) and the specific knowledge you have about how people use smartphones in order to build an application that is intuitive and easily understood by users (Smith, 2012).

6.3.3. Process Ontologies

These are used to describe the operations of a system. For example, a process ontology might be used to describe a system that processes data and produces results in an efficient way. A process ontology typically consists of three major components: input, process, and output. Inputs are any entities that enter into the system; outputs are anything produced by the system; and processes are the interactions between inputs and outputs. Inputs can be either physical or abstract. Physical inputs include things like energy sources and materials (e.g., wood), while abstract inputs include information (e.g., measurements). Processes can also be either physical or abstract. Physical processes include things like chemical interactions, while abstract processes include biological ones such as cell division or photosynthesis. The output of a given process will determine what kind of entity comes out at the end of it—either a physical entity such as wood or an abstract one like data about wood (Bunge, 2012) (Figure 6.5).

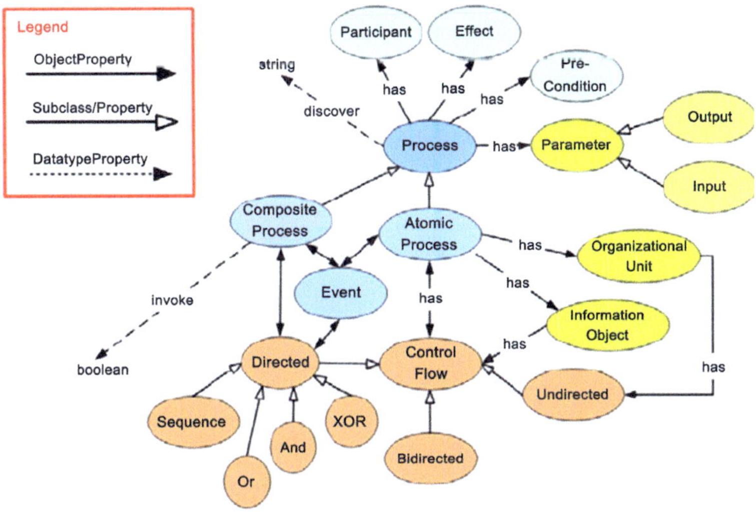

Figure 6.5. *The composition of the top-level process ontology.*

Source: Mondorf, & Herborn, (2008); Scientific figure on ResearchGate. Available from: https://www.researchgate.net/figure/The-composition-of-the-top-level-process-ontology_fig5_221508638.

6.3.4. Taxonomic Ontologies

Taxonomic ontologies are one type of ontology that is commonly used in system theory. Taxonomic ontologies organize knowledge into a hierarchical structure based on class-subclass relationships. At the top of the hierarchy is a root node, which represents the most general concept in the ontology. Below the root node are one or more child nodes, which represent more specific concepts that are subclasses of the root node. Each child node can have its own child nodes, creating a branching structure that represents the relationships between different concepts. Taxonomic ontologies are useful in system theory because they provide a way to organize and classify knowledge about a particular domain. By using a hierarchical structure, taxonomic ontologies make it easy to navigate and search for information within the ontology. For example, if we have an ontology of different types of animals, we can use the hierarchy to quickly find all the different types of birds, mammals, or reptiles. Taxonomic ontologies can also be used to infer new knowledge based on the relationships between different concepts. For example, if we know that all birds have feathers and can fly, we can infer that any new bird species we discover will also have these characteristics. This can be useful in system theory for predicting the behavior or characteristics of new systems based on their classification within the ontology (Smith, 2012).

One limitation of taxonomic ontologies is that they can be rigid and inflexible. Once a hierarchy has been established, it can be difficult to modify or expand the ontology without disrupting the existing structure. This can be a problem in dynamic or rapidly changing domains where new concepts or relationships may need to be added to the ontology frequently. Another limitation of taxonomic ontologies is that they may not capture all the nuances or complexities of a particular domain. For example, if we have an ontology of different types of cars, we may classify them based on their size, shape, or engine type. However, this may not capture other important characteristics of cars, such as their safety features or environmental impact.

Taxonomic ontologies are an important type of ontology used in system theory. They provide a way to organize and classify knowledge about a particular domain based on class-subclass relationships. Taxonomic ontologies are useful for navigating and searching for information within the ontology, as well as for inferring new knowledge based on the relationships between different concepts. However, taxonomic ontologies may be inflexible and may not capture all the nuances or complexities of a particular domain (Bunge, 2012).

6.3.5. Spatial Ontologies

Spatial ontologies are another type of ontology used in system theory. They are used to represent and organize knowledge about the spatial relationships between objects in a particular domain. Spatial ontologies can be used to represent both physical and abstract spaces, and can be used to model a wide range of systems, from geographic information systems to social networks. Spatial ontologies organize knowledge into a structure that represents the relationships between different spatial entities. The entities can be organized into a hierarchy based on their spatial relationships, such as containment, adjacency, or proximity. For example, if we have an ontology of a city, we can organize the entities based on their spatial relationships, such as neighborhoods, streets, buildings, and landmarks.

Spatial ontologies are useful in system theory because they provide a way to represent and reason about the spatial relationships between objects in a particular domain. By using a structured representation, spatial ontologies make it easy to navigate and search for information within the ontology. For example, if we have an ontology of a city, we can use the hierarchy to quickly find all the buildings in a particular neighborhood or all the landmarks within a certain distance of a particular location. Spatial ontologies can also be used to infer new knowledge based on the spatial relationships between different entities.

For example, if we know that two buildings are adjacent to each other, we can infer that people or goods can easily move between them. This can be useful in system theory for predicting the behavior or interactions between different objects based on their spatial relationships.

One limitation of spatial ontologies is that they can be complex and difficult to construct. Spatial ontologies may require a large amount of domain-specific knowledge and may need to be customized for different applications or domains. This can be a challenge in domains where the spatial relationships between objects are not well understood or are constantly changing. Secondly, they may not capture all the nuances or complexities of a particular domain. For example, if we have an ontology of a city, we may classify buildings based on their use, such as residential, commercial, or industrial. However, this may not capture other important characteristics of buildings, such as their age, architectural style, or historical significance. Spatial ontologies are useful for navigating and searching for information within the ontology, as well as for inferring new knowledge based on the spatial relationships between different entities. However, spatial ontologies may be complex and difficult to construct, and may not capture all the nuances or complexities of a particular domain (Smith, 2012).

6.4. ONTOLOGY DEVELOPMENT PROCESS FOR SYSTEM THEORY

Ontology development is a complex process that involves the creation of a structured representation of knowledge about a particular domain. In system theory, ontologies are used to represent and organize knowledge about the components, relationships, and behavior of systems. The ontology development process for system theory involves several stages, including conceptualization, specification, implementation, and evaluation.

- **Conceptualization:** The first stage of ontology development is conceptualization, which involves identifying the scope and purpose of the ontology and defining the concepts and relationships that will be represented. This stage involves a thorough analysis of the domain and the identification of the key concepts and relationships that are relevant to the system being modeled. The conceptualization stage may involve the use of various tools, such as mind maps, concept maps, or domain analysis techniques, to help organize and structure the knowledge about the domain.
- **Specification:** The second stage of ontology development is specification, which involves defining the formal structure of the ontology and specifying the relationships between the concepts. This stage involves selecting an appropriate ontology language, such as OWL or RDF, and defining the classes, properties, and axioms that will be used to represent the concepts and relationships in the ontology. The specification stage may involve the use of various tools, such as ontology editors or protégé, to help define and formalize the ontology.
- **Implementation:** The third stage of ontology development is implementation, which involves creating the ontology in the chosen ontology language and populating it with data. This stage involves translating the formal specification of the ontology into a machine-readable format, such as an OWL file or a SPARQL endpoint, and importing data from various sources into the ontology. The implementation stage may involve the use of various tools, such as reasoners, query engines, or data integration tools, to help populate and maintain the ontology (Bunge, 2012).
- **Evaluation:** The final stage of ontology development is evaluation, which involves assessing the quality and usefulness of the ontology. This stage involves evaluating the ontology against various criteria, such as completeness, consistency, coherence, and usability, and identifying any issues or limitations that need to be addressed. The evaluation stage may involve the use of various tools, such as ontology metrics, quality assurance frameworks (QAFs), or user feedback surveys, to help assess the ontology.

This process involves a systematic and iterative approach to representing and organizing knowledge about a particular domain. The process involves several stages, including conceptualization, specification, implementation, and evaluation, and may involve the use of various tools and techniques to help organize, formalize, and evaluate the ontology. The ontology development process is an ongoing process, and the ontology may need to be revised and updated as new knowledge and data become available (Smith, 2012).

6.5. APPLICATION OF ONTOLOGIES IN SYSTEM MODELING AND SIMULATION

Ontologies are a powerful tool for modeling and simulating complex systems. An ontology is a formal specification of a shared conceptualization, which can be used to represent knowledge about a particular domain. In the context of system modeling and simulation, an ontology can be used to represent the structure and behavior of a system, as well as the relationships between its components. There are several key benefits to using ontologies in system modeling and simulation. First, ontologies provide a standardized way of representing knowledge about a system. This can help to ensure that all stakeholders involved in the modeling and simulation process are using the same terminology and concepts, which can reduce confusion and improve communication (Figure 6.6).

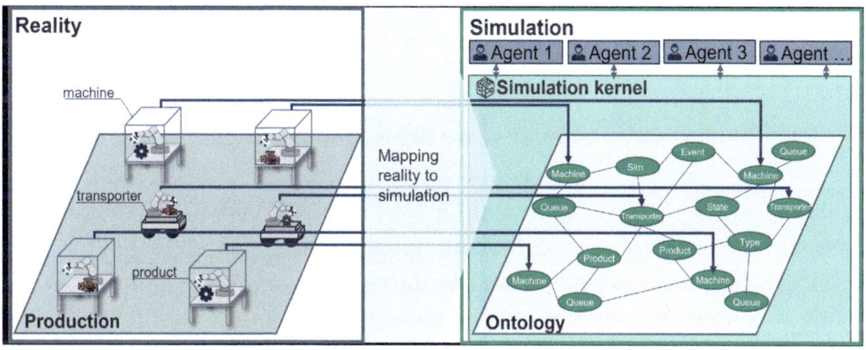

Figure 6.6. *Ontology-based production simulation.*

Source: May, Kiefer, Kuhnle, & Lanza, (2022); http://dx.doi.org/10.3390/app12031608.

Second, ontologies can help to capture the complexity of a system in a structured way. By representing the system as a set of interrelated concepts, an ontology can provide a comprehensive view of the system that can be used to guide the modeling and simulation process. Third, ontologies can help to facilitate reuse of models and simulations. By representing systems in a standardized way, ontologies can make it easier to reuse existing models and simulations across different projects and domains. There are several different approaches to using ontologies in system modeling and simulation. One approach is to use ontologies to define the structure and behavior of the system itself. For example, an ontology might be used to represent the components of a manufacturing system, their relationships, and their interactions.

Another approach is to use ontologies to represent the knowledge and expertise of domain experts. For example, an ontology might be used to represent the knowledge of a team of engineers who are designing a new system. This ontology could capture information about the design process, the requirements of the system, and the constraints that must be considered. A third approach is to use ontologies to represent the simulation itself. For example, an ontology might be used to represent the parameters and inputs of a simulation, as well as the outputs and results that are generated. This ontology could be used to guide the simulation process and to ensure that the results are accurate and reliable (Bunge, 2012).

6.5.1. Ontology-Driven Decision Support in System Simulation

Ontology-driven decision support in system simulation refers to the use of ontologies to guide the decision-making process during system simulation. An ontology is a formal specification of a shared conceptualization, which can be used to represent knowledge about a particular domain. In the context of system simulation, an ontology can be used to represent the structure and behavior of a system, as well as the relationships between its components. The use of ontologies in decision support can help to ensure that decisions are based on a comprehensive understanding of the system being simulated. By representing the system as a set of interrelated concepts, an ontology can provide a comprehensive view of the system that can be used to guide the decision-making process.

There are several key benefits to using ontology-driven decision support in system simulation. First, ontologies can help to ensure that decisions are based on accurate and reliable information. By representing the system in a standardized way, ontologies can help to ensure that all stakeholders involved in the decision-making process are using the same terminology and concepts, which can reduce confusion and improve communication. Second, ontologies can help to facilitate the integration of different types of data and knowledge. By representing the system and its components in a structured way, ontologies can help to integrate data from different sources and to ensure that all relevant information is considered in the decision-making process. Third, ontologies can help to improve the transparency and traceability of the decision-making process. By representing the decision-making process in a structured way, ontologies can help to ensure that decisions are based on clear and well-defined criteria, and that the rationale behind each decision is documented and can be traced back to the underlying data and knowledge (Smith, 2012).

6.6. ONTOLOGY-BASED KNOWLEDGE REPRESENTATION IN SYSTEM THEORY

Ontology-based knowledge representation in system theory refers to the use of ontologies to represent knowledge about complex systems. The use of ontologies in knowledge representation can help to ensure that knowledge is represented in a standardized and structured way. By representing the system as a set of interrelated concepts, an ontology can provide a comprehensive view of the system that can be used to guide the analysis and design of the system.

There are several key benefits to using ontology-based knowledge representation in system theory. First, ontologies can help to ensure that knowledge is represented accurately and consistently. By providing a standardized way of representing knowledge, ontologies can help to ensure that all stakeholders involved in the analysis and design process are using the same terminology and concepts, which can reduce confusion and improve communication. Second, ontologies can help to facilitate the integration of different types of knowledge. By representing the system and its components in a structured way, ontologies can help to integrate knowledge from different sources and to ensure that all relevant information is considered in the analysis and design process (Smith, 2012).

Third, ontologies can help to improve the traceability and transparency of the analysis and design process. By representing the analysis and design process in a structured way, ontologies can help to ensure that the rationale behind each decision is documented and can be traced back to the underlying data and knowledge. By providing a standardized way of representing knowledge about complex systems, ontologies can help to ensure that all stakeholders have a comprehensive understanding of the system being analyzed and designed, and that all relevant information is considered in the process (Bunge, 2012).

6.6.1. Semantic Interoperability in System Theory

Semantic interoperability in system theory refers to the ability of different systems to exchange and interpret data and information in a way that is meaningful and understandable to all parties involved. It involves the use of common standards and shared understanding of the meaning of data and information. In system theory, semantic interoperability is crucial for effective communication and collaboration between different systems. It enables the exchange of information and knowledge between systems, which is essential for decision-making and problem-solving. Semantic interoperability ensures that the data and information exchanged between systems are not only syntactically correct but also semantically meaningful.

One of the key challenges of achieving semantic interoperability is the heterogeneity of data and information sources. Different systems may use different data models, formats, and terminologies, which can lead to inconsistencies and misunderstandings. To overcome this challenge, system theorists use ontologies to represent the shared conceptualization of a particular domain. By using ontologies, system theorists can ensure that all stakeholders involved in the communication and collaboration process are using the same terminology and concepts, which can reduce confusion and improve communication.

Another challenge of achieving semantic interoperability is the need for standardization. To ensure that different systems can exchange and interpret data and information, it is essential to establish common standards for data models, formats, and terminologies. This requires collaboration and coordination between different stakeholders, including system designers, developers, and users. Semantic interoperability has several benefits in system theory. First, it enables effective communication and collaboration between different systems, which is essential for decision-making and problem-solving. Second, it promotes the reuse of data and information, which can reduce the cost and time required for system development. Third, it improves the accuracy and reliability of information, which is essential for effective decision-making.

6.6.2. Ontology-Based Knowledge Acquisition in System Theory

Ontology-based knowledge acquisition in system theory refers to the process of using ontologies to acquire and represent knowledge about complex systems. The process of ontology-based knowledge acquisition involves several steps. First, the domain of interest is identified, and the scope of the ontology is defined. This involves identifying the key concepts and relationships that are relevant to the domain and determining the level of detail required to represent the domain adequately (Smith, 2012).

Second, the ontology is developed by defining the concepts, relationships, and axioms that are required to represent the domain accurately. This involves using formal languages such as OWL or RDF to specify the ontology and ensuring that it is consistent and coherent. Third, the ontology is populated with knowledge by acquiring information from various sources, such as experts, databases, and documents. This involves mapping the knowledge to the ontology by identifying the relevant concepts and relationships and specifying their properties. Fourth, the ontology is refined and validated by testing it against real-world scenarios and ensuring that it accurately represents the domain of interest. This involves checking the ontology for completeness, consistency, and coherence and making any necessary adjustments.

Ontology-based knowledge acquisition has several benefits in system theory. First, it enables the capture and representation of complex knowledge in a structured and standardized way. This ensures that the knowledge is consistent and can be easily shared and reused. Second, it facilitates the integration of knowledge from different sources and domains. By providing a shared conceptualization of the domain, ontologies can help to integrate knowledge from different sources and to ensure that all relevant information is considered. Third, it supports the development of intelligent systems that can reason and make decisions based on the knowledge represented in the ontology. By providing a formal and structured representation of knowledge, ontologies can be used to develop intelligent systems that can reason and make decisions based on the knowledge represented in the ontology (Bunge, 2012).

6.7. ONTOLOGY MAPPING AND INTEGRATION IN SYSTEM THEORY

Ontology mapping and integration in system theory is the process of aligning and integrating different ontologies within a system. Ontologies are structured knowledge representations that define the concepts and relationships within a specific domain. System theory, on the other hand, is a multidisciplinary approach that seeks to understand the behavior of complex systems. Ontology mapping and integration is essential in system theory because it enables the integration of knowledge from different domains and disciplines. This integration is crucial in understanding complex systems, which often involve multiple domains and disciplines. For example, understanding the behavior of an ecosystem requires knowledge from biology, ecology, and environmental science. Ontology mapping and integration involves several steps, including ontology alignment, ontology mediation, and ontology merging. Ontology alignment involves identifying the common concepts and relationships between different ontologies. Ontology mediation involves resolving any inconsistencies or conflicts between the ontologies. Ontology merging involves combining the ontologies into a single, IO (Smith, 2012) (Figure 6.7).

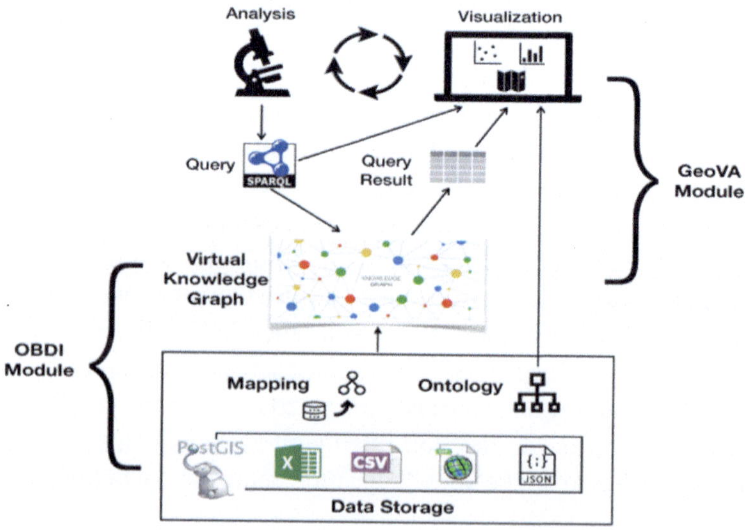

Figure 6.7. *A framework uniting ontology-based geodata integration and geovisual analytics.*

Source: Ding, Xiao, Calvanese, & Meng, (2020); Retrieved from http://dx.doi.org/10.3390/ijgi9080474.

One of the challenges of ontology mapping and integration is the heterogeneity of ontologies. Ontologies may use different vocabularies, taxonomies, and semantics, making it difficult to align and integrate them. However, several approaches have been proposed to overcome this challenge, including ontology matching, ontology transformation, and ontology learning. Ontology matching involves identifying the correspondences between the concepts and relationships in different ontologies. This approach uses various techniques, including lexical, structural, and semantic matching. Lexical matching involves comparing the labels or names of the concepts in the ontologies. Structural matching involves comparing the structure or hierarchy of the ontologies. Semantic matching involves comparing the meaning or semantics of the concepts in the ontologies (Smith, 2012).

Ontology transformation involves converting the concepts and relationships in one ontology to match those in another ontology. This approach is useful when the ontologies have different structures or semantics. Ontology learning involves automatically extracting the concepts and relationships from unstructured data sources, such as text documents or databases. Ontology mapping and integration have several applications in system theory, including knowledge management, decision support, and data integration. In knowledge management, ontology mapping and integration enable the sharing and reuse of knowledge across different domains and disciplines. In decision support, ontology mapping and integration provide a unified view of the data and knowledge needed to make informed decisions. In data integration, ontology mapping and integration enable the integration of data from different sources and formats (Bunge, 2012).

6.7.1. Ontology Alignment

Ontology alignment is a critical step in ontology mapping and integration in system theory. It involves identifying the common concepts and relationships between different ontologies. Ontology alignment is essential because ontologies from different domains and disciplines may use different vocabularies, taxonomies, and semantics. Therefore, ontology alignment aims to identify the correspondences between the concepts and relationships in different ontologies to enable their integration. Ontology alignment can be achieved using various techniques, including lexical, structural, and semantic matching.

- Lexical matching is a simple approach that involves comparing the labels or names of the concepts in the ontologies. This approach is useful when the ontologies have similar vocabularies or taxonomies. However, lexical matching may not be sufficient when the ontologies have different semantics or when the labels are ambiguous.

- Structural matching involves comparing the structure or hierarchy of the ontologies. This approach is useful when the ontologies have similar structures or when the relationships between the concepts are important. Structural matching can be achieved using various techniques, including graph-based algorithms, tree-based algorithms, and logic-based algorithms.
- Semantic matching involves comparing the meaning or semantics of the concepts in the ontologies. This approach is useful when the ontologies have different vocabularies or taxonomies. Semantic matching can be achieved using various techniques, including knowledge-based methods, machine learning methods, and hybrid methods (Smith, 2012).

6.7.2. Ontology Mediation

Ontology mediation is another critical step in ontology mapping and integration in system theory. It involves resolving any inconsistencies or conflicts between the ontologies being integrated. Ontology mediation is necessary because ontologies from different domains and disciplines may have overlapping or conflicting concepts and relationships. Therefore, ontology mediation aims to resolve these inconsistencies or conflicts to enable the integration of the ontologies. Ontology mediation can be achieved using various techniques, including ontology merging, ontology transformation, and ontology mapping.

6.7.3. Ontology Merging

Ontology merging is a key technique in ontology mapping and integration in system theory. It involves combining two or more ontologies into a single, IO. Ontology merging is necessary when ontologies from different domains or disciplines need to be integrated to enable knowledge sharing or interoperability. Ontology merging can be achieved using various techniques, including manual merging, semi-automatic merging, and automatic merging (Bunge, 2012).

CHAPTER

7 Technologies and Systems for Managing Metadata

Contents

7.1. INTRODUCTION

Data has developed into the cornerstone of corporations, governments, and organizations across a wide range of industries in the continuously changing digital landscape. It could be challenging to organize, search, and fully utilize the data given its size and complexity. Metadata management becomes essential in this situation. Metadata, or "data about data," makes it simpler to manage and analyze data in an efficient manner by supplying context, descriptions, and relationships. We'll examine the systems and technologies that have developed to aid in the efficient administration of metadata in this article (Riley, 2017) (Figure 7.1).

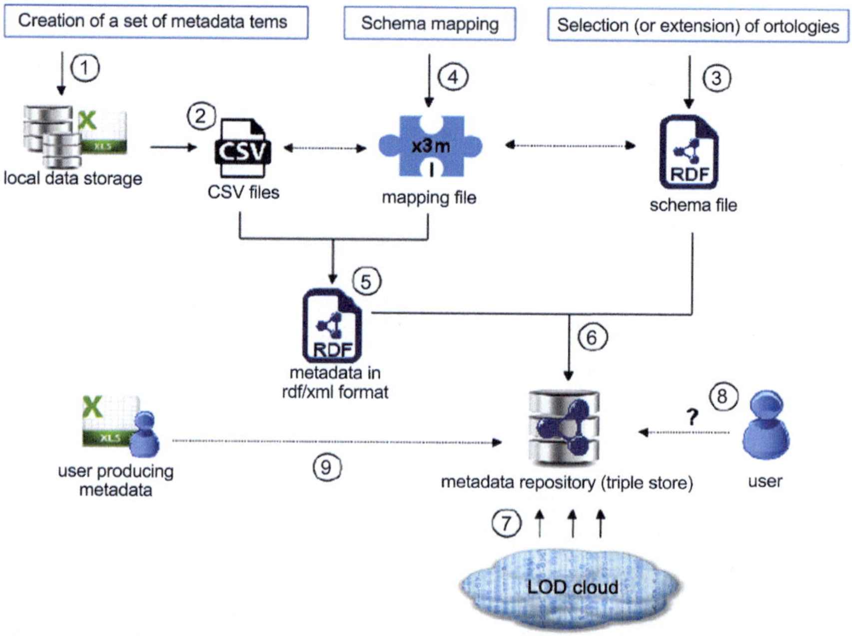

Figure 7.1. *Schema of the steps involved in creating the metadata management system.*

Source: Minadakis, Faulwetter, Doerr, Arvanitidis, & Keklikoglou, (2015). Scientific figure on ResearchGate. Available from: https://www.researchgate.net/figure/Schema-of-the-steps-involved-in-creating-the-metadata-management-system-Numbers-in_fig2_276418246.

Metadata can be thought of as the basic building blocks of data. Users may successfully analyze and interpret data thanks to the crucial information it provides on the traits and relationships of datasets. Data types, formats, definitions, and the place of origin of the data are all included in metadata. Metadata serves as an essential building component for data governance, data integration, and data analytics by classifying and organizing data.

It is impossible to emphasize the significance of metadata management. Organizations encounter a variety of difficulties when attempting to unlock the full potential of their data assets without adequate management. Data silos, inconsistent data definitions, data duplication, and trouble locating pertinent data are some of these issues. These issues are addressed by metadata management, which provides a methodical method of managing and organizing data assets.

Organizations use a variety of technologies and systems that were created specially to handle the challenges of managing metadata to do so efficiently. These technologies include a wide range of topics, including metadata extraction, repositories, standards, visualization, and management systems. Each of these technologies is essential for enabling businesses to effectively manage their metadata and unleash the potential of their data.

To store, arrange, and manage metadata assets, centralized databases known as metadata repositories are used. They give a thorough overview of an organization's metadata, making it simple to access and manage. Relational databases, graph databases, and distributed systems like Hadoop and Apache Cassandra are a few examples of different kinds of metadata repositories. Organizations can efficiently store and retrieve metadata thanks to these repositories, which form the foundation of metadata management (Froeschl, 2013).

Technologies for harvesting and extracting information allow for the automatic extraction of metadata from diverse data sources. Organizations can extract metadata from unstructured data sources including documents, photos, and videos using technologies like optical character recognition (OCR), machine learning, and natural language processing (NLP). By automating the extraction procedure, metadata is preserved as accurate and current while saving time and effort (Riley, 2017)

For the seamless integration and sharing of metadata across various systems and sources, metadata standards and interoperability are essential. A uniform language for metadata is provided by standards like Dublin Core, Metadata Object Description Schema (MODS), and the Resource Description Framework (RDF), promoting interoperability and consistency. Regardless of the system or application used, these standards guarantee that metadata stays consistent and simple to comprehend.

Users can get insights into the relationships and structure of metadata using visualization and exploration tools for metadata. Organizations may visualize complicated metadata landscapes using tools like network graphs, tree maps, and tag clouds, which makes it simpler to comprehend and traverse the metadata ecosystem. By allowing users to spot patterns, linkages, and anomalies within their metadata assets, visualization tools play a crucial part in metadata management.

Metadata management systems offer comprehensive solutions for enterprises to oversee and maintain metadata integrity in addition to these technologies. As a single source of truth for metadata, master data management (MDM) solutions put a strong emphasis on ensuring accurate and consistent metadata throughout an organization's data sources. On the other side, data catalogs serve as centralized repositories that let users find, comprehend, and access metadata assets. Users can more easily take advantage of metadata by using these catalogs, which offer search functionality, data lineage information, and data quality details (Froeschl, 2013).

Overall, an organization's data management strategy must include key elements for managing metadata, such as technology and systems. They make it possible for effective data governance, precise data analysis, and quick data integration. In today's data-driven world, organizations may improve decision-making, operational efficiency, and competitive advantage by utilizing these technologies to unleash the power of metadata and fully utilize their data assets.

7.2. UNDERSTANDING METADATA MANAGEMENT

Metadata is crucial to data management because it gives data context, structure, and meaning. Metadata, also known as "data about data," contains crucial details on the traits and relationships of datasets. It serves as a link between uninterpreted raw data and its interpretation, empowering people to find, comprehend, and efficiently utilize data. It is essential to examine metadata's primary components and its function throughout the data lifecycle in order to fully appreciate its importance in data management (Riley, 2017).

7.2.1. Components of Metadata

Numerous properties that define and characterize data are included in metadata. These qualities can be divided into many sorts, such as:

- **Descriptive metadata:** This kind of metadata offers details about the nature, setting, and qualities of data. It contains information like titles, descriptions, keywords, and subject headings. Users can comprehend the content of the data and its applicability to certain use cases thanks to descriptive metadata.
- **Structural Metadata:** Structural metadata specifies how a dataset's data items are arranged in a hierarchy, and organized. It outlines the connections between various elements, including tables, columns, and records. For database management systems, structural information is especially crucial since it facilitates effective data retrieval and manipulation.
- **Administrative Metadata:** The technical and operational facets of data management are covered by administrative metadata. It contains details like the data source, the date of creation, the owner, the rights of access, and data quality indicators. Such metadata aids in data governance, compliance, and data integrity assurance (Froeschl, 2013).
- **Technological Metadata:** Technical metadata is concerned with the details and qualities of data's technological nature. It contains information on data formats, data kinds, encoding techniques, and storage needs. Technical information is essential for data integration since it guarantees the efficient processing and blending of data from various sources.

7.2.2. Role of Metadata in Data Management

As a crucial building block for efficient data management throughout its lifecycle, metadata. Here are a few crucial functions that metadata performs:

- **Data Discovery and Identification:** Users can find and recognize pertinent data assets inside huge repositories thanks to metadata. The use of descriptive metadata, such as titles, keywords, and tags, facilitates search and retrieval and enables users to find the precise information they require for analysis or decision-making.
- **Understanding and Interpreting Data:** Metadata gives data vital context and meaning. While structural metadata supports in understanding the relationships and arrangement of data elements, descriptive metadata helps consumers grasp the substance and purpose of data. For correct data interpretation and efficient data usage, this understanding is crucial.

- **Data Integration and Interoperability:** The integration of data from diverse sources is made easier by metadata standards and interoperability. Organizations may make sure that data can be easily merged, shared, and exchanged between various systems and platforms by adhering to standard metadata models and formats. Interoperability and easy data integration are encouraged by this.
- Administrative metadata is essential to data governance processes, according to data governance and compliance. Establishing data ownership, access restrictions, data lineage, and data quality standards is made easier by this. Organizations can enforce data policies, adhere to legal obligations, and guarantee data privacy and security by using metadata.
- **Data Lineage and Provenance:** Metadata keeps track of the origin, modifications, and history of data, recording its lineage and provenance. This knowledge is essential for determining the trustworthiness of the data, evaluating its dependability, and comprehending the alterations made to the data during its existence.
- **Decision-making and Data Analytics:** Metadata offers the required information for efficient decision-making and data analysis. It enables analysts to comprehend the shortcomings, biases, and quality of the data they are using. In order to ensure precise and trustworthy conclusions, metadata also directs the selection of appropriate data sets and qualities for particular analytical tasks.

Metadata, which provides the context, arrangement, and structure necessary to fully exploit the potential of data assets, is the cornerstone of data management. By understanding the components and functions of metadata, organizations can easily find, grasp, integrate, and manage their data throughout its lifecycle. With effective metadata management, businesses may get useful insights, make intelligent decisions, and gain a competitive edge in the data-driven world (Riley, 2017).

7.3. METADATA MANAGEMENT CHALLENGES

While efficient metadata management is essential for managing data effectively, developing and sustaining strong metadata management practices can be difficult for enterprises. These difficulties can make it more difficult for the company to get the most out of its data assets. The following are some typical issues that businesses have with metadata management:

- **Data silos:** When various departments or business units within a company independently develop and maintain their own metadata repositories without enough collaboration, data silos result. As a result, metadata becomes dispersed and inconsistent throughout the company, which makes it challenging to align and integrate information for complete data management.
- Metadata that is insufficient or erroneous can have a significant negative effect on the accuracy and dependability of data assets. Essential information may be missing from incomplete metadata, making it difficult to comprehend the context and applicability of the data. On the other hand, inaccurate information might deceive users, leading to wrong interpretations or judgments based on the data.
- **Lack of Standardization:** The integration and interoperability of data can be hampered by inconsistent and nonstandard information formats, naming conventions, and classification schemes. It becomes difficult to distribute, aggregate, and analyze data across many systems, platforms, or organizations without standardized metadata.
- **Metadata Governance:** Adequate governance procedures are necessary for efficient metadata management. The process of managing and preserving metadata assets requires defining roles, responsibilities, and procedures. Inconsistent metadata definitions, unapproved changes, and issues assuring metadata correctness and quality can result from a lack of governance (Froeschl, 2013).
- **Scalability and complexity:** Managing metadata becomes more difficult as data volumes and diversity continue to rise. It is challenging to manage and preserve metadata at scale since large businesses frequently deal with a great number of data sources, systems, and metadata attributes. To keep up with changing data environments, metadata management strategies must be scalable and adaptable.
- **Data security and privacy:** Metadata frequently includes private information about the owners, sources, and access privileges of data. To prevent unauthorized access, data breaches,

and compliance violations, it is essential to ensure that suitable data privacy and security measures are in place for metadata. To protect metadata, organizations must employ the proper access controls, encryption, and data masking strategies.

- **Metadata Maintenance:** Keeping track of and cataloging existing metadata can be difficult, especially if information is dispersed among numerous systems and repositories. It takes specialized resources and tools to locate pertinent metadata, capture it accurately, and retain it consistently. Organizations may find it difficult to maintain metadata that is current and relevant without effective metadata discovery and maintenance practices.
- **Integration with Legacy Systems:** Legacy systems are those that have been in use for a long time but were not originally created with metadata management in mind. It can be difficult and time-consuming to include metadata management procedures into these systems. To extract and map metadata from historical systems into a consolidated metadata repository or catalog, extensive work may be needed.
- **Cultural and Organizational Challenges:** Changing an organization's culture is frequently necessary for metadata management. It entails encouraging accountability, cooperation, and metadata knowledge among many stakeholders. The adoption and efficacy of metadata management strategies can be hampered by resistance to change, a lack of awareness of metadata, and inadequate training.
- **Technology Limitations:** The accessibility and capability of tools and systems for managing metadata might be problematic. Some businesses could have trouble locating the right technologies to meet their particular metadata management needs. Additionally, it can be difficult and requires careful planning and execution to integrate metadata management solutions with current infrastructure and systems (Riley, 2017).

Effective data management must address a number of issues before organizations can fully benefit from metadata management. In order to manage metadata effectively, it is important to eliminate data silos, ensure accurate and complete metadata, standardize metadata formats, implement governance practices, address scalability and complexity issues, ensure data privacy and security, streamline metadata discovery and maintenance, integrate with legacy systems, address cultural and organizational challenges, and use the right technologies. Organizations can develop sound metadata management procedures and realize the full potential of their data assets by overcoming these difficulties (Froeschl, 2013).

7.4. TECHNOLOGIES AND METADATA MANAGEMENT

By giving data assets context, structure, and meaning, metadata management is essential to efficient data management. Adopting the right technology is crucial for effective metadata management as organizations work to maximize the value of their data and maintain data governance. Advanced capabilities to acquire, store, integrate, control, and use metadata across many data environments are provided by these technologies. This article will examine various important technologies that give businesses the ability to manage their metadata effectively and make the best use of their data assets.

7.4.1. Metadata Repositories and Catalogs

Catalogs and Metadata Repositories: Catalogs and Metadata Repositories are centralized systems for managing and storing Metadata. These tools offer a uniform view of metadata assets, enabling businesses to consistently collect, arrange, and maintain metadata. Users can quickly find, comprehend, and access metadata thanks to features like data lineage tracking, metadata versioning, and search capabilities provided by metadata repositories and catalogs (Figure 7.2).

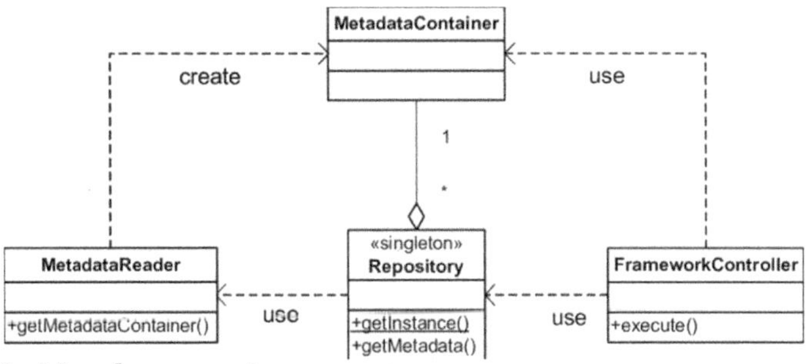

Figure 7.2. *Metadata repository structure.*

Source: Guerra, Souza, & Fernandes, (2009); Scientific figure on ResearchGate. Available from: https://www.researchgate.net/figure/Metadata-Repository-structure_fig3_228820397.

These technologies are vital in making it easier to discover, comprehend, integrate, and regulate data. Let's delve deeper into the main features and advantages of metadata repositories and catalogs:

- The management and storage of metadata assets can be done in a centralized location thanks to metadata repositories and catalogs. They act as the only reliable source of metadata, maintaining consistency and lowering the possibility of fragmented or inconsistent metadata across numerous systems and data sources. Organizations can build a consistent and dependable basis for information management by collecting all of their metadata in one place.
- Organization and capture of metadata are made possible by metadata repositories and catalogs, which give businesses an organized, standardized way to collect and arrange metadata. They offer ways to record crucial metadata properties like data descriptions, data source details, data formats, data ownership information, and data usage rights. These technologies enable the classification and categorization of metadata, enabling effective metadata asset organization and retrieval.
- Search and discovery capabilities are provided by metadata repositories and catalogs, which enable users to find and access pertinent metadata quickly and simply. On the basis of metadata elements like keywords, tags, data kinds, or data source names, users can conduct searches. The usage of advanced search features, such as full-text search, faceted search, and filtering tools, allows users to target their searches and precisely discover particular metadata assets. These speeds up the metadata discovery process and facilitates effective data exploration and analysis (Riley, 2017).
- Versioning and lineage tracking capabilities are frequently included in metadata repositories and catalogs. Organizations can keep a historical record of changes made to metadata over time by using versioning. Users can now follow the development of metadata assets, comprehend the context of changes, and make sure data governance principles are being followed. On the other side, lineage tracking records the connections between metadata assets, illustrating the flow and changes in data throughout the course of its existence. Impact analysis is made easier by using

metadata lineage, which also improves data governance and quality initiatives.

- Collaboration and Knowledge Sharing: Metadata repositories and catalogs encourage communication and information exchange between users and stakeholders in the metadata industry. They offer tools for user feedback, metadata annotation, and comments, letting people add their own thoughts, explanations, and suggestions to the information assets. Through collaboration, the company may better comprehend its data assets as a whole and advance data literacy. By exchanging knowledge and providing context, users can improve the overall quality and usability of metadata (Froeschl, 2013).
- Metadata repositories and catalogs are essential for supporting data governance activities in terms of data governance and compliance. They enable organizations to enact policies, guidelines, and best practices for metadata management. The tools for determining data ownership, access restrictions, and metadata usage rights are provided by metadata repositories. They also make it easier to validate metadata, making sure that it follows established standards and principles. Organizations can keep an extensive inventory of their information assets using metadata catalogs, ensuring compliance with legal obligations and easing audits.
- Data integration platforms, data lakes, data warehouses, and data governance tools are just a few examples of the other data management technologies and systems that metadata repositories and catalogs can interact with. Integration facilitates efficient metadata interchange between many systems and permits workflows and automation that are driven by metadata. In order to enable various data management tasks, such as data integration, data quality management, and data analytics, it makes sure that metadata is accessible and available.

The key technology for handling metadata within companies are metadata repositories and catalogs. These solutions help enterprises to implement efficient metadata management practices by offering centralized storage, effective organization, search capabilities, versioning and lineage tracking, collaborative features, and integration with the data management ecosystem. Utilizing metadata repositories and catalogs enables organizations to more efficiently discover, comprehend, regulate, and use their data assets, which in turn leads to better decision-making and increases the value of their data.

7.4.2. Metadata Integration and Interoperability Tools

Tools for metadata integration and interoperability make it possible for metadata to be seamlessly exchanged and integrated across various systems and platforms. Employing these technologies enables businesses to construct mappings between distinct metadata models, harmonize metadata from various sources, and align metadata formats. Organizations can create a comprehensive view of their data assets by fostering interoperability, which allows them to incorporate metadata from various systems, databases, and apps (Riley, 2017).

These techniques are essential for solving the problems caused by fragmented, inconsistent, and non-interoperable metadata. These technologies help businesses better understand their data, improve data governance, and realize the full potential of their data assets by supporting the seamless integration of information. Let's examine the main features and advantages of tools for metadata integration and interoperability in more detail:

- **Harmonization of metadata:** Tools for metadata integration make it easier to combine metadata from many systems, sources, and formats. These technologies offer the ability to map and transform metadata attributes to a shared model or standard. Organizations can guarantee consistency and compatibility across various metadata sources by harmonizing metadata structures, naming conventions, and classification schemes. The ability to combine and evaluate data from diverse systems and platforms is improved by metadata harmonization, which also aids data integration efforts.
- **Exchange and Sharing of Metadata:** Tools for metadata interoperability make it possible for metadata to be shared and exchanged between various systems and organizations. Extensible Markup Language (XML), RDF, and Metadata Object Description Schema (MODS) are just a few examples of the protocols and industry standards that these tools enable for the exchange of metadata. A standardized format for exchanging metadata can guarantee seamless system integration and interoperability. This

makes it easier for various departments and stakeholders to collaborate on data integration and information exchange.

- Integration of metadata from different systems and platforms, such as databases, data warehouses, enterprise resource planning (ERP) systems, customer relationship management (CRM) systems, and content management systems (CMS), is made possible through the usage of metadata integration tools. Each system's metadata attributes are extracted by these tools, who then incorporate them into a centralized metadata catalog. Users are given a thorough understanding of data assets thanks to cross-system metadata integration, which enables them to comprehend the connections, interconnections, and context of data across various systems (Froeschl, 2013).
- **Data Lineage and Impact Analysis:** The tracking of data lineage and impact analysis is made easier by technologies for metadata integration and interoperability. Data lineage illustrates the movement of data through various phases of its lifecycle by establishing linkages and dependencies between metadata assets. Impact analysis aids businesses in understanding the possible repercussions of modifications to metadata or data formats on ancillary systems and procedures. These technologies support data governance, data quality management, and change management projects by offering insights into data lineage and impact.
- **Federated Metadata Search and Discovery:** Metadata interoperability tools are used to federate metadata across different systems and repositories. Using federated search capabilities, users can simultaneously search for metadata attributes across numerous metadata sources. By eliminating the need to use several systems separately, this saves time and effort. Federated metadata search enhances data discovery by enabling users to find relevant metadata assets across different sources and have a thorough grasp of the data that is available.
- The functionality of mapping and changing metadata attributes between various metadata models or schemas is provided by metadata integration tools. By allowing companies to specify mappings between source and target metadata attributes, these technologies make it easier to align and transform metadata. The integration and consistency of understanding of metadata

from diverse sources is ensured through metadata mapping and transformation. When transferring data between systems or for data integration initiatives, this is extremely helpful (Riley, 2017).

- **Interoperability with Data Governance and Data Management Tools:** Data governance and data management technologies such as data cataloging tools, data lineage tools, data integration platforms, and data quality management tools are all compatible with metadata integration and interoperability tools. By integrating these solutions, metadata is synchronized and used effectively across the entire data management ecosystem. It helps data integration, data quality management, and data analytics projects and enables metadata-driven automation. It also improves data governance processes.

The issues brought on by fragmented and inconsistent metadata must be resolved using tools for metadata interoperability and integration. By enabling the harmonization, exchange, and integration of data from many sources, these solutions assist enterprises in creating a single view of their data assets. Through the facilitation of metadata harmonization, cross-system integration, information exchange, and interoperability, these solutions enhance data comprehension, collaboration, and governance. Organizations may fully appreciate the value of their data assets and deliver greater insights and decisions by utilizing technology for metadata integration and interoperability.

7.4.3. Metadata Extraction and Harvesting Tools

There are tools for automating the extraction and harvesting of metadata from numerous sources, including databases, files, and applications. These technologies automatically gather metadata attributes by using crawling, scanning, and parsing techniques. By eliminating manual work, ensuring broad coverage, and reducing the chance of inaccurate or incomplete metadata, organizations can efficiently collect metadata (Froeschl, 2013).

These programs use data mining, crawling, scanning, and parsing techniques to automatically extract metadata attributes. Metadata extraction and harvesting technologies streamline the gathering and maintenance of metadata by removing manual labor, assuring thorough coverage and lowering the risk of inaccurate or incomplete metadata. Let's explore the main features and advantages of metadata extraction and harvesting technologies in more detail:

- **Automated metadata collection:** Tools for harvesting and extracting metadata from a variety of data sources are used to collect metadata automatically. To find and collect metadata attributes, these programs can search databases, file systems, document repositories, webpages, and other data repositories. These solutions reduce time and effort by automating the metadata collection process, which is especially useful for processing huge amounts of data and metadata.
- **Comprehensive Metadata Coverage:** Metadata extraction and harvesting techniques make sure that all metadata attributes are covered completely. Technical metadata (such as file formats, data types, and schema details), descriptive metadata (such as titles, descriptions, and keywords), administrative metadata (such as creation dates, data ownership, and access permissions), and structural metadata (such as relationships, hierarchies, and data mappings) are just a few of the types of metadata that can be extracted by these tools. These technologies provide a comprehensive view of data assets by capturing a wide variety of information elements.
- **Integration of Multi-Source Metadata:** Metadata extraction and harvesting techniques can combine metadata from several sources into a single catalog or repository. They are able to collect metadata from a variety of systems, databases, applications, and file formats and organize it uniformly. Data integration, analysis, and governance are made easier for companies thanks to this integration's ability to provide a consolidated view of metadata from diverse sources.
- **Metadata enrichment:** Tools for metadata extraction and harvesting frequently have this feature available. These programs can improve extracted metadata by adding supplementary data from outside sources. To add further context and descriptive qualities to the collected metadata, they might retrieve and combine metadata from external databases, APIs, or reference sources, for instance. Enhancing the quality and value of metadata will increase data comprehension and discovery (Riley, 2017).
- **Scalability and Efficiency:** Metadata harvesting and extraction techniques are made to work effectively with massive amounts of data and metadata. These technologies can quickly process

and extract metadata from tens of thousands or millions of files, records, or documents. Organizations may manage metadata across enterprise-wide or large data environments thanks to its scalability, which guarantees that metadata is gathered and updated on time.

- Tools for metadata extraction and harvesting can enhance the quality and consistency of metadata. These solutions minimize the possibility of human error by automating the extraction process, resulting in accurate and trustworthy metadata. They uphold universal metadata extraction policies and guidelines, improving the consistency and dependability of metadata across various sources and data types.
- **Metadata Extraction and Harvesting Tools:** Metadata extraction and harvesting tools make it easier to find and search for metadata. Users can search for and find relevant metadata assets based on features like keywords, data kinds, or source systems once metadata has been retrieved and incorporated into a centralized repository. Finding particular metadata assets is made easier as a result, and data exploration and analysis are improved (Froeschl, 2013).
- **Regulatory Compliance and Data Governance:** Tools for extracting and harvesting metadata are helpful for these endeavors. They guarantee that the metadata related to private or regulated data is properly gathered and managed. Through the extraction of metadata pertaining to data sensitivity, access restrictions, or compliance mandates, these tools can enforce data classification and retention standards. This makes it possible for enterprises to follow legal and regulatory requirements.

Tools for automating metadata extraction and harvesting ensure thorough coverage and consistency by automating the process of obtaining metadata from various sources. These solutions increase metadata quality, save time and effort by automating information gathering, and make it easier to integrate and explore metadata. Utilizing technologies for metadata extraction and harvesting enables businesses to effectively manage and use their information assets, improving governance, analysis, and data comprehension processes.

7.4.4. Data Profiling and Quality Tools

To evaluate data quality, find anomalies, and pinpoint data-related problems, data profiling and quality tools examine metadata and underlying data. These technologies look at metadata properties like data consistency, correctness, and completeness to reveal information about the caliber and dependability of data assets. Organizations can spot data problems early and take action to improve data integrity by utilizing data profiling and quality technologies. Organizations can obtain insight into the condition of their data, maintain data accuracy, completeness, and consistency, and make educated decisions based on trustworthy and high-quality data by utilizing data profiling and quality technologies. Let's explore the main features and advantages of data profiling and quality tools in more detail:

- **Data Profiling:** To comprehend a data set's structure, content, and features, data profiling technologies look at it. Such features as data kinds, value distributions, data patterns, and data completeness are analyzed by these technologies. Data profiling reveals information about the integrity and quality of data, reveals data abnormalities, and points out potential data quality problems. It aids organizations in comprehending the data they have, its general caliber, and its applicability to particular use cases (Riley, 2017).
- **Data Quality Evaluation:** Using predetermined metrics and criteria, data quality technologies evaluate the quality of the data. These techniques assess the degree to which data is accurate, complete, consistent, valid, and timely. They validate data, locate data problems, and determine data quality ratings. In order to successfully handle data concerns, businesses can quantify the quality of their data and set priorities for change.
- **Data Standardization and Cleansing:** Tools for data quality frequently have the ability to standardize and cleanse data. Anomalies, inconsistencies, and inaccuracies in the data are automatically detected and corrected by these programs. They are able to eliminate duplicate records, fix typos, format data values, and uphold data standards. Data standardization and cleansing increase data uniformity, correctness, and adherence to established standards and guidelines.
- **Data Profiling Visualization:** To provide data profiling results in an intuitive and user-friendly way, data profiling solutions

frequently offer visualizations. Histograms, frequency diagrams, data distributions, and data quality dashboards are a few examples of these representations. The features and quality issues of the data are more easily understood and addressed by users when data profiling results are shown visually.

- Data profiling and quality tools interact with metadata repositories and catalogs to take advantage of metadata in the evaluation of data quality. Additional context on data qualities, sources, and business processes is provided through metadata. These tools improve data profiling and quality analysis by adding metadata, allowing users to comprehend the significance and application of data features and enabling more precise and thorough assessments of data quality (Froeschl, 2013).
- **Data Validation and rule Enforcement**: Organizations can design and implement data validation rules and business rules thanks to data quality solutions. To assure data integrity and compliance with business needs, these technologies validate data in comparison to specified rules. They can compare data to domain-specific rules, referential integrity restrictions, and regulations compliance standards. Organizations are assisted in maintaining data consistency, accuracy, and compliance via data validation and rule enforcement.
- **Monitoring and Alerting for Data Quality:** Data quality technologies offer features for ongoing monitoring and alerting for data quality. These systems keep an eye on data sources in real-time, identify data quality problems, and alert or notify users when data quality thresholds are crossed. By ensuring that data issues are quickly detected and resolved, data quality monitoring helps to reduce the negative effects that bad data can have on corporate operations and decision-making.

Data profiling and quality technologies produce reports and documentation that are used to convey the findings of data quality assessments. These reports give information on the general data quality, point out particular data problems, and monitor the development of measures to increase data quality. Data quality reports aid in communicating with stakeholders, promote data governance initiatives, and provide evidence for legal compliance.

Organizations can evaluate, examine, and enhance the quality of their data assets with the aid of data profiling and quality technologies. Utilizing these technologies, companies can evaluate data quality, establish data cleansing and standardization processes, and obtain insights into data structures and features. These technologies help organizations better comprehend data, increase data accuracy, and improve data governance procedures, which in turn enables them to make decisions based on trustworthy and high-quality data (Riley, 2017).

7.4.5. Data Lineage and Impact Analysis Tools

Tools for tracking and visualizing data and metadata flow throughout its lifecycle include data lineage and impact analysis tools. These instruments aid organizations in comprehending the provenance, modifications, and interdependencies of data assets. Impact analysis enables companies to evaluate the prospective effects of changes to data structures or metadata on downstream systems and processes, whereas data lineage gives a historical record of data and metadata transformations.

Let's explore the main features and advantages of data lineage and impact analysis tools in more detail:

- The end-to-end journey of data, including its source systems, transformations, and target systems, is captured and documented by data lineage tools. They monitor data flow, spot data pipelines, and record connections between data components and systems. To chart the movement of data within the organization's data environment, data lineage technologies frequently use techniques including metadata extraction, data integration, and data flow analysis (Froeschl, 2013).
- Data lineage tools offer visual representations of data lineage, making it simpler for users to comprehend the journey and changes that data goes through. These visualizations may take the form of lineage trees, flowcharts, or graphical data pipelines. Users can better grasp complicated data flows, spot bottlenecks, and comprehend how data is used by various systems and processes by using data lineage visualization.
- Exploration of Data Lineage: Interactive exploration and navigation of Data Lineage information is made possible by Data Lineage tools. To understand the data sources or destinations for a particular data element, users can trace the data lineage back

or forward. Users can trace data transformations, discover the systems and processes that consume or produce particular data items, and identify the sources of data through this interactive exploration.

- Impact Analysis: Tools for data lineage and impact analysis evaluate how changes to data, systems, or procedures will affect data assets farther down the line. They aid businesses in comprehending the effects that a change in one data attribute, schema, or system may have on other data elements, reports, analytics, and business procedures. Impact analysis enables businesses to assess potential effects of changes, reduce risks, and guarantee data consistency and integrity across the entire data ecosystem.
- Tools for analyzing the lineage and impact of data are helpful for regulatory compliance and data governance projects. They assist organizations show data lineage for compliance requirements by giving visibility into the flow and transformations of data. These technologies help in developing data governance frameworks and meeting legal requirements by assisting in identifying data dependencies, assuring data accuracy and integrity, and providing data traceability.
- Data lineage technologies assist with data lifecycle management by collecting data lineage data at various stages of the data lifecycle. They provide a full picture of the evolution and use of data by documenting its generation, ingestion, transformation, storage, and consumption. Organizations can use data lineage technologies to track changes, understand the lifecycle of data, and make educated decisions about data preservation, archival, or erasure (Riley, 2017).
- Tools for data lineage and impact analysis are essential for managing the quality of the data. Understanding data lineage enables companies to track out the origins of data quality problems, identifying the underlying causes and implementing corrective actions. Impact analysis supports data cleaning, data validation, and data quality improvement projects by assessing the potential effects of data quality concerns on downstream systems and processes.
- Data lineage and impact analysis tools support informed decision-making among many stakeholders and foster

collaboration between them. These tools enable communication and collaboration between business users, data analysts, data stewards, and IT teams by fostering a shared knowledge of data flows, relationships, and effect. By providing accurate and trustworthy information about the history and effect of data, they enable stakeholders to make data-driven decisions.

Tools for tracking the origins, transformations, and effects of data throughout an organization's data ecosystem are known as data lineage and impact analysis tools. These tools give organizations visibility into the journey of data. These solutions enable enterprises to support regulatory compliance, enable data governance, assure data integrity, and make educated decisions based on a thorough understanding of data lineage and impact (Froeschl, 2013).

7.4.6. Metadata Governance and Data Stewardship Tools

The design and enforcement of metadata management policies and standards are made easier by technologies for metadata governance and data stewardship. These technologies give enterprises the ability to specify metadata governance frameworks, delegate tasks, and guarantee regulatory compliance. They assist with tasks like metadata validation, change management, and access restrictions, advancing the security, accuracy, and consistency of metadata.

7.4.7. Machine Learning and Artificial Intelligence

To automate jobs and improve processes connected to metadata, machine learning and AI approaches are being used more and more in metadata management. These technological advancements can help with metadata classification, enrichment, and recommendation. Machine learning algorithms can assess metadata usage patterns, learn from user interactions, and offer individualized recommendations for finding and utilizing metadata.

7.4.8. Cloud-based Metadata Management platforms

Organizations looking to manage metadata in distributed and dynamic contexts can take advantage of the flexible and scalable solutions provided by cloud-based metadata management platforms. These platforms offer scalable infrastructure, centralized metadata repositories, and collaboration tools for managing metadata assets. Organizations can benefit from flexibility, scalability, and accessibility with the help of cloud-based solutions, which also guarantee metadata governance and consistency (Riley, 2017). Technologies for metadata management give businesses the tools and capabilities they need to deal with the difficulties in managing metadata. These technologies enable organizations to effectively capture, integrate, govern, and use metadata across various data environments. They range from metadata repositories and catalogs to metadata integration tools, data profiling and quality tools, data lineage and impact analysis tools, metadata governance and data stewardship tools, machine learning and AI, and cloud-based platforms. Organizations may make the most of their data assets by utilizing these technologies, which will enable them to make wise decisions that will lead to economic success.

7.5. METADATA MANAGEMENT SYSTEMS

Systems for managing metadata are essential for efficiently collecting, compiling, storing, and utilizing metadata within an organization. These solutions give businesses a consolidated platform for managing metadata assets, allowing them to better comprehend data, control data better, and maximize decision-making based on data. We shall examine the essential elements, characteristics, and advantages of metadata management systems in this post (Froeschl, 2013) (Figure 7.3).

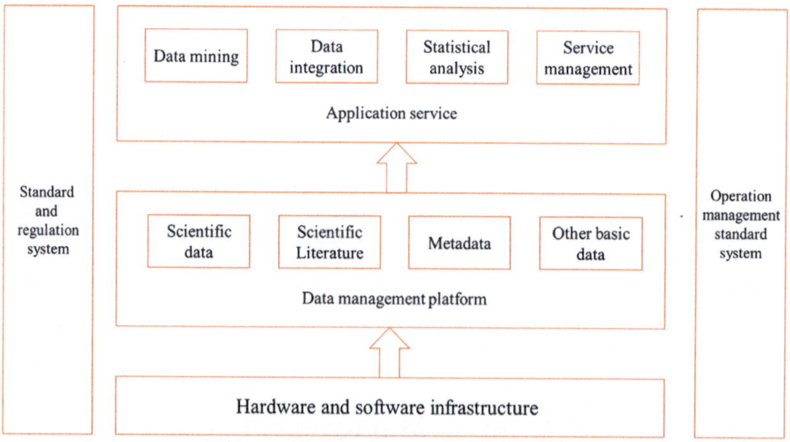

Figure 7.3. *Architecture of metadata management system based on scientific data and scientific literature.*

Source: Wang, Chen, & Li, (2018); Scientific figure on ResearchGate. Available from: https://www.researchgate.net/figure/Architecture-of-metadata-management-system-based-on-scientific-data-and-scientific_fig2_329479311.

7.5.1. Components of Metadata Management Systems

Repositories for metadata serve as a central location for storing metadata assets in metadata management systems. Technical metadata (such as data structures and database schemas), business metadata (such as data definitions and business glossaries), and operational metadata (such as data usage and data lineage) are all stored in these repositories. To facilitate effective search, retrieval, and analysis, metadata repositories offer a standardized and organized framework for recording and managing metadata.

Metadata management systems make it possible to collect metadata from a variety of sources, including databases, files, programs, and platforms for data integration. These systems have the ability to automatically extract, parse, and import metadata, which saves time and ensures thorough coverage. By building mappings between various metadata sources, addressing errors, and aligning various metadata formats, they also facilitate metadata integration (Riley, 2017).

Management of metadata models and schemas is made possible by the tools that metadata management systems offer. With the use of these tools, businesses can design taxonomies and metadata structures that are tailored to their particular requirements and industry. By providing uniform definitions, properties, and relationships, metadata modeling enables consistent representation of metadata assets. The definition of metadata hierarchies, relationships, and dependencies with the use of schema management features improves metadata organization and retrieval.

Search and discovery capabilities for metadata are provided by efficient metadata management systems. With the help of these functionalities, users may browse and find particular metadata assets using criteria like keywords, data elements, tags, or categories. The effective navigation and retrieval of metadata is made possible by metadata search capabilities, facilitating data discovery, impact analysis, and data lineage understanding. Users can filter and rank search results using advanced search capabilities like relevance ranking and faceted search.

Data Lineage and Impact Analysis: Metadata management systems usually include data lineage and impact analysis functions. As it tracks the movement of data and information over the course of its existence, data lineage keeps track of transformations, derivations, and relationships between data assets. Impact analysis tools enable organizations to understand the potential consequences of changes to data structures, metadata definitions, or data sources. Data lineage and impact analysis are tools that support data governance, compliance, and decision-making processes (Froeschl, 2013).

7.5.2. Benefits of Metadata Management Systems

Metadata management systems enhance data comprehension by giving descriptive information about data assets. Users are therefore better equipped to use the data efficiently and make decisions because they have a greater understanding of its structure, context, and quality. By leveraging substantial metadata, organizations may better grasp the meaning, history, and linkages of their data, which helps to eliminate ambiguity and improve data comprehension (Riley, 2017).

Metadata management technologies are crucial for data governance activities. The standardization, uniformity, and regulatory compliance of metadata are made easier by these technologies. By using metadata governance frameworks, organizations may ensure data integrity, respect data policies, and enhance data security. Metadata management systems support data stewardship by providing mechanisms for metadata ownership, accountability, and collaboration.

Organizations can integrate and harmonize metadata from many sources and systems thanks to metadata management tools. These systems support data integration and interoperability by establishing mappings, addressing inconsistencies, and aligning metadata formats. In order to create a comprehensive picture of data assets and support data-driven efforts, this enables enterprises to mix data from various systems, databases, and apps.

Data discovery and lineage analysis are made easier because to the robust search and discovery capabilities provided by metadata management systems. Users may rapidly locate data pieces, data sources, and related metadata with the use of metadata search tools. Organizations can track the beginnings, transformations, and dependencies of data using features for data lineage analysis, which also supports data lineage documentation, impact analysis, and regulatory compliance (Froeschl, 2013).

In conclusion, in the digital age, metadata management is crucial for maximizing the value of data. Organizations can boost data analytics capabilities, enable effective data governance, and improve data quality by utilizing technologies and systems created expressly for managing metadata. To fully utilize their data assets in the ever-evolving technological environment, organizations must keep up with the most recent developments and best practices in metadata management (Riley, 2017).

CHAPTER

8 Ontologies and Ontology Languages

Contents

8.1. INTRODUCTION

In recent years, the Internet has grown tremendously. However, there are unresolved issues that are preventing the Web from expanding even faster. There are primarily two technical constraints on the Web's impact on our world. On the one hand, computing power has the potential to limit the potential and implementation of novel concepts and applications. On the other hand, the expressiveness of the formalism that surrounds computer science may limit its potential for growth and impact. However, neither appears to be a significant barrier at the moment. Increasing computing power pushes the bounds of physics further and further each year. On the other hand, new, increasingly complex applications are developed to test and advance computers' expressiveness and capabilities (Spear, 2015).

The Semantic Web concept and idea were created specifically to improve the expressiveness of computer science formalisms. The current Web can be roughly described as a collection of linked, hypertext documents that run over the Internet and are distinguished primarily by the static and syntactic nature of the codified information. This means that only a human reader can comprehend and decipher the available information. As a result, current Web technology can only use a very small portion of the available information. Furthermore, the full potential of modern computers' information processing abilities has yet to be realized. They only function as information rendering tools, displaying content in a human-readable format.

To overcome these constraints, more expressive methods that take advantage of everything that computer science and computing have to offer are required. These are the Semantic Web's specific goals. The Semantic Web is the next generation of the World Wide Web, in which data has semantics that computers can process and understand. The Semantic Web is a growing Web extension that allows content to be expressed in ways that software agents can understand, interpret, and use. This facilitates the discovery, sharing, and integration of information by software agents. This cutting-edge technology, which is not a new Web but rather an addition to the existing one in which information is given a clear meaning, essentially provides structure to the Web's meaningful content.

The fundamental idea behind the Semantic Web is the representation of data in a machine-readable format. Ontologies make it easier to realize such representations. They define formal and congruent conceptualization specifications as providing agents (organizations, people, and software) with a shared and common understanding of a domain via machine-processable data and information semantics. Ontologies provide tools for describing the fundamental categories and relationships of things by defining entities and types of entities within their framework.

Ontologies combine two critical components required to improve the Web with semantic technology. They accomplish this by outlining formal information semantics, which provides machine processability first and foremost. Second, because of their ability to define real-world conceptualization, they enable machine-human comprehension. Ontologies connect machine-processable content with human meaning by using a common terminology as a connecting element (Noy, 2012).

Indeed, some ontological concepts, such as how they relate to knowledge bases, how to distinguish a lightweight ontology from a heavyweight ontology, or what it means to use or extend an ontology—these concepts are known as "ontological commitments"—are not always obvious to the user. As a result, more explanation is required.

A class of technologies known as Semantic Web Languages now enables ontology modeling and ontology authoring. These languages provide varying degrees of expressivity and inference capabilities depending on the logic formalism used. To select the best one for the intended application domain, it is sometimes necessary to strike a balance between the first two factors and the tools available. To try to solve this problem, we will go over the most important ones in this chapter (Spear, 2015).

8.2. A METADATA GLOSSARY FROM CONTROLLED VOCABULARIES TO ONTOLOGIES

This section describes the main characteristics and distinguishing features of controlled vocabularies, taxonomies, thesauri, and ontologies. The goal is to provide the reader with the knowledge needed to assess the application and use of each paradigm.

8.2.1. Controlled Vocabularies

A controlled vocabulary is a collection of predefined words used to speed up content retrieval. Controlled vocabularies, in contrast to natural language vocabularies, are made up of pre-defined, authorized terms. Controlled vocabularies can be used to define database schemas, create labeling systems, and categorize content, among other things. A catalog contains a controlled vocabulary.

8.2.2. Taxonomy

Taxonomy refers to the science of classification. The term is derived from the Greek words taxis (order) and nomos (law or science). In our context, the best definition of a taxonomy is a set of controlled vocabulary terms. Each vocabulary word is referred to as a taxon. Taxa identify discrete pieces of meaningful content in a specific domain. Taxonomies are typically organized hierarchically, classifying various types of items into an order (for example, an alphabetical list). The Wikispecies project, which aims to compile a species directory, is an excellent example of taxonomy. The "Taxonavigation" diagram depicts the taxonomic pathway that leads to the species.

8.2.3. Thesaurus

The Latin word for thesaurus was derived from an ancient Greek word that serves as its etymological foundation. In both cultures, thesaurus was used to refer to a repository of words as well as a storehouse or treasury. A thesaurus is similar to a dictionary in this regard, with the exception that it does not provide word definitions, its scope is limited to a specific domain, entry terms are single-word or multi-word entries, and it only allows for limited cross-referencing among the contained terms, such as synonyms and antonyms (Spear, 2015).

A thesaurus is not intended to be a comprehensive glossary. Instead, they are intended to aid in distinguishing between similar meanings so that the best one can be chosen for the intended purpose. Scope notes, which are textual annotations that help define terms and explain their context, are also included in thesauri. A thesaurus is a taxonomy expressed in natural language that reveals a specific set of relationships between the codified terms.

8.2.4. Ontologies

In philosophy, ontology is the study of being or existence. It is the fundamental topic of metaphysics, which focuses on the types and structures of objects, properties, events, processes, and relations associated with each component of reality to systematize the explanation of existence. Ontologies, like taxonomies, represent relationships between terms; this is why the term "ontology" was only recently adopted in the field of computer science. Ontologies, on the other hand, offer a far more robust mechanism for representing the relationships between concepts such as terms and attributes.

This is because they are currently the preferred mechanism for representing knowledge. There are numerous ontology definitions. An ontology defines the fundamental terms and relations that comprise a topic area's vocabulary, as well as the rules for combining terms and relations to define vocabulary extensions. In his 1991 book Enabling Technology for Knowledge Sharing, Neches provided one of the earliest definitions of ontologies. Studer and Fensel clarified and improved the definition in 1998. The authors define an ontology as "a formal, explicit specification of a shared conceptualization" in their work. The formal requirement for an ontology is to be machine-readable. The term explicit refers to the explicit definition of the concepts used as well as the constraints placed on their use. Reflects the notion that ontology captures consensual knowledge, i.e., that it is not the sole domain of one person but is accepted by a group. The process of identifying the relevant concepts for a phenomenon to create an abstract model of that phenomenon (Noy, 2012).

8.2.4.1. Ontologies and Knowledge Bases

The relationship between ontologies and knowledge bases is debatable. It is unclear whether an ontology can contain both concrete manifestations of abstract concepts and abstract schema (for example, concept Person). When attempting to draw a clear distinction between abstract schema definitions and the instance level, one encounters the issue that, in some circumstances, instances are required to specify abstract concepts. The definition of "New Yorker" as the concept of people who live in New York is an example of this problem because, in this case, the city instance "New York" is required to specify the concept. Several authors have addressed this issue, determining the boundaries and connections between preexisting definitions. Guarino and Giaretta's article Ontologies and Knowledge Bases: Towards a Terminological Clarification laid the groundwork for clarifying the relationship between ontologies and knowledge bases by depicting an ontology as a logical theory. "A logical theory that provides a clear, albeit incomplete, explanation of a conceptualization." Guarino refined his definition in 1998, emphasizing that an ontology is an engineering artifact composed of a set of logical axioms. "A collection of logical precepts designed to explain the intended meaning of a vocabulary."

Ontologies can be classified as heavyweight or lightweight based on their axiomatization richness. Ontologies that are heavyweights rely heavily on axioms to model knowledge and constrain domain semantics. Lightweight ontologies, on the other hand, use few or no axioms to model knowledge and define the meaning of domain-specific concepts. Heavyweight ontologies are a subset of lightweight ontologies. They usually concentrate on taxonomies, have few logical relationships between classes, and few cross-taxonomy connections (also known as "properties") (Spear, 2015).

8.2.4.2. Ontological Obligations

Ontologies are typically engineering artifacts that provide the domain vocabulary as well as some assumptions about the vocabulary's meaning. They are used to communicate by the participants in a specific interaction. Participants can only communicate effectively if they have already agreed to use common ontologies. This assumes that they use the vocabulary consistently and coherently with the definitions provided in the common ontology.

As a result, ontological commitments are agreements to use a shared lexicon logically and consistently. They promise consistency but not complete ontology. This entails making as few assertions as possible about the world being modeled and allowing the parties involved to specialize in the ontology as needed. Gruber's (1995) five ontological commitments are as follows:

- **Clarity:** An ontology should communicate the intended meaning of a defined term. Definitions should be objective. A full definition (defined by both necessary and sufficient conditions) is preferable to a partial definition (defined only by necessary or sufficient conditions), and definitions can be stated on formal axioms. Every definition should be described using natural language.
- **Minimal Encoding Bias:** The conceptualization should be specified at the knowledge level rather than relying on a specific symbol-level encoding.
- **Extensibility:** Using the existing vocabulary, one should be able to define new terms for specialized purposes without changing the definitions of the existing terms.
- **Coherence:** To be coherent, an ontology must allow for inferences that are consistent with the definitions. If a conclusion drawn from the axioms contradicts a definition or informal example provided, the ontology is illogical (Noy, 2012).

Because ontological commitment is based on the consistent use of vocabulary, ontological commitment can be kept to a bare minimum by defining only those terms that are required for the communication of knowledge that is consistent with the theory.

8.3. ONTOLOGY LANGUAGES

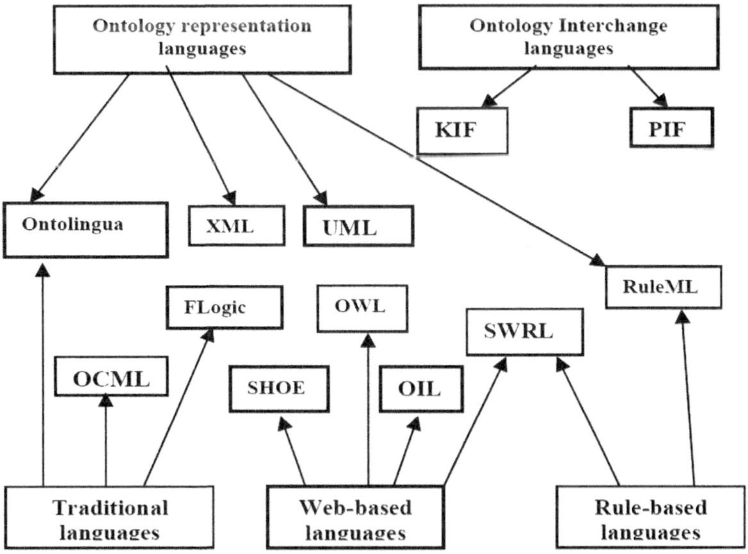

Figure 8.1. *Classification of ontology languages.*

Source: Yordanova, & Stefanov, (2006); Scientific figure on ResearchGate. Available from: https://www.researchgate.net/figure/Ontology-languages-classifications_fig1_32231413.

The following section provides a comprehensive review of the most important ontology languages currently in use. RDF(S), OWL, WSML, and SKOS are examples of these languages. For the sake of completeness, we also briefly review the early languages OIL and DAML+OIL (Spear, 2015) (Figure 8.1).

8.3.1. Resource Description Framework

RDF, a general-purpose language, is used to represent data about Web resources. The Resource Description Framework Schema (RDFS) provides a mechanism for defining the semantics of RDF modeling primitives. RDF(S) is an abbreviation for RDF and RDFS. RDF(S) is not a semantic language per se, but rather a general-purpose language for describing metadata on the Web (Figure 8.2).

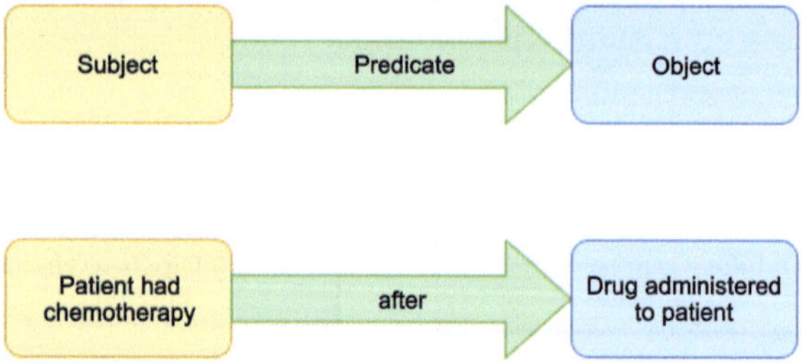

Figure 8.2. *Resource description framework (RDF) triple example.*

Source: Chen, Du, Song, Liu, Jiang, & Tao, (2018); Scientific figure on ResearchGate. Available from: https://www.researchgate.net/figure/Resource-Description-Framework-RDF-triple-example_fig1_323348519.

The RDF(S) data model provides a syntax-neutral, binary relations-based method of representing expressions. The language is based on the idea that resources can be described by making statements that specifically specify the properties and values of the resources. To represent the various components of a statement in RDF(S), the terms subject, object, and predicate are combined into triples. In a nutshell, subjects denote the object of the statement, predicates denote the quality of the object of the statement, and objects denote the amount of the quality to which the predicate refers. As shown in the following example:

www.ontogame.org is written by Katharina Siorpaes. "author" is the subject, "www.ontogame.org" is the predicate, and "Katharina Siorpaes" is the object.

Notably, RDF(S) now includes a reification mechanism that allows the definition of statements about statements. The language includes a useful set of primitives for modeling ontologies, such as sub-classing relationships for expressing subsumption. As a result, the language can be said to be expressive enough for the purpose for which it was designed (Noy, 2012).

8.3.2. The Web Ontology Language

The DAML+OIL language gave rise to the OWL ontology language. It is divided into three language varieties: OWL DL, OWL Lite, and OWL Full, each with a different level of expressivity and reasoning.

OWL Lite is the least expressive and logically complex variant. It is intended for users who only need basic constraints and a classification hierarchy. While supporting, cardinality constraints restrict the use of only the numbers 0 and 1. Rapid language adoption is facilitated by tool development and the ease of migration from thesauri and other taxonomies.

The description's logic variant OWL DL provides maximum expressivity while maintaining full computational completeness and decidability. Under the restrictions on language construct usage imposed by this variant, a class cannot be an instance of another class.

Full OWL Full combines RDF's syntactic flexibility with the greatest amount of expressiveness while providing no computational guarantees, such as completeness and decidability (Spear, 2015).

8.3.3. Web Service Modeling Language

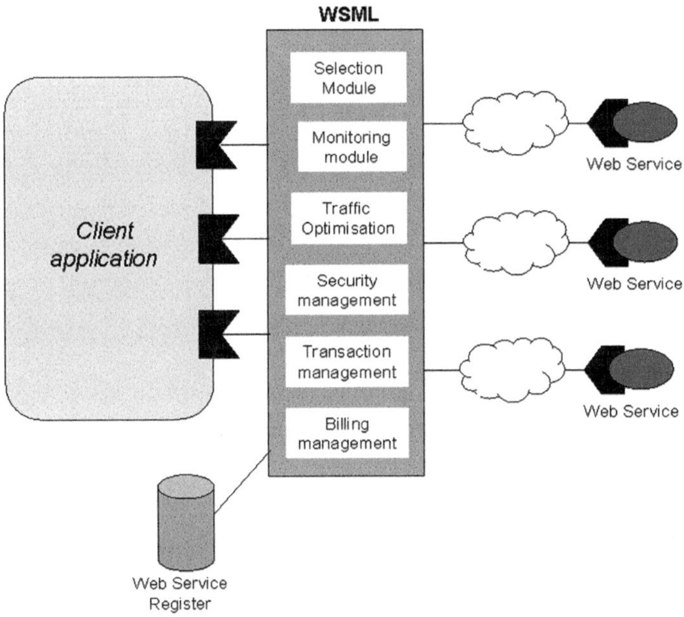

Figure 8.3. *General architecture of the WSML.*

Source: Vanderperren, Suvee, Verheecke, Cibrán, & Jonckers, (2005); Scientific figure on ResearchGate. Available from: https://www.researchgate.net/figure/General-architecture-of-the-WSML_fig3_221014711.

The WSML provides formal syntax semantics for the web service modeling ontology (WSMO). The three formalisms on which WSML is based are logic programming, first-order logic, and description logic. The significant number of WSML variants available can be tailored to the application's and the targeted application domain's needs. These are the WSML-Full, WSML-DL, WSML-Flight, WSML-Core, and WSML-Rule specifications. The WSML language family includes a human-readable syntax as well as XML, RDF, and an OWL mapping for machine-to-machine communication (Figure 8.3).

- **The WSML-Core:** Because it is built on top of OWL Lite, a constrained version of OWL Lite, WSML-core is fully compliant with this OWL subset. The formalism used precisely satisfies the intersection of Horn Logic and Description Logic (without function symbols and equality) with the addition of data type support. This language can model classes, attributes, binary relationships (class and relation hierarchies), and instances. WSML-core is the preferred language for practical applications because it has the best computational properties despite having the least expressive power of the WSML family languages. WSML-Core is extended in the areas of Description Logics, Programming with WSML-DL, and WSML-Flight, in that order.
- **WSML-DL:** WSML-DL syntactically and semantically extends WSML-Core to a full-fledged Description Logic paradigm, namely, SHIQ, thereby efficiently implementing a portion of OWL. WSML-DL extends WSML-Core's functionality by providing a less constrained syntax. The use of Description logics causes the majority of restrictions on the use of WSMD-DL syntax in this direction (Noy, 2012).
- **The WSML-Flight:** WSML-Flight is a robust language that extends WSML-Core in the direction of logic programming. It provides a wide range of attribute modeling primitives, including integrity and value constraints. WSML-Flight is semantically equivalent to Datalog when inequality and (locally) stratified negation are present. It enables effective defensible reasoning while also incorporating a full rule language.
- **The WSML-Rule:** WSML-Rule creates a full-fledged Logic Programming language by adding Logic Programming functionality to WSML-Flight. It allows the use of function symbols and unsafe rules and does not restrict the use of variables in logical expressions.
- **WSML-Full:** In WSML-Full, the non-monotonic extension of WSML-Rule unites all WSML-DL and WSML-Rule variants under a single First-Order framework.

8.3.4. Easy Knowledge Management System

The SKOS4 initiative is focused on developing specifications for knowledge organization systems such as thesauri, folksonomies, and lightweight ontologies. Wilson et al. (2009) describe SKOS core, as an RDF vocabulary that can express the content and structure of concept schemes. Concept schemes include thesauri, classification schemes, glossaries, taxonomies, and ontologies, all of which use a controlled vocabulary. The SKOS core meta-model is extremely compact, describing only the bare minimum of classes and properties required to express knowledge in simple structures such as taxonomies (Spear, 2015).

If SKOS does not meet the domain requirements, its RDF vocabulary status allows for very flexible use with other RDF vocabularies. SKOS core contains the most important components required to define controlled vocabularies. The most important components of SKOS are concepts as mental units, which are analogous to labeled classes in OWL. SKOS also supports the expression of semantic relationships, such as "broader," "narrower," or "related." Furthermore, SKOS supports the use of constructs for concept mapping, whether precise or fuzzy. SKOS extensions make it easier to declare relationships between concepts with more precise semantics (Noy, 2012).

8.3.5. Oil, DAML + Oil Fensel

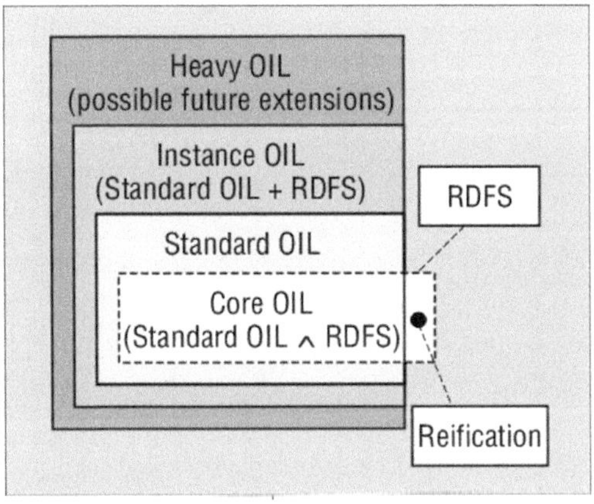

Figure 8.4. *OIL's layered language model.*

Source: Fensel, Harmelen, Horrocks, Mcguinness, & Patel-Schneider, (2001); Scientific figure on ResearchGate. Available from: https://www.researchgate.net/figure/OILs-layered-language-model_fig2_3453918.

Van Harmelen, et al. (2001) describe OIL, which is based on RDFS and aims to express semantics on the Web. It combines description logic approaches' formal semantics and reasoning support with XML syntax, modeling primitives from the frame-based knowledge representation paradigm, and modeling primitives. In addition to the XML syntax, OIL has a presentation syntax. Daml+OIL, on the other hand, has supplanted OIL as a dynamic language. DAML+OIL employs both XML and RDF elements. It incorporates components from frame-based systems based on description logics. It was replaced by the OWL language family (Figure 8.4).

8.4. COMPONENTS OF ONTOLOGY

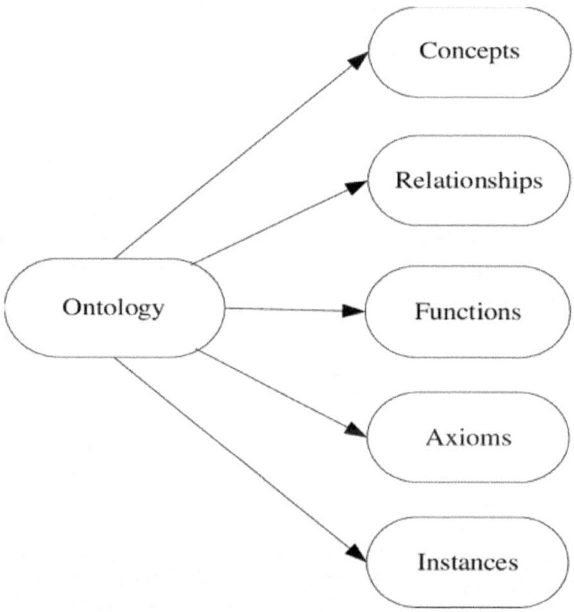

Figure 8.5. *Components of ontology.*

Source: Castilho, & Lopes, (2009); Scientific figure on ResearchGate. Available from: https://www.researchgate.net/figure/Main-components-of-an-ontology_fig1_226525271.

8.4.1. Classes as a Core Component of Ontology

Classes are the fundamental building blocks and core elements of ontology that aid in the organization of knowledge representation. They are necessary for organizing the field of study, defining concepts, and classifying entities.

This comprehensive explanation delves into the concept of classes, their significance, and their role in the construction of ontologies (Figure 8.5).

8.4.1.1. Definition and Conceptualization

Classes in ontology represent concepts or categories within a domain. Through abstract representations of those entities, they define a group of entities with related characteristics, traits, or behaviors. By capturing the fundamental characteristics that entities belonging to their share, classes enable classification and grouping based on commonalities.

When conceptualizing classes, domain experts identify and define the key concepts and categories relevant to the domain. The representation of these concepts as classes in ontology creates a shared understanding of the domain's structure and content. Classes must be named, their attributes and relationships defined, and a description of their meaning and function provided (Spear, 2015).

8.4.1.2. Hierarchical Class Organization

A taxonomic structure formed by the hierarchical organization of classes in an ontology is known as a class hierarchy. The hierarchy represents the relationships between classes, including those between superclasses (parent classes) and subclasses (child classes). This hierarchical organization, which allows for entity classification and sub-classification, allows for a more detailed representation of knowledge.

Subclasses represent concepts that are more specialized or specialized, whereas superclasses represent concepts that are more general or abstract. Superclasses define the shared traits and properties that subclasses inherit. In an ontology of animals, for example, "Animal" could be a superclass, and "Mammal" and "Bird" could be subclasses. Mammals and birds are organisms with animal characteristics such as multiple cells, the ability to move, and the need for food (Noy, 2012).

The class hierarchy enables the ontology's reasoning and inference capabilities. Moving through the hierarchy allows you to infer properties and relationships for entities based on their position in the hierarchy. For example, if an entity belongs to the "Bird" subclass, it can be assumed that it has characteristics unique to birds, such as the ability to fly.

8.4.1.3. Characteristics and Traits of a Class

Classes have traits and qualities that define their behaviors and traits. These characteristics describe the traits and characteristics associated with entities belonging to a specific class. Attributes can be both object and data properties.

Object properties define class or instance relationships. For example, in an ontology describing a university, the class "Student" may have an object property called "isEnrolledIn," which connects the student to the class "Course."

Data properties assign values or constraints to instances. To indicate an individual's age, the data property "age" of the class "Person" may contain values such as 25, 30, or 40.

Classes may also have additional characteristics such as limitations or constraints. These restrictions define the requirements or guidelines that entities must follow to be classified. Constraints can be expressed using formal languages such as OWL, allowing for the precise and logical specification of class membership.

8.4.1.4. Knowledge Representation and Reasoning

Classes are the primary unit of knowledge representation in ontologies. They provide a structured and ordered representation of concepts and categories within a domain, making it easier for various entities and systems to share and exchange knowledge. Ontologies use classes to capture the semantics and connections between entities, allowing computers to reason and draw conclusions.

Knowledge reasoning is the process of inferring new knowledge from previously known information within an ontology. Using logical rules and inference mechanisms, machines can infer implicit relationships, draw conclusions, and respond to complex questions. Classes and their hierarchical relationships are heavily used in this reasoning process. By traversing the class hierarchy, machines can infer properties, relationships, and classifications for entities based on their positions within the hierarchy.

8.4.2. Properties

As a core component in the ontology domain, property plays a critical role. Properties in an ontology are used to describe the attributes, traits, or connections associated with classes and instances. They enable the representation of complex knowledge and ease inference and reasoning by allowing the structure of an ontology to be defined (Spear, 2015).

- **Types of Property:** Ontologies have two types of properties: object properties and data properties. Object properties specify how different entities are related or connected, which establishes class or instance relationships. In an ontology that represents a social network, for example, an object property called "isFriendOf" could be used to establish a friendship between two people. Data properties, on the other hand, impose constraints or values on instances. They provide more information and describe the characteristics or traits of the instances. The "age" data property, for example, can be linked to a specific instance to represent that instance's age.
- **Characteristics of Properties**: A property's behavior and ontology usage is defined by several significant characteristics, including:
  - **Domains and Ranges:** Domains and ranges are associated with properties. The domain identifies the class or instance to which the property applies, whereas the range specifies the permitted values or classes that the property may take. The property "hasColor" in an ontology representing fruits, for example, would have the domain "Fruit" and the range "Color" to indicate that it relates to instances of fruits and accepts values from the domain of colors.
  - **Cardinality:** The number of instances that can be linked to a property is denoted by the term "cardinality." It specifies whether a property has only one value (cardinality one) or multiple values (cardinality many). Cardinality constraints help define relationships between instances and increase an ontology's precision. The property "hasChild" in a family ontology may have a cardinality of many, indicating that a person may have more than one child.
  - **Symmetry and Asymmetry:** A property can exhibit various symmetry traits. In contrast to asymmetric properties, symmetric properties are true in both directions. The symmetric property "isMarriedTo" indicates that if John and Mary are married, Mary is also married to John. In contrast, "hasChild" is an asymmetric property because

it does not always follow that if John is the parent of Mary, Mary is the parent of John.

  - **Transitivity:** The transitivity of a property is determined by its transitivity. According to the transitive property assumption, any instance related to the second instance is also related to the first instance through the same property if there is a relationship between two instances through that property. Because the property "isAncestorOf" is transitive, if John is an ancestor of Mary and Mary is an ancestor of Alice, then John is also an ancestor of Alice (Noy, 2012).

- **The significance of Properties in Ontology:** Properties are critical to ontology development and knowledge representation for a variety of reasons.
  - **Knowledge Structuring:** Properties provide a means of describing the attributes, characteristics, and connections of classes and instances, which aids in the structuring of knowledge within an ontology. They aid in the organization and classification of information, allowing for a more in-depth understanding of the subject.
  - **Semantic Enrichment:** By capturing the relationships between entities, properties improve an ontology's semantics and expressiveness by allowing for the expression of complex relationships, dependencies, and constraints.
  - **Inference and Reasoning:** Properties play an important role in inference and reasoning. They enable automated reasoning systems to derive new knowledge from pre-existing ontologies. By defining properties and their characteristics, inference mechanisms can classify instances, identify inconsistencies, and infer implicit relationships.
  - **Integration and Interoperability:** The properties of ontologies make it easier for them to integrate and interact with one another. By defining properties with shared meanings and traits, ontologies from various sources can be aligned, merged, and used together. Properties provide a common language for communication and knowledge sharing among various systems and domains.
  - **Contextual Representation:** The properties of an ontology allow for the contextual representation of knowledge. By

connecting properties to specific domains or instances, ontologies can represent the specific attributes and characteristics relevant to those entities. Because of this contextual representation, knowledge modeling becomes more specialized and focused (Spear, 2015).

8.4.3. Instances as a Core Component of Ontology

Instances are the foundation of an ontology and are required for knowledge representation and semantic modeling. By using instances, which represent specific objects, entities, or people within a domain, ontologies can capture the actual entities and their characteristics.

- **Instances' Definition:** Instances, also known as individuals, are concrete members of classes in ontology. They act as stand-ins for specific objects in the domain being modeled. Instances can be physical objects, conceptual ideas, or even events or processes. Apple, Orange, and Banana are just a few examples of instances in an ontology representing the domain of "Fruits." Instances are created using class templates, and they inherit the relationships and properties associated with those classes.
- **Characteristics of Instances:** A variety of factors influence the representation and use of instances in ontologies. These characteristics are as follows:
    - Identity: Each instance is identified by a unique identifier that distinguishes it from other instances. Use this identifier to refer to and interact with the instance within the ontology.
    - Instances have properties or attributes that describe their characteristics. These attributes can be explicitly added to an instance or inherited from the class to which they belong. A "Person" instance, for example, could have attributes such as "name," "age," and "gender."
    - Instances within the ontology may be connected to other instances or classes. Relationships establish ties, reliances, or associations between various entities. For example, an instance of the class "Book" may be related to instances of the classes "Author" and "Publisher."
    - Classification: Instances are classified into different classes within the ontology. The class to which an instance belongs represents the category or concept that it embodies.

Classification enables the organization and categorization of entities based on shared characteristics and connections.

- **The Role of Instances in Knowledge Representation:** Instances are critical when representing knowledge in an ontology. They increase the breadth and specificity of the data being represented. Some important aspects of how instances affect knowledge representation are as follows:
  - Instances enable the mapping of real-world entities to ontologies. Ontologies can model entities and their properties by modeling specific instances, providing a structured representation of the domain.
  - Contextualization: Instances provide context-specific information. They allow the ontology to record the specific traits, qualities, and connections of the domain's entities. Contextualization improves the accuracy and precision of the knowledge being represented.
  - Examples as Instances: Instances are examples or exemplars of the concepts defined by classes. Because they provide concrete examples of abstract ideas, both humans and machines can relate to and comprehend them better.
  - Instances as Data: An instance can store data values that correspond to attributes associated with it. This data can be used for a variety of purposes, including classification, deductive reasoning, and decision-making. Using instances, data can be stored and used within an ontology (Noy, 2012).
- **Using Instances to Reason and Infer:** Ontologies' reasoning and inference abilities are influenced by instances. By using instances, ontologies can support various types of reasoning, such as classification, deduction, and induction. Instances are important in the following aspects of reasoning:
  - The ontology's entities are categorized and classified using instances. By assigning instances to specific classes, the ontology can categorize similar entities and infer their shared traits and relationships.
  - Instances aid inference by providing specific examples and data. Based on preexisting ontology axioms and rules, reasoning engines can use these examples to conclude, discover hidden connections, and generate new knowledge.

- Data-driven reasoning can be applied to instances that have associated data values. By examining the values of instance attributes, ontologies can make judgments, perform calculations, and generate new knowledge based on the data available (Spear, 2015).

8.4.4. Axioms

Axioms are an important part of ontology because they provide a formal and logical framework for knowledge representation. Axioms are statements that express constraints, rules, or facts within an ontology, allowing for accurate and unambiguous knowledge representation.

- **Axioms: What They Are and Why They Matter:** Axioms are logical assertions that describe the relationships, characteristics, and constraints found in an ontology. They contribute to the evolution of ontologies in a variety of ways. Axioms are important because they ensure clarity and consistency in knowledge representation by defining the semantics and meaning of classes, instances, and properties. They define the conditions under which concepts can be classified, examples can be generated, and connections can be made. Axioms can also be used to automate ontology inference and reasoning. Axioms aid deductive reasoning by providing a set of logical constraints and rules that allow the ontology to infer new information or establish implicit relationships between entities. Axioms serve as the foundation for logical reasoning engines for tasks such as consistency checking, classification, subsumption, and other inferential tasks.
- **Types of Axioms:** Axioms are classified into several types based on their function and the aspects of ontology they address. The following are examples of typical axiom types:
  - **Axioms of Class:** The class axioms, which specify relationships between classes, define the taxonomic hierarchy within an ontology. For example, the subclass axiom "Bird" "Animal" states that the class "Bird" is a subclass of the class "Animal." Other class axioms are disjointness axioms (such as "Cat" "Dog," indicating that cats and dogs are disjoint classes) and union axioms (such as "Bird" "Ostrich" "Penguin," indicating that a bird is either an ostrich or a penguin).

- **Property Axioms:** A property axiom in an ontology describes the qualities and connections between properties. For example, the domain axiom "hasChild Person" states that only instances of the class "Person" can have the property "hasChild" applied to them. Range axioms specify the permissible classes or values for a property, such as "hasAge xsd:integer," which specifies that the property "hasAge" should only have integer values.
- **Individual Axioms:** Individual axioms specify the characteristics and connections of specific instances within an ontology. For example, "John hasAge 30" assigns the value 30 to the property "hasAge" for the specific instance "John." Individual axioms provide concrete knowledge of specific entities, enabling precise instance representation and reasoning.
- **Logical Axioms:** Logical axioms define the logical relationships and constraints in an ontology. These axioms use formal logic languages, such as the OWL, to express logical rules and conditions. According to the equivalence axiom "Person (Human hasChild.Person)," a person is equivalent to a human who has at least one child who is also a person.

- **Axioms' Importance in Ontology**: For a variety of reasons, axioms are crucial to the development and application of ontologies. Axioms, first and foremost, improve the expressivity and accuracy of ontologies. They provide a formal and logical structure to the ontology while capturing the intricate relationships, constraints, and laws that exist within a domain. Ontology designers can use axioms to represent knowledge in a way that is both machine and human-processable (Noy, 2012).

Axioms also allow for automated inference and reasoning in ontologies. By specifying the logical rules and constraints, axioms enable reasoning engines to perform tasks such as consistency checking, classification, and subsumption reasoning. They allow the ontology to draw conclusions, infer relationships, and identify discrepancies within the represented domain.

Axioms also aid in the integration and interoperability of ontologies. By adhering to standardized axiom languages such as OWL, ontologies can be shared, merged, and aligned with other ontologies, facilitating knowledge integration and exchange across various domains. Axioms provide ontology developers with a common language and framework for establishing consensus and ensuring consistency in knowledge representation.

- **Problems and Considerations When Creating an Axiom:** Axiom development in ontologies can be difficult and time-consuming. To begin with, axiom development necessitates domain knowledge and a thorough understanding of the represented domain. To ensure the validity and utility of the ontology, axioms should accurately capture the semantics and relationships within the domain (Spcar, 2015).

Second, it is critical to select the appropriate axiom language and expressivity level. The chosen language should be compatible with the ontology's requirements as well as the tools' reasoning capacity. Expressivity and simplicity must be balanced to avoid unnecessary complexity or performance issues.

Ontology evolution complicates axiom development even more. As knowledge advances and novel insights are discovered, axioms may need to be updated or expanded. It is critical to consider how changing an axiom affects previously held knowledge, as well as how the modified axiom interacts with ontologies that use or are aligned with it.

8.4.5. Relationships

Relationships are an important part of ontology because they define the connections and interactions between entities within a domain. Relationships are critical for capturing the semantics and dependencies between various concepts and instances.

- **Types of Relationship and Definition:** The associations or connections between entities are referred to as relationships in ontology. They define how things relate to one another and can be classified into different types based on how they behave. N-ary relationships contain more than two entities, whereas binary relationships contain only two. Asymmetric (one entity has a different role or characteristic than the other) or symmetric (both entities share the same relationship) relationships are also possible (Noy, 2012).
    - Semantic Expressiveness: Relationships improve their semantic expressiveness by providing ontologies with a way to represent intricate relationships between entities.

They allow ontologies to capture the domain's dynamic and interdependent nature, as well as the attributes and characteristics of individual entities. Relationships allow for the representation of dependencies, hierarchies, compositions, and a variety of other patterns of connectivity, which improves knowledge representation and allows for more complex reasoning.

- Identifying Interactions and Dependencies Ontologies with well-defined relationships provide a framework for capturing entity interactions and dependencies. They allow you to simulate how different entities within a domain influence, rely on, or interact with one another. Relationships, for example, can be used in a medical ontology to represent the connections between symptoms, illnesses, and treatments, allowing for more thorough knowledge representation and assisting decision-making.
- Making Inference and Reasoning Possible: For inference and reasoning within ontologies, relationships are critical. By defining relationships between entities, ontologies enable logical inferences and the creation of new knowledge. Rationality engines can use relationships to infer implicit relationships, draw conclusions, and respond to difficult questions. If an ontology specifies a relationship between "parent" and "child," for example, the reasoning engine can make an implicit assumption about the relationship between "grandparent" and "grandchild" without explicitly defining it.
- Taxonomies and Hierarchical Relationships: Hierarchical relationships, a common type of relationship in ontologies, form taxonomies that organize concepts into hierarchical structures. These relationships allow entities to be grouped based on shared characteristics and traits. Hierarchies facilitate more effective knowledge organization, search, and navigation, making it easier to retrieve and explore information within a domain (Noy, 2012).
- Relationship Properties and Cardinality: Relationships can have characteristics that help to define them. Among these properties are cardinality constraints, which define the

number of entities in a relationship. Cardinality constraints can limit the types of associations that can be formed between entities, such as "one-to-one," "one-to-many," or "many-to-many" relationships.

There are several challenges in designing and managing relationships in ontologies. The appropriate granularity and specificity of relationships must be considered to ensure accurate and thorough knowledge representation. Important considerations include the consistency and coherence of relationships, as well as conformity to the overall structure of the ontology. Furthermore, striking a balance between expressivity and complexity is critical to avoid developing overly complex ontologies that impair understanding and reasoning (Spear, 2015).

8.4.6. Inference Mechanisms

Inference mechanisms, which are critical to ontology, enable the ability to derive new knowledge and infer implicit relationships. Through logical reasoning and deduction, these computational methods improve the expressiveness and functionality of ontologies.

- **The Importance of Inference Mechanisms:** Because of inference mechanisms, ontology can reason and draw logical conclusions from previously known information. They allow for the automatic inference of new knowledge that is implicit in the ontology. This capability improves the strength and utility of ontologies in a variety of domains. Inference mechanisms enable systems to draw conclusions, verify claims, and fill information gaps, improving knowledge sharing, integration, and decision-making.
- **Types of Inferences:** A variety of computational techniques known as inference mechanisms enable various types of inferences within an ontology. The following are examples of key types of inferences:
  - Class Subsumption: Inference mechanisms can determine class relationships such as subsumption and superclass relationships. By examining the relationships between classes, these mechanisms can determine whether two classes are equivalent or whether one class is a subclass of another.

- Instance Classification Inference mechanisms allow for the automatic classification of instances into appropriate classes based on their properties and relationships. They can determine which classes the instance belongs to by looking at the class definitions and the properties associated with it.
- Property Reasoning: Inference mechanisms can infer instances' implicit or missing properties using information already present in the ontology. For example, if an ontology states that "All mammals give birth to live young," the inference mechanism can infer that a specific instance of the class "Dog" has the property "gives birth to live young" even if it is not explicitly stated.
- Checking for Consistency: Inference mechanisms help ensure the coherence and consistency of ontologies by identifying inconsistencies or conflicts within the knowledge represented. Identifying instances or properties that defy the stated axioms or rules can help to resolve inconsistencies (Spear, 2015).

• **The Advantages of Inference Mechanisms:** Ontology can benefit from inference mechanisms in a variety of ways:
  - Improved Knowledge Representation: Inference mechanisms enrich ontology knowledge by inferring implicit relationships and generating new knowledge. They go beyond the explicitly stated information, allowing for a more thorough understanding of the domain and the facilitation of more precise and accurate knowledge representation.
  - Intelligent Reasoning: Inference mechanisms enable intelligent reasoning within ontologies, allowing systems to arrive at deductively sound conclusions. Intelligent agents, decision support systems, and semantic search engines all rely on this capability.
  - Efficient Knowledge Integration: Inference mechanisms make it easier to integrate different ontologies or knowledge sources by harmonizing and aligning the represented knowledge. By resolving discrepancies, locating commonalities, and inferring relationships between

ontologies, they enable seamless knowledge exchange and interoperability.

- Adaptability and flexibility Ontologies can evolve and change over time thanks to inference mechanisms. As new information becomes available or the domain knowledge changes, these mechanisms can automatically update the ontology, infer new relationships, and ensure the consistency of the represented knowledge.

- **Considerations and Challenges:** Despite their benefits, inference mechanisms are not without challenges and considerations. Some of these difficulties include scalability issues, computational complexity, and the tension between expressivity and efficiency. It is critical to design scalable and effective inference mechanisms for dealing with massive ontologies and real-time reasoning. Furthermore, because highly expressive inference can be computationally costly, striking a balance between expressive reasoning and practical efficiency is critical.

Furthermore, due to the complexity of ontologies and the inherent uncertainty in real-world domains, inference mechanisms may encounter difficulties. Ontology engineering researchers are currently working on handling uncertainty, probabilistic reasoning, and dealing with ambiguous or incomplete information (Noy, 2012).

8.4.7. Challenges in Designing and Utilizing Ontology Components Effectively

A variety of issues and factors must be carefully considered for ontology components to be designed and used effectively. Ontologies are a powerful tool for knowledge representation, but creating and using them can be difficult.

- **Domain Expertise: To** create ontologies that accurately represent a specific domain, the domain must first be thoroughly understood. Knowledge engineers and other domain experts, such as subject matter experts, are critical to ontology development. Cooperation between domain experts and ontology engineers is required to ensure that the ontology components accurately capture the domain's concepts, relationships, and semantics. Inadequate or inaccurate representations may result from a lack of domain knowledge, reducing the ontology's usefulness (Spear, 2015).

- **Granularity:** Choosing the appropriate level of granularity for ontology components is difficult. Granularity refers to the degree of specificity with which concepts, properties, and relationships are defined. If the ontology is too coarse-grained, it may lose important distinctions and nuances. On the other hand, if it is too fine-grained, the ontology may become overly complicated to manage. To keep the ontology useful and maintainable, the ideal balance of granularity and simplicity must be found.
- **Expressivity vs. Efficiency:** Ontologies' expressiveness varies, with more expressive ontologies supporting more sophisticated reasoning capabilities but potentially requiring more computational resources. When designing ontologies, expressivity and efficiency must be balanced. Complex reasoning is enabled by highly expressive ontologies, such as those built on Description Logics, but the corresponding inference mechanisms may be computationally expensive. Based on the application's requirements, it is critical to select an appropriate level of expressivity that maximizes both reasoning power and computational efficiency.
- **Ontology Scalability:** Managing large ontologies can be difficult. As ontologies grow in size and complexity, problems with organization, storage, and retrieval become more important. Effective indexing and retrieval mechanisms are required to handle large ontologies effectively. Reasoning engines must be optimized for scalability and responsiveness when performing inference on large ontologies. Scalability considerations are critical for avoiding performance bottlenecks and making ontology components usable.
- **Ontology Alignment and Integration:** To facilitate knowledge transfer and interoperability between different systems or domains, ontologies must frequently be aligned and integrated. Integrating ontologies from various sources with varying terminology and structures can be difficult. Overcoming semantic heterogeneity, resolving disputes, and creating mappings between ontologies are examples of complex tasks. For ontology alignment and integration to be effective, semantic gaps between ontologies must be filled using ontology matching methods, alignment algorithms, and mediation techniques (Noy, 2012).

- **Ontology Evolution:** Ontologies are dynamic systems that evolve to account for new information, domain changes, and changing requirements. Controlling ontology evolution, on the other hand, can be difficult. Updating ontologies while maintaining consistency and backward compatibility is difficult. To manage ontology updates, track changes, and maintain version control, strong strategies, and tools are required. The consequences of ontology changes on existing applications and systems must also be carefully managed.

It is critical to assess the quality, efficacy, and suitability of ontologies for a given purpose. Some evaluation criteria include correctness, completeness, clarity, and usability. Ontologies can be evaluated to identify areas for improvement, validate the ontology against the target domain, and ensure its utility in real-world applications. Ongoing research is being conducted to develop comprehensive evaluation methods and metrics for assessing the worth and performance of ontology components (Spear, 2015).

8.5. TYPES OF ONTOLOGY

Domain Ontology

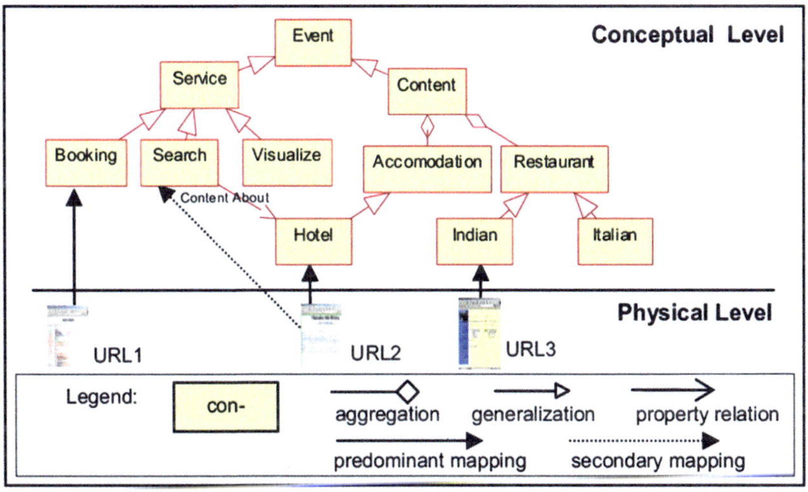

Figure 8.6. *An example of domain ontology.*

Source: Vanzin, Becker, & Ruiz, (2005); Scientific figure on ResearchGate. Available from: https://www.researchgate.net/figure/Domain-ontology-example_fig3_221017457.

A domain ontology (also known as a domain-specific ontology) represents concepts that fall under a specific term. Domain ontology specifies the meanings of terms used in that domain. For example, the word "card" has several meanings. The term's "playing card" connotation would be represented by an ontology pertaining to the "poker" domain (Figure 8.6).

Domain ontologies are frequently incompatible due to the very specific and frequently eclectic ways in which they represent concepts. As the number of systems that rely on domain ontologies grows, it becomes necessary to combine them into a more comprehensive representation. Different ontologies in the same domain result from language differences, ontologies' intended applications, and perceptions of the domain (based on cultural background, educational attainment, ideologies, and so on).

Upper Ontology:

An upper ontology, also known as a foundation ontology, is a representation of universally applicable common objects found in many domain ontologies. It typically employs a core glossary containing terms and descriptions of related objects as they appear in various relevant domain sets (Noy, 2012).

Many upper ontologies, including Dublin Core, have been standardized and can be used.

- Hybrid Ontology

  Higher-level and domain ontologies are combined in a hybrid ontology.

- Ontology Editor

To aid in the creation or manipulation of ontologies, applications called ontology editors are developed. They frequently express ontologies using one of the many ontology languages. A few provide export to various ontology languages (Spear, 2015).

When choosing an ontology editor, one of the most important factors to consider is how far the editor abstracts from the actual ontology representation language used for persistence, as well as the possibilities for visual navigation within the knowledge model. Support for meta-ontologies such as OWL-S, Dublin Core, and others, as well as integrated inference engines and information extraction tools, are critical features. Another critical feature is the ability of foreign knowledge representation languages for ontology matching to be imported and exported. Ontologies are designed with a specific use and application in mind.

Ontology Learning

Ontology learning is the automatic or semi-automatic development of ontologies, including the extraction of domain terms from natural language text. Because manually creating ontologies takes a lot of time and effort, there is a need to automate the process. Information extraction and text mining techniques have been investigated to automatically link ontologies to documents (Noy, 2012).

CHAPTER

9 Using Metadata for E-Learning

Contents

9.1. INTRODUCTION

E-learning environments are considered a crucial component in the field of education as they facilitate students in accomplishing their academic tasks and meeting graduation requirements within the stipulated time frame. The implementation of the ideas, techniques, and strategies that have been recently introduced in various scholarly works to enable the creation of e-learning platforms that are accessible and foster digital inclusivity poses a formidable task. The incorporation of accessibility metadata in this particular context serves to not only enrich the depiction of modified educational resources but also facilitates the identification of said resources by students, particularly those with disabilities, by their unique requirements and inclinations. The present investigation involved a methodical examination aimed at ascertaining the existing level of understanding concerning the utilization of accessibility metadata in e-learning settings (Kameas, 2015) (Figure 9.1).

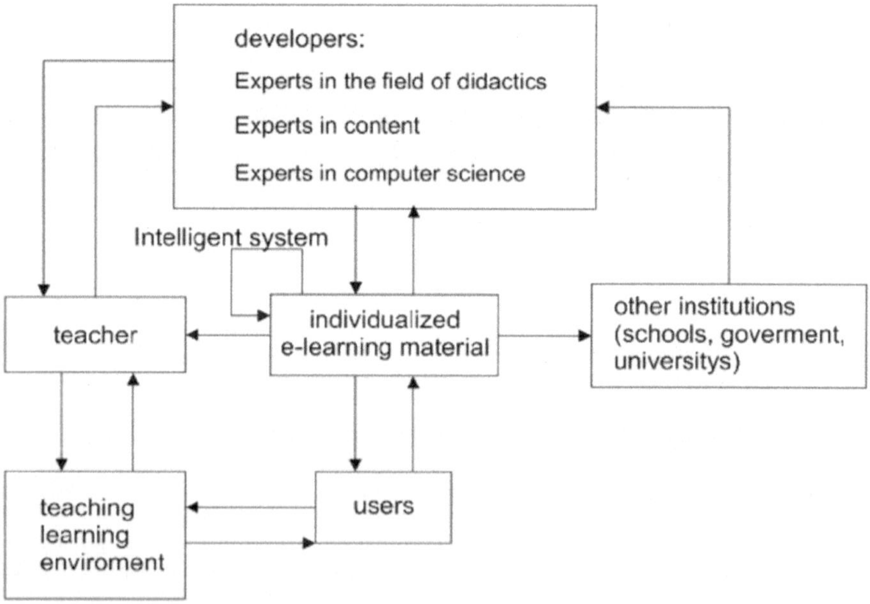

Figure 9.1. *Use of metadata obtained in individualized e-learning material.*

Source: Dolenc, Pesek, & Abersek, (2013); Scientific figure on ResearchGate. Available from: https://www.researchgate.net/figure/Use-of-metadata-obtained-in-individualized-e-learning-material_fig3_271852557.

The swift advancement of technology mandates intricate and specialized proficiencies that require periodic updating. As a result, the importance of ongoing education and perpetual learning is on the rise. E-learning is a suitable option for individuals seeking to pursue further education as it allows for simultaneous completion alongside other commitments. Consequently, academic institutions are faced with novel challenges, including the implementation of a robust e-learning framework and the integration of digital course materials. Furthermore, e-learning systems must be designed in a manner that enables convenient access to both courses and course materials. The provision of information about courses and other relevant factors serves to enhance accessibility. In the absence of an ontology that provides a framework for interpreting metadata, the value of basic metadata is negligible. The present chapter aims to furnish a comprehensive outline of the application of ontologies and metadata in e-learning systems. Furthermore, an analysis will be conducted on the educational metadata prerequisites, along with an evaluation of the implementation of ontologies and metadata in three distinct e-learning systems (Garcia, 2010).

9.2. CONTENT ORGANIZATION AND CATEGORIZATION

Metadata consists of more than just the identifiers after blog posts. It is ostensibly "data about data," so it is content data in terms of content data. The structural information defines the components and relationships of a page's content. It makes it easy to insert a content block into a different template and maintains content and design distinct by defining the page's components. When structural information is in place, it's easier to construct content based on user interactions, behavior patterns, and preferences. This type of data enables personalization as well as content analytics and data-driven insights.

This is related to the content model because I am confident that when a visitor selects one of the challenges listed in the designated area, he will be directed to the correct page. Consequently, the descriptive metadata optimizes the material's relationships and logic. A crucial aspect of a content management system is its search function. A content management system's primary objective is to make content accessible, as this enables you to take action, make business decisions, conduct research and development, etc.

The primary challenge for discoverability is determining how to anticipate users' future information inquiries. Categorization is advantageous in this situation. The discoverability of any item of content depends on how well it has been categorized. Ideally, effective labeling will increase the durability of the material. You might believe that if you do something correctly the first time, you can forget about it until it's time to retire it. Nevertheless, the reality often appears to be quite distinct. One strategy is to use technology to automatically classify content. It consistently applies laws to individuals. The process is more expedient. It is less expensive because it relieves people of labor-intensive tasks. It can also classify groups or entire document collections, either immediately or later (Kameas, 2015).

Utilizing concept-based categorization facilitated by an analytics engine incorporated into the content management system can yield these benefits. These systems generate concepts for categorizing additional texts based on a mathematical analysis of the example documents you provide. They can determine significance that eludes keywords and other traditional taxonomy approaches by discovering hundreds of keywords for each item. They may make connections that one would otherwise overlook.

The practice of hoarding items "just in case" is no longer prevalent. Due to cost and risk exposure concerns, organizations must only retain essential information, particularly as the volume and variety of content grow. For effective content management, cost management, and exposure control, effective categorization and marking systems are necessary. As a consequence of obsolete and superfluous documents, every company's content repositories grow. There are multiple duplicates of the same or very similar information throughout the organization. According to some estimates, this makes up at least 20% of a company's content. Effectively eliminating this content will reduce active and backup storage, bandwidth, cloud storage for off-site disaster recovery, and archive volume by 20%. Such components can be identified through comprehensive and effective labeling, thereby reducing the company's costs and risk to any applicable legal and regulatory obligations. Effective content management reduces risk and reduces content management costs. Nonetheless, there are additional reasons to enhance classification besides this one.

Superior categorization based on conceptual analysis increases operational efficiency by facilitating rapid, accurate, and exhaustive data collection. Reduced time spent searching for information is a significant advantage for any organization, as it permits more time to be spent on actual work. It is essential for businesses whose revenue relies on consumers receiving quality information quickly and readily (Garcia, 2010). Conceptual analytics systems have two advantages over traditional taxonomies and human categorization. Because it generates a mathematical index, it is ineffective for discovering confidential information or indications about the company. Additionally, it is repeatable and predictable. It consistently yields the same result, making it indispensable for legal and regulatory activities. The concept-based analysis automatically categorizes content based on knowledge gleaned from provided sample documents, making it discoverable and actionable regardless of language. Using unstructured information, one of the firm's most valuable assets, the business becomes more competitive both internally and externally.

9.3. SEARCH AND DISCOVERY

Metadata facilitates the process of locating and searching for feline images, irrespective of whether a particular feline is being sought. What is the methodology for retrieving images through a search engine? What specific keywords do you plan to utilize to optimize your search outcomes? Articulating our desired visual elements in a photograph can present a formidable task. It can be challenging to communicate the intricate network of visual components within a singular image through the use of search queries. It is possible to mentally visualize the appearance of an image even in the absence of conscious awareness of its existence. The absence of individuality is evident in search engines. At present, the ordinary human intellect surpasses the capabilities of all computer-based technologies. Liqun Luo from Stanford University asserts that although the brain is significantly slower than a computer when performing basic computational steps, humans excel over computers in a wide range of real-world tasks. These tasks include identifying a bicycle or a specific pedestrian on a busy city street, as well as smoothly reaching for and moving a cup of tea to one's lips. Additionally, humans outperform computers in the areas of conceptualization and creativity (Kameas, 2015).

The disparity between the interpretation of the content of a digital image by a machine and a human, commonly referred to as the semantic gap, often poses a challenge to the accuracy and efficacy of such searches. Search engines encounter challenges in comprehending the context, semantics, and entities embedded in an image exclusively through pixel information. Despite the visual appearance of search results being influenced by the content of an image, it is the associated textual information, commonly known as "metadata" among librarians that determines the outcome of the search rather than the image per se. The execution of this process may present challenges in cases where the digital representation of an image comprises a limited quantity of textual information, where the textual descriptions are of a subjective nature, or where the descriptions lack reliability.

The advent of AI-powered visual search tools is already causing a transformation in this regard. For iPhone users, it is possible to observe a lack of precision in the search results when searching for basic terms such as "dog" or "food" in their photo gallery. This is evidenced by the occurrence of inaccurate search results, such as the retrieval of images of cats and shoes when searching for "dog." The Amazon Lens feature enables users to capture images of nearby items and conduct a search for comparable merchandise. It is expected that the increasing size of training datasets will lead to greater prevalence and accuracy of image recognition, object detection, and enhanced information extraction technologies. Instead of relying on human-generated text to associate with an image, these techniques facilitate the computer to autonomously generate metadata directly from the image. The integration of AI technology has the potential to enhance image search functionality by streamlining the process, increasing its logical coherence, and improving its capacity to accurately interpret and align with user queries. Subtle variations in hue, viewpoint, lighting, or arrangement can pose a challenge in identifying images that share comparable aesthetic attributes through commonly accessible methodologies. Artificial intelligence (AI) envisions a future where the process of identifying photographs with similar visual attributes is simplified (Garcia, 2010).

The correlation between search queries and visual information is a crucial factor in the process of identifying photographs. Currently, the efficacy of photo retrieval is contingent upon the degree of concordance between search terms and image metadata. Occasionally, depictions of the visual elements within an image are incorporated, although this is not consistently the case. Queries that fail to visually represent the intended results are deemed ineffective. The potential for AI tools to mitigate the gap between our visual expectations and their realization is a promising prospect. However, the acquisition of knowledge regarding metadata and its effective implementation are crucial factors in the ongoing pursuit of image discovery (Kameas, 2015).

9.4. PERSONALIZED RECOMMENDATIONS

With the development of data collection and capture technologies, the importance of information filtering to make recommendations has increased. Online shoppers have far too many options to choose from. Effective user recommendations have become a significant obstacle in e-commerce. Over the past decade, researchers and practitioners have become increasingly interested in the study of methods for generating dependable personalized recommendations. User preferences are typically expressed in terms of ratings or stars assigned to each object on a continuum. However, implicit feedback only indicates user-object interactions. Implicit quantitative or binary feedback may exist. Quantitative implicit feedback based on frequency demonstrates a user's engagement with an item. In binary implicit feedback, a 1 indicates user engagement with the item, while a 0 indicates non-interaction. Since a 0 in the data may represent either undetected interaction or negative feedback, implicit feedback is regarded as notably incoherent. In this investigation, we employ binary implicit feedback to provide the top N suggestions. The absence of unambiguous user interest signals makes the recommendation task more difficult when using binary implicit.

We use neighborhood-based and model-based collaborative filtering algorithms to generate concepts from binary implicit inputs. Because there are insufficient explicit user indications of apathy and insufficient training data sets, the accuracy of recommender systems may be low. The content-based method generates feature vectors for the proposed items using the properties of the items in real-world scenarios, these feature vectors are frequently sparse and of high dimension, which reduces the utility and accuracy of the content-based strategy. Recently, researchers have sought to leverage item meta-information to address the problem of sparse feedback data. They constructed the heterogeneous information network (HIN) using the meta-information of the commodities. In the case of an online bookstore, meta-information such as the book's category, discipline, subject, course for which it is appropriate, author(s), etc., would be included. In the context of an online store, this meta-data may be used to derive the HIN for books (Garcia, 2010).

Online personalized recommendations are pertinent suggestions generated by a recommendation engine (also known as a recommender system) that employs an algorithm to select options based on information about the customer's on-site navigation. • What search terms have they inserted as suggestions? How long have they been searching? What are their recent acquisitions? What additional items might complement what they have been viewing? What additional products have other customers purchased in addition to what they appear to desire? What items are in their purchasing cart? Have they abandoned it? Have they shared anything on social media about a product? What films have they viewed on the online movie subscription site model? Before recommendation engines can make accurate predictions regarding what to recommend, they must examine all available data. Three significant focus areas are highlighted: This form of recommendation engine collects and analyzes data on user preferences and behaviors to determine what a user prefers based on their similarities with other users. It is important to note that the content of the product, novel, or film is not evaluated. This method makes predictions based on past behavior by analyzing user preferences among individuals with similar interests. A matrix-based algorithm directs it (Kameas, 2015).

There are two methods to perform collaborative filtering: model-based and memory-based

Memory-based collaborative filtering identifies user clusters and analyzes user activity to predict the interactions of similar users. It also identifies groupings of things that user A has rated and uses those groupings to predict how user A would interact with an item B that is comparable. The development of prediction models through machine learning and data mining is the foundation of model-based collaborative filtering. For instance, it may predict preferred items based on interactions with a particular item. It can recommend more items to more individuals. If you see the phrase "If you like that, you might also like this," or if you viewed an item a few weeks ago and now receive a recommendation for a similar item, the filtering is content-based. When creating content-based recommendations, comparable products are categorized by their features. The algorithms that generate suggestions take into consideration client preferences and item parameters (such as genre, category, and color). The success or failure of your website could be determined by the quality of the recommendations provided. When you can use big data to impress and retain contented customers, you have attained the elusive goal of engagement. Sustained engagement leads to an improvement in site performance.

Better conversion rates will ultimately result from your consistent efforts to understand your customers' needs from the moment they begin searching until they reach the checkout page, regardless of whether they abruptly end their shopping spree or purchase several additional suggested items before returning the following day to look for more. Personalized recommendations ultimately benefit both enterprises and customers.

9.5. COMPETENCY MAPPING

Strategic route planning is necessary for effective navigation to save trip time. Similar to using a DAM platform. The digital asset management (DAM) system's search functionality is greatly aided by metadata. Without it, one's whole collection of things would be vulnerable to irreparable loss and made useless. It is understood that entering data might be a time-consuming operation. What steps may be done to guarantee the accurate entry of metadata? the metadata correlation. Although it is possible to make changes to each metadata field independently, doing so can be tedious and time-consuming. Different uploading methods demand various metadata management methodologies. A method called metadata mapping enables the automatic, continuous, or one-time allocation of substantial metadata from many sources (Garcia, 2010).

The goal of this discourse is to examine the best configuration for one's metadata mapping.

- Finding out where your data is right now is the first step. The next step is to decide the cartographic category or categories you will use in collaboration with your DAM team. It is crucial to determine the metadata's underlying structure before mapping. May I be of any help to you? Establish a metadata taxonomy for your system in collaboration with your team by evaluating the metadata options available to you. Gathering metadata from your institution's current databases and technologies is a good place to start the process. By your framework, start the process of charting your method. It is advised that when creating your mapping process, you consider the following factors.
- Determine where your data is right now. Although your current sources and systems include a sizable amount of information, the word "metadata" may not have been used yet. Whether you are using self-made movies or stock photos, it is likely that the materials you are using already include information. Utilizing metadata from other tools, such as a product information management (PIM) system or an internal content system, may help standardize information across platforms and get rid of discrepancies. Finding pre-existing data might help you allocate assets in your DAM system efficiently and avoid making unnecessary efforts (Kameas, 2015).
- Decide which type (or types) of mapping will be used. There

are several approaches available for mapping information. Understanding the source of one's data makes it easier to concentrate on the best answers. Single-use imports are frequently used to change metadata on assets that have already been imported into a DAM system or to move metadata across DAM solutions. A spreadsheet in the XLS or CSV format is used to import data once, often using the asset's file name as the unique identification. This import function allows for the completion of a large number of tasks in advance. The metadata fields and values are simultaneously filled in after preparation, making it a good substitute for customized metadata encoding.

Documents are imported into the system based on their IDs. An automated script incorporated into your DAM system may permanently and autonomously correlate metadata with associated files by using a consistent file name convention and standard metadata values. The procedure entails listing values in an XLS spreadsheet and then translating those values to the elements.

When working with digital photographers who use Adobe Bridge, Lightroom, and Photoshop, the use of automated imports can produce notable time savings. The existent XMP, IPTC, or Exif information is immediately sent to the DAM system upon picture upload. Photographers have the option to add more information to picture editing software, which may then be quickly connected to pre-existing fields in a DAM system. Since they input all pertinent information into their editing software, which then sends the data to the DAM system, this technique is beneficial for managing freelance photographers. The administrator in charge of DAM may be able to save time by doing this and make it simpler to find specific information about a picture.

Because they may be tailored to a business's unique tools and needs, API imports are incredibly flexible. Teams may use API import to build custom integrations that allow real-time data changes from other sources, such as PIM systems and CMSs. Teams can decide the frequency of data imports based on their own internal rules. Through this type of import, data synchronization across all instruments used by an entity may be accomplished in the simplest way possible. It is recommended to keep an eye out for opportunities to simplify and hasten the metadata mapping process. Determine the most effective solutions that will improve your present processes and procedures by working with other tools. This ensures the continued use of your data and speeds up the completion of your goal

(Garcia, 2010). For effective content retrieval inside a DAM system, high-quality information must be provided within the metadata. Utilize the best methods for handling picture information and other productivity-boosting concepts, such as restricted lexicon inventories. Relevant content can also be held by your DAM system's manufacturer. Widen, a DAM system has a metadata importer tool that makes it possible to simultaneously add information to several assets. It is possible to maintain simplified and effective metadata by being aware of your alternatives.

9.6. PROGRESS TRACKING AND REPORTING

Effective metadata management tools offer comprehensive contextual information to facilitate a deeper understanding of the data. Their contributions serve to augment the pertinence and caliber of the data. This allows for the optimization of the commercial possibilities inherent in the data. In the context of expanding and decentralized data, the utilization of metadata is imperative for several reasons. Firstly, metadata enables the discovery of data. Secondly, metadata facilitates the recognition of data linkages. Thirdly, metadata allows for the monitoring of data usage. Lastly, metadata enables the assessment of both the advantages and disadvantages of data utilization (Kameas, 2015).

The utilization of these methods is crucial in attaining the desired outcome. Thus, effective management of metadata plays a crucial role in facilitating the process of digital transformation and realizing the objectives of a Chief Data Officer. The efficacy of a metadata management system is enhanced through the utilization of AI and machine learning. Intelligent systems that are "active" have the potential to be enhanced with human knowledge, as well as other applications and data analytics software, to yield novel data insights. As a result, the management of large volumes of data has become increasingly intricate and fluid, necessitating the development of sophisticated systems, applications, and techniques. The administration of metadata necessitates the adaptation to the diverse range of data that exists across the entire organization. The given width has been bisected. An essential capability is the ability to gather metadata from both on-premises and cloud-based sources that are distributed throughout the enterprise. The subsequent diagram depicts the four distinct classifications of metadata that necessitate proper management:

The inclusion of technical data, comprising of database schemas, mappings, and code, alongside quality assurance procedures. The metadata about the business context, including but not limited to glossary vocabulary, governance procedures, and application metadata. The metadata that is relevant to the operations and infrastructure encompasses various metrics such as volume, run-time statistics, time stamps, and system and location data. Metadata of usage, including user evaluations, comments, and usage trends. As alluded to in the preceding segment, active metadata pertains to metadata that has undergone enhancement through the utilization of AI and machine learning. Active metadata management and predictive data intelligence go beyond providing support for metadata analysis and instead, promote or suggest actions to be taken by users. Upon identifying any absent or inaccurate content, the information can be automatically reinstated and enhanced through the process of restoration. This facilitates the improvement of analytical processes, the mitigation of expensive mistakes, and the optimization of decision-making capabilities. The four aforementioned categories of metadata constitute the fundamental elements of a standardized metadata framework. Intelligent metadata management technologies utilize a diverse range of capabilities to establish a shared foundation (Garcia, 2010).

- Collect metadata from both on-premises and cloud-based business data systems, such as data lakes and data warehouses. Tools and processes such as databases and filesystems, data integration tools, and workflows are instrumental in facilitating the data fitness of data analytics and data science tools.
- Become a curator. Utilizing a compendium of lexicon, principles, and methodologies, explicate the commercial outlook of the information. The inclusion of metadata is imperative in the context of commercial activities. Gather user input through the means of ratings, reviews, and certifications. This aids in ascertaining the usefulness of data assets for other users.
- To infer is to draw a conclusion or make an educated guess based on available information or evidence. Employ cognitive abilities to infer connections that were not disclosed by the assemblage of metadata. This section pertains to the topics of data provenance and lineage, data similarity, and the categorization of the most precise data sets for diverse user groups and applications.
- Optimal approaches for managing metadata.

By adhering to the recommended guidelines for metadata management, it is possible to establish a sophisticated data management system that is well-suited for the contemporary multi-cloud and hybrid data landscape. One crucial step is to establish a coherent metadata framework. Establishing a standardized metadata framework enables the provision of comprehensive insight and intelligence across all data management procedures. Employ the four primary categories of metadata. To optimize the worth of one's data, it is recommended to employ metadata intelligence for the four principal categories of metadata, namely technical, business, and operational/infrastructure, and usage/social. Utilize AI and machine learning techniques to enable the activation of your metadata. To enhance the intelligence and dynamism of all cloud data management activities, it is recommended to integrate AI and machine learning techniques in the unification of metadata management.

Leveraging an AI-driven data catalog, enhance the accessibility and usability of metadata for all users of data. To foster a culture of data appreciation within an organization, it is imperative to gather corporate data and furnish a pertinent business context. An AI-driven data catalog is capable of examining, arranging, and categorizing data to enhance the accessibility, comprehension, and trustworthiness of pertinent information throughout an enterprise (Kameas, 2015).

It is imperative to ensure that the management of metadata possesses the appropriate scope, depth, and scale to adequately fulfill the demands of the present data ecosystem. Effective metadata management necessitates the ability to extract comprehensive metadata, comprehend intricate data lineage (such as by interpreting database code), and manage a vast number of metadata assets, potentially numbering in the hundreds of millions. Implementing model governance is crucial for ensuring the responsible and ethical use of AI and machine learning. The process of operationalizing AI/ML models involves the acquisition and preservation of metadata that is specific to the model. By avoiding algorithmic bias, it is possible to effectively manage the performance of AI/ML models by business Key Performance Indicators (KPIs). It is recommended to incorporate metadata stewards who possess the proficiency to execute advanced metadata management principles into your data governance team. This is commonly regarded as a crucial determinant of a proficient metadata management approach (Garcia, 2010).

9.7. INTEGRATION WITH LEARNING MANAGEMENT SYSTEMS

The Learning Object Repository (LOR) is a well-organized concept that allows educators to share, manage, and utilize educational resources more easily. This method has grown in popularity among academic and research institutions all around the world. To be interoperable and scalable, learning object repositories (LORs) rely heavily on a variety of standards and protocols, including LOM, SCORM, and others. Learning management systems (LMS), which make it simpler to enroll for courses offered by prestigious academic institutions at a distance, have considerably assisted the growth of e-learning. However, there is no established technique for merging these two e-learning systems and assuring their successful collaboration at the moment. The current study describes the process of importing data linked to learning objects onto the Open class platform (Kameas, 2015) (Figure 9.2).

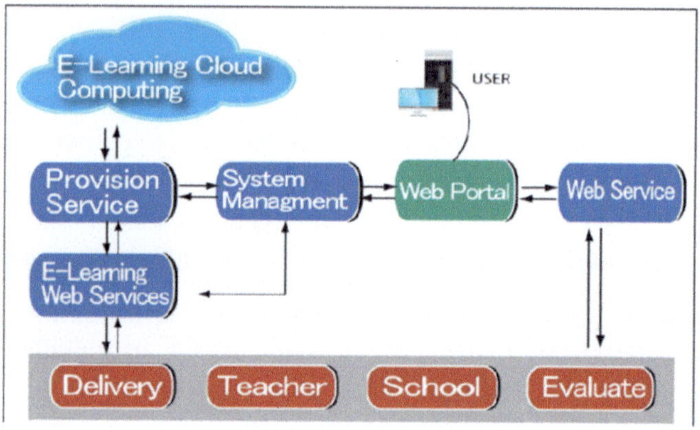

Figure 9.2. *Model of integrated learning management system.*

Source: Kaewkiriya, & Utakrit, (2012); Scientific figure on ResearchGate. Available from: https://www.researchgate.net/figure/Model-of-integrated-learning-management-system_fig5_301223525.

A consistent framework, the dissemination of metadata mappings, and the development of bridge languages were all aims of previous research on educational system interoperability. To index content from LMS, a LOR should be employed (Kameas, 2015). Many LMSs do not yet support automated content import from learning object repositories (LORs). Even when such functionality is provided, it is typically weak and confined to a few specific repositories. Inconsistencies in metadata standards and concerns regarding interoperability appear to be having a significant influence on the current situation. An example of this is the development of a customized plugin for the Moodle LMS that allows for the selective transfer of educational content solely from the MERLOT learning repository. The LUISA initiative, which was supported by the European Union, later established a framework for integrating Learning Object Repositories (LOR) with a Learning Content Management System (LCMS). By employing semantic technologies, the aforementioned solution effectively addressed the critical issue of ensuring interoperability in Digital Rights Management (DRM) (Garcia, 2010).

Higher education organizations interested in implementing asynchronous remote learning may find the Open e-Class platform, which is both free and customizable, useful. Furthermore, the Greek Academic Network, or Gunet, has implemented a system to deliver asynchronous e-learning services to institutions. The aforementioned organization is mostly responsible for the Gunet Asynchronous eLearning Group's inception, growth, and maintenance. It is unknown which specific standards and protocols are included in the e-class platform's architecture. This part aims to define the E-Class platform's metadata schema, show how it links to the LOM standard, and identify the various specifications and standards that comprise its infrastructure. Furthermore, we outline how we want to map to other repositories. Section 2 discusses additional criteria as well as the mapping of Learning Object Metadata (LOM).1. LOM standard developed by the Institute of Electrical and Electronics Engineers (IEEE) is extensively used for defining educational resources and content (Kameas, 2015).

Given the growing number of these resources, utilizing metadata to characterize them is an effective method to avoid the issues of identifying, organizing, and reusing them. Prior research indicates that creating specified definitions for learning material aspects increases sharing efficiency and breadth, management clarity and universality, and seeking precision and accuracy. As the need for educational metadata inclusion grows, there is a larger need for the development and implementation of metadata management systems that can effectively and efficiently carry out several operations on educational information. In terms of clarifying teaching materials. These systems have the potential to be employed anywhere. Web-based learning content repositories may be accessed, managed, and supported. These technologies make it simpler to index, store, retrieve, and utilize previously stored data. Lrmmss stands for Learning Resource Metadata Management Systems. The primary goal of developing educational materials among the aims of metadata-based systems is interoperability among linked systems and simplifying the reuse of stored and controlled information, both at the level of description and organization and at a more granular level of technical representation. The first aim is met by employing standard exchange technologies such as Extensible Markup Language (XML), and the second purpose is met by conforming to educational technology criteria.

Despite the availability of the IEEE Learning Object Metadata (LOM) [2, a widely acknowledged standard for identifying educational resources], many Learning Resource Management Systems (Lrmmss) continue to employ non-IEEE standards or out-of-date IEEE standards. Because of the existence of mechanisms designed to support the exploration, assessment, adaptability, and manipulation of learning resources in a context characterized by cultural and linguistic diversity (as identified by CEN/ISSS [3] as an issue of internationalization), it is also possible that two educational systems using identical metadata standards will encounter interoperability difficulties (Garcia, 2010).

9.8. QUALITY ASSURANCE AND CONTENT EVALUATION

The provision of quality information is anticipated to be a crucial and fundamental value-added service offered by worldwide portals and international gateways. The quality of metadata is a crucial aspect of acquiring knowledge on content sharing and distribution. The selection of high-quality metadata that encompasses information about content quality is a crucial aspect of this process, as it significantly influences the accessibility of information resources, as well as the recall and precision of search outcomes. Ensuring the quality of metadata is of particular significance for exceptional assets that are exclusively accessible through specialized digital repositories. An illustration of distinctive and precious commodities is represented by digitized historical patents. The present article presents a case study on the management of metadata for a digitized compilation of United States patents that were published during the 19th and early 20th centuries. Additionally, the article outlines forthcoming research goals. Additionally, this report presents the findings of a metadata change assessment aimed at enhancing the quality assurance of the metadata for this particular collection. The anticipated outcome of the project is to enhance understanding of metadata management, metadata quality control, and the impact of metadata modification on these procedures (Kameas, 2015).

In contrast to conventional cataloging practices, a digital library initiative typically involves making determinations regarding the treatment of novel formats, diverse resource types, and a range of techniques for implementing innovative, dynamic metadata standards tailored to distinct communities with diverse needs and expectations. In the context of metadata development, developers must tackle novel responsibilities such as administration, provenance, rights management, and preservation. Furthermore, they must also contend with interoperability concerns that may emerge in the aggregated setting. Consequently, within this advanced setting, the quality of metadata is evaluated based on a significantly wider spectrum of operational requirements beyond mere compliance with established conventions and criteria for conventional descriptive and subject cataloging. The assessment of metadata quality is significantly impacted by the functional viewpoint on the quality of information. The effectiveness of metadata in facilitating user tasks and services is contingent upon its quality. However, to determine the necessary data elements for supporting said tasks and services, it is imperative to establish a set of universally recognized dimensions for measuring metadata quality. The three most frequently employed metrics for assessing metadata quality encompass coherence, precision, and entirety. To achieve comprehensiveness, metadata ought to delineate every distinct entity by utilizing all the necessary components that enable unrestricted entry to the content of that particular object in digital repositories. The completeness of digital collections is significantly influenced by the characteristics of different resource categories or the nature of the individual collections in question. In certain local contexts, regulations and standards may specify the essential data components required to create thorough metadata records for workflow and functionality. This may include metadata production, information access, and services. In certain cases, an element that is obligatory or conditionally mandatory for a particular resource type may be deemed optional for another resource type.

The concept of accuracy pertains to the degree to which the data content of a metadata element aligns with the particular items it is describing and how it is intended to be presented. The scope of coverage includes incorrect or missing data input, as well as spelling and typographical errors. The precise application of metadata has the potential to yield erroneous data values. The 10th reference is required to complete the list of sources cited in the document.

The assessment of consistency at the conceptual/semantic and structural levels can be facilitated through the utilization of data values. The level of conceptual or semantic consistency in resource descriptions is influenced by the degree to which identical data values or elements are utilized to depict interconnected concepts. Structural consistency pertains to the degree to which a uniform data structure or format is employed for the representation of selected metadata elements. Modifying how an individual's name is documented, such as presenting the surname followed by the given name and middle initial or listing the surname followed by the initials of the given and middle names, could potentially result in issues about the management of authoritative entities and irregular employment of data. The 11th reference is being requested. According to Caplan and other researchers, ensuring consistency in metadata quality is a challenging task in digital archives, primarily due to the presence of conceptual ambiguities and semantic overlaps among different information elements. This difficulty is further compounded by the heterogeneous and scattered nature of digital archives. The present annotation pertains to the topic of Quality Assurance Mechanisms (Kameas, 2015) (Figure 9.3).

Figure 9.3. *Metadata quality assurance.*

Source: Wagner, & Henzen, (2022); http://dx.doi.org/10.3390/ijgi11060334.

Numerous initiatives have been undertaken to integrate quality assurance measures into the metadata generation process, in light of recognized challenges in maintaining metadata quality. Application profiles, which are also referred to as metadata standards and best practices guides, represent a crucial approach to enhancing the quality of metadata. Metadata standards typically include various components such as names, identifiers, definitions or descriptions, comments, content rules, and examples for each metadata element. The purpose of these guidelines is to provide metadata authors with a set of regulations that delineate and explicate the appropriate usage of particular metadata schemes in the context of digital collections. One potential application in this instance is the integration of metadata guidelines within a metadata generation system. The system has the potential to aid metadata creators in generating superior quality metadata through the utilization of textual guidelines on a web-based form or by capitalizing on tools like pop-up windows and drop-down menus. Nevertheless, it seems that these metadata recommendations generally encompass discrete criteria for different information systems. Digital repositories' reference metadata systems prioritize flexibility and simplicity to effectively manage the vast amount of digital content available. Heery and Patel noted in their scholarly article on application profiles that metadata creators tend to adapt metadata schemas to suit their individual needs, rather than constructing a universal data model that can serve as a mediation mechanism throughout the information generation process. Park and Lu observed significant variations in the interpretation and communication of local metadata regulations, despite the implementation of a uniform standard such as the Dublin Core (DC) metadata system in digital archives. Distinct labels and regional variations were employed by each guideline to delineate digital resources specific to the locality. The task of generating collective metadata and procuring pertinent search outcomes from a heterogeneous assortment of metadata inputs furnished by distinct entities may pose a formidable challenge. Moreover, the norms that are defined at a local level are often not disclosed to the general public to enhance the exchange and compatibility of data. The fifteenth citation (Kameas, 2015).

Several scholars have researched various semi-automatic methods for generating metadata to enhance the efficiency and uniformity of metadata utilization. Several systems can retrieve a webpage, automatically produce metadata, and subsequently facilitate online form editing for the resultant data. Several studies have shown the development of a computer-assisted system that employs automatic indexing and data extraction techniques to generate descriptive and other metadata values from digital objects. This system takes into account the context of the objects, including their usage, user profiles, metadata repositories, and domain ontologies. Nevertheless, a thorough examination of the feasibility and expandability of these research outcomes in an actual metadata production setting remains outstanding (Garcia, 2010).

9.9. ACCESSIBILITY CONSIDERATIONS

In the perspective of embracing human variety, "accessibility" and "adaptability" are frequently used interchangeably. The environment must be flexible enough to accommodate each user's particular requirements and preferences. The phrase "individualized adaptability and accessibility in e-learning, education, and training" describes the degree to which a good, service, setting, or installation may be utilized by people with various levels of expertise. On the other side, adaptability refers to a digital resource or delivery system's ability to change its appearance, control strategies, structure, access mode, and user assistance to meet the demands of the user. This definition is based on the body of previous research. Flexibility, customization, universality, usability, interoperability, reusability, and navigability are examples of accessibility features that are intended to make it easier to produce and use a variety of goods.

Even in the absence of a long-lasting or transitory handicap, some people may have trouble obtaining information. As a consequence, various accessibility principles increase everyone's efficacy, especially in situations where they are limited. The ability of mobile device users to access the Internet in situations of both high and low lighting, such as direct sunshine or poorly lit locations, is facilitated by ensuring enough color contrast. In a variety of settings, including tumultuous and peaceful circumstances, such as medical facilities and educational institutions, captions serve a useful role. Despite their unwillingness to label them as "disabilities," age-related functional limits are a real reality that older people face. These aforementioned issues are included in the accessibility problem.

A continual effort in the creation and application of technology in education is the ongoing investigation of increasingly adaptable inventions. To enable the thorough educational and technical process, an assessment must be developed. To meet the needs of learners, several institutions and nations have worked to develop certification and quality standards in e-learning situations. As an instance, it is essential that emphasizes the variety of distant learning strategies used by many Asian nations to create an excellent culture through hierarchical protocols. The aforementioned tactics are intended to increase the professionals' capacity for accepting responsibility and level of unswerving commitment. In this specific setting, accessibility is of utmost significance and demands a complex strategy that incorporates educational, social, and cultural elements. The ideas of inclusion, accessibility, and diversity are intertwined in a variety of ways. These include moral considerations that go beyond self-interest, a social engagement that fosters diversity and reaches a wider audience, political participation in society, and economic implications that could result in a loss of customers. According to current data, almost 15% of the world's population, or about 1 billion individuals, have a handicap of some kind. In developing nations, the prevalence of impairment is particularly evident. As the infrastructure for healthcare, rehabilitation, and educational institutions that support diversity among pupils is still in its infancy, the aforementioned tendency might prove to be detrimental. Therefore, it is crucial to design evaluation processes to support educational inclusion (Kameas, 2015) (Figure 9.4).

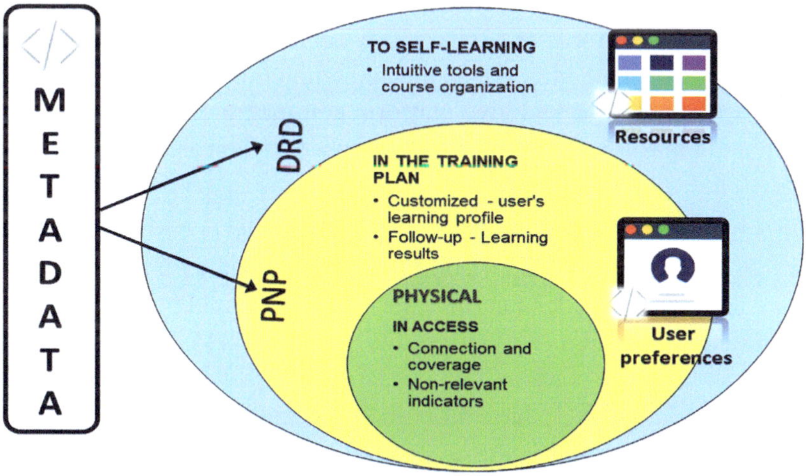

Figure 9.4. *Data accessibility.*

Source: Ingavélez-Guerra, Otón-Tortosa, Hilera-González, et al., (2023); https://doi.org/10.1007/s10209–021–00851-x.

Governments must ensure that every kid has access to a top-notch education in light of the prevalence of exclusion, discrimination, and educational inequality. The right of people with disabilities to acquire education is acknowledged in Article 24 of the Convention on the Rights of Persons with Disabilities and Optional Protocol. The States Parties should build a thorough educational system that encourages lifelong learning and is inclusive at all levels to maintain justice and impartiality. In its 2012 Paris Declaration, UNESCO urged its member states to support the improvement of Open Educational Resources (OERs) by highlighting their value, assuring their dependability, and putting them through peer review. This is done to support the creation of frameworks for evaluating and verifying learning outcomes that are obtained from OERs. Through the Incheon Declaration and the Education 2030 Framework of Action, the world conference on Education reaffirmed its commitment to the idea of "education for all" in 2015. According to the Incheon Declaration, fairness and inclusion in education are the cornerstones of a revolutionary education strategy. It is crucial to remember that every educational goal should be attained by everyone, without exception. Therefore, it is essential to give preference to evaluation strategies that promote educational inclusion. Technology is fundamental to both online learning and e-learning settings in this particular situation. Texts, videos, animated images, interactive exercises, simulations, audio files, downloaded papers, evaluation examinations, and communication tools are only a few of the digital resources used in e-learning. Typically, LMSs are connected with courses to provide students access to their materials and give platform administrators a way to monitor, instruct, and measure the progress of their users (Kameas, 2015).

According to the ISO/IEC 25000 System and Software Quality Requirements and Evaluation (SQuaRE) standards, accessibility must be taken into account as a crucial component when evaluating the quality of software products. Understanding the relationship between technology and instructional design, as well as the pervasiveness of computers and their interaction with various concurrent devices and systems, is crucial for developing a cutting-edge and effective pedagogical approach. This is because the teaching and learning process goes beyond the simple use of technology tools.

The importance of accessible online learning is growing since it is essential to enable the full integration of people with impairments. By clarifying the accessibility of the provided information and services within an electronic learning environment, the addition of metadata relevant to accessibility has the potential to increase the adaptability of OERs (Garcia, 2010).

CHAPTER

10 Methodologies for the Creation of Semantic Data in Libraries

Contents

Academic libraries face numerous challenges in managing and organizing vast amounts of information and providing effective access to their resources. One promising solution to these challenges is the implementation of semantic data methodologies. This chapter explores various methodologies that academic libraries can employ to create semantic data, enabling enhanced discovery, interoperability, and knowledge organization.

10.1. UNDERSTANDING SEMANTIC DATA

Semantic data, also known as linked data or the Semantic Web, holds immense potential for transforming the landscape of academic libraries. By enhancing the meaning and interconnectivity of information, semantic data enables more sophisticated search capabilities, improved resource discovery, and enhanced user experiences (Brilakis, 2016).

10.1.1. Definition and Characteristics of Semantic Data

Semantic data enhances information retrieval and search capabilities by providing contextualized and more precise results. Subsequently, semantic data enables data integration and interoperability, facilitating seamless sharing and exchange of information across different systems and platforms. This interoperability enhances collaboration and resource sharing among academic libraries, leading to improved resource discovery and access for users (Tischendorf, 2015).

Furthermore, semantic data enables the creation of knowledge graphs, which provide a visual representation of interconnected concepts and relationships. These knowledge graphs can aid in exploring complex topics and identifying hidden connections between different academic disciplines. Semantic data can be defined for its use in visualizing the relationships between academic papers, facilitating interdisciplinary research and discovery. Characteristically, semantic data emphasizes the use of standard vocabularies and ontologies, enabling consistent and structured representation of data. This standardization promotes data reusability and enhances the discoverability of resources across different library collections.

Moreover, semantic data incorporates the principles of linked data, enabling the establishment of meaningful connections between different datasets. These connections enable a rich web of relationships, facilitating the discovery of related resources and supporting serendipitous exploration (Brilakis, 2016) (Figure 10.1).

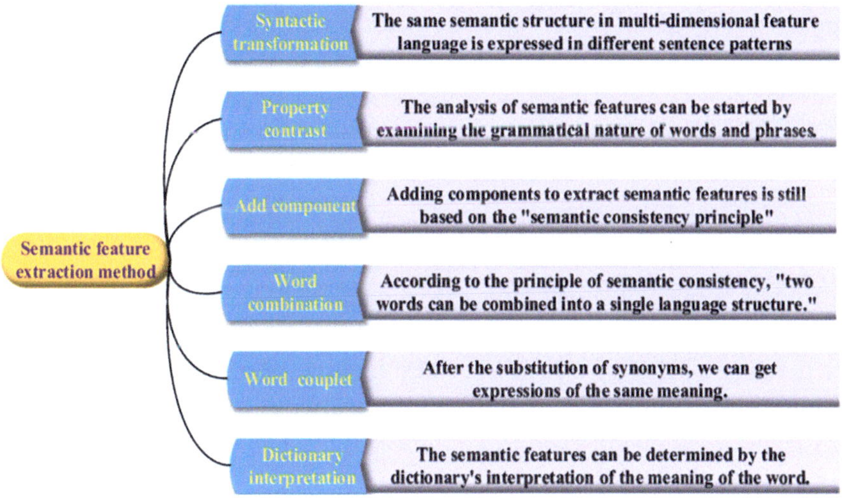

Figure 10.1. *Characteristics and meaning of semantic data.*

Source: Lou, & Zhang, (2020); Scientific figure on ResearchGate. Available from: https://www.researchgate.net/figure/Classification-and-meaning-of-semantic-feature-extraction-method_fig4_336831211.

However, implementing semantic data in academic libraries requires a systematic approach. Libraries can start by adopting standard vocabularies, such as Dublin Core and Library of Congress Subject Headings (LCSH), to enhance data consistency and interoperability. Additionally, libraries can leverage semantic technologies, such as Resource Description Framework (RDF) and SPARQL (SPARQL Protocol and RDF Query Language), to create linked data representations of their collections and enable more advanced search functionalities (Brilakis, 2016).

One example of successful implementation is the BIBFRAME (Bibliographic Framework) initiative, which aims to transform traditional Machine-Readable Cataloging (MARC) records into linked data representations. The Library of Congress has been actively working on implementing BIBFRAME, allowing for more flexible and interconnected bibliographic data.

Semantic data offers significant advantages for academic libraries, including improved information retrieval, enhanced interoperability, and the ability to create knowledge graphs. By adopting standard vocabularies and semantic technologies, academic libraries can harness the power of semantic data to address challenges such as information overload, resource discovery, and interdisciplinary research. However, successful implementation requires careful planning, collaboration, and ongoing maintenance to ensure the quality and accuracy of the semantic data ecosystem within academic libraries.

10.1.2. Importance of Semantic Data in Academic Libraries

Academic libraries have long been at the forefront of knowledge dissemination and preservation, serving as crucial resources for students, researchers, and educators alike. However, in today's digital age, these institutions face numerous challenges, including information overload, user demands for personalized services, and the need to adapt to evolving technological landscapes. In this subtopic, we critically discuss the significance of semantic data as a solution to these problems, drawing upon insights from the literature.

Academic libraries are inundated with vast amounts of information from various sources, making it increasingly challenging for users to discover relevant resources efficiently. Semantic data, by organizing and linking data through meaningful relationships, enables enhanced discovery mechanisms. By extracting semantic meaning from metadata, such as titles, abstracts, and subject headings, users can navigate the extensive resources more effectively (Tischendorf, 2015).

Meeting the diverse needs of users has become a primary concern for academic libraries. Semantic data offers a way to personalize services and enhance user experiences. Through semantic analysis, libraries can gain insights into user preferences, behavior, and interests, allowing them to tailor recommendations and suggest related resources. Therefore, implementation of semantic technologies in building intelligent systems can recommend relevant scholarly articles based on the semantic similarity of content, ensuring that users discover relevant materials aligned with their interests and research goals.

Academic libraries house a plethora of resources, ranging from books and journals to digital archives and multimedia content. Ensuring seamless integration and interoperability of these diverse resources is a crucial challenge. Semantic data enables the creation of linked data repositories, where different resources are connected through semantic relationships. This allows for enhanced resource discovery and interoperability.

Nevertheless, the implementation of apt methodologies for creation of semantic data is a challenging task for academic endeavors with the fast evolving digital era. Therefore, it is appropriate for academic libraries to evaluate the appropriate methodologies for creation of semantic data and evolution of semantic digital libraries as a solution to problems facing digital libraries (Brilakis, 2016) (Figure 10.2).

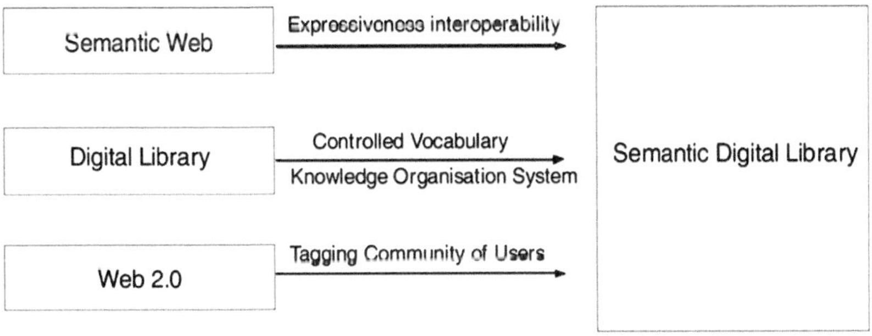

Figure 10.2. *Creation of semantic digital libraries.*

Source: Roy, & Arora, (2011); Scientific figure on ResearchGate. Available from: https://www.researchgate.net/figure/Formation-of-semantic-digital-libraries_fig3_267847204.

10.2. METHODOLOGIES FOR SEMANTIC DATA CREATION

The methodologies for semantic data creation offer valuable solutions to the challenges faced by academic libraries in managing and providing access to their vast knowledge resources. These methodologies provide a framework for organizing, integrating, and retrieving information in a more efficient and meaningful way. By employing these methodologies, libraries can enhance resource discovery, improve interoperability, and offer users a more comprehensive and meaningful access to academic information.

Knowledge Organization Systems, which entails the development and management of controlled vocabularies and thesauri, The Linked Data Approach methodology, which links structured data from various online sources, and Semantic Web Technologies, which entails the creation and enrichment of the web with machine-readable semantic data, are the methodologies for creating semantic data.

These approaches are related and complement one another. The Linked Data method can benefit from the basis that Knowledge Organization Systems give for consistent and standardized descriptions. In consequence, Semantic Web technologies enable the development of a network of linked resources that may be further enhanced with semantic data. By enabling effective organization, integration, and retrieval, these approaches help academic libraries to overcome the difficulties of handling massive volumes of information. By using these approaches, libraries may promote interoperability, increase resource discovery, and provide users more thorough and relevant access to knowledge resources. The interconnectedness of these techniques enables a comprehensive strategy for properly managing and using academic knowledge (Tischendorf, 2015).

10.2.1. Knowledge Organization Systems

Knowledge Organization Systems serve as valuable tools for effectively managing and retrieving knowledge and information within academic libraries. These systems encompass a range of components, including subject headings, thesauri, classification schemes, and ontologies. KOSs have a long history of development and usage across diverse communities and contexts. The fundamental elements of knowledge organization involve both knowledge organization processes and knowledge organization systems. KOPs encompass activities such as abstracting, indexing, cataloging, subject analysis, and classifying, while KOSs are the tools that facilitate these processes.

In a broader sense, KOSs encompass various organizational structures and systems beyond traditional library systems. They can include encyclopedias, bibliographic databases, conceptual systems, disciplines, cultures, and social divisions of labor. This broader perspective recognizes the relationship between knowledge and organization in multiple spheres of society. For example, the organization of knowledge within a discipline involves the establishment of key concepts, theories, and methodologies that guide research and academic discourse. Similarly, cultural perspectives and social organization influence the way knowledge is structured and disseminated.

On the other hand, KOSs can also be understood in a narrower sense, referring specifically to the functional tools designed for organizing knowledge and information. These tools are essential for academic libraries in ensuring efficient access to resources. For instance, subject headings and classification schemes help categorize and group similar resources, allowing users to locate relevant materials more easily. Thesauri, on the other hand, provide controlled vocabularies that aid in precise and consistent indexing and retrieval of information (Brilakis, 2016). Epistemological considerations also play a significant role in understanding KOSs. Different philosophical beliefs about knowledge, such as realism or relativism, can shape approaches to knowledge organization. These beliefs influence the design and implementation of KOSs, impacting the way information is organized and presented. For example, a realist perspective may prioritize a hierarchical classification system based on objective relationships between concepts, while a relativist perspective may prioritize a more flexible and context-dependent approach to knowledge organization.

Furthermore, KOSs reflect fundamental human cognitive processes of categorization and classification. The hierarchical and associative links utilized in KOSs mirror the mental patterns employed by individuals to make sense of information. However, it is important to acknowledge that the way these mental patterns are coded and transformed into meaningful classifications is culturally biased. Western classificatory thinking, influenced by philosophers such as Plato and Aristotle, differs from other cultural perspectives, such as Chinese classificatory thinking.

When considering KOSs as semantic tools, it becomes essential to recognize their cultural specificity and potential imposition of a particular worldview on collections and items. Classification systems embedded with cultural biases raise questions about their compatibility with different cultures and their ability to represent marginalized items within a culture. For instance, certain classification schemes may overlook or underrepresent resources from non-Western or marginalized perspectives, limiting access and perpetuating inequalities within knowledge organization (Tischendorf, 2015).

Various typologies have been proposed to classify KOSs, providing an inventory of different types and aiding in understanding their characteristics and applications. These typologies include thesauri, classification schemes, subject headings, taxonomies, and ontologies. Each type serves a specific purpose and offers unique benefits within the knowledge organization process. Thesauri, for instance, offer controlled vocabularies that facilitate precise indexing and retrieval of information, while ontologies provide formal representations of concepts and their relationships, enabling more advanced semantic querying and inference (Figure 10.3).

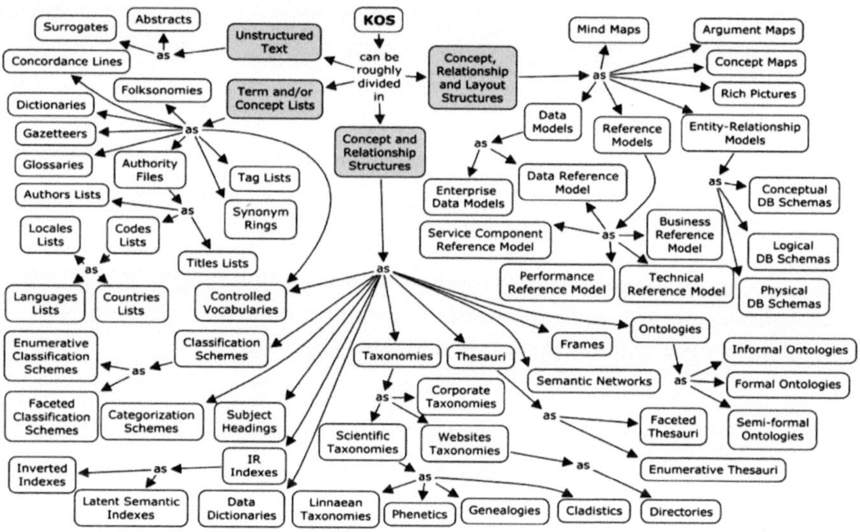

Figure 10.3. *Ontologies as a type of knowledge organization system.*

Source: Farinelli, (2017); Scientific figure on ResearchGate. Available from: https://www.researchgate.net/figure/Ontologies-as-type-of-knowledge-organization-system_fig2_324993820.

The development and implementation of knowledge organization systems within academic libraries is an ongoing and evolving process. As information environments shift towards digital platforms and the internet, it becomes imperative to reassess and adapt KOSs to meet the changing needs of users. This involves considering the theoretical foundations upon which these systems are built, acknowledging their cultural specificity, and addressing the potential biases and limitations they may introduce. Building controlled vocabularies and thesauri is an essential aspect of knowledge organization, enabling precise and consistent indexing and retrieval of information within academic libraries while promoting equitable access to diverse resources (Brilakis, 2016).

10.2.1.1. Building Controlled Vocabularies, Thesauri and Taxonomies

Knowledge organization systems, such as controlled vocabularies, thesauri, and taxonomies, play a crucial role in addressing the complex challenges faced by academic libraries. These systems offer structured approaches to organizing and categorizing information, thereby significantly improving information retrieval, indexing consistency, and user guidance. Let's explore these ideas further, providing specific examples to support our arguments.

Controlled vocabularies are restricted lists of predetermined terms used for indexing or categorizing information within a specific subject area. They ensure consistency in indexing by providing a standardized set of terms that indexers must adhere to. For academic libraries, controlled vocabularies are of utmost importance in cataloging resources and guiding users to relevant materials. Let's take the example of a library catalog focused on art history. By employing a controlled vocabulary, all items related to art history can be consistently indexed under the appropriate term, such as "art history," making it easier for users to find relevant resources without being hindered by inconsistent or ambiguous terminology (Tischendorf, 2015).

Taxonomies, with their hierarchical classification systems, provide an essential organizational framework for categorizing information. Although traditionally used for classifying plants and animals, taxonomies now encompass any controlled vocabulary with a hierarchical structure. In academic libraries, taxonomies play a crucial role in organizing vast amounts of information, enabling efficient retrieval. Let's examine a taxonomy of academic disciplines as an example. It could have broader categories such as "natural sciences," "social sciences," and "humanities," and narrower categories like "chemistry," "sociology," and "literature." Such taxonomies aid in classifying research materials, allowing users to browse resources by subject area or interdisciplinary connections. If a student is interested in interdisciplinary research between sociology and literature, they can explore resources under both the broader categories and identify materials that bridge the two disciplines.

Thesauri, being more structured versions of controlled vocabularies, offer additional benefits in knowledge organization systems. They provide synonyms, alternative expressions, and detailed relationships between terms. For instance, a thesaurus might include hierarchical relationships like "broader term" and "narrower term," associative relationships, and equivalence relationships. This comprehensive information assists both indexers and literature searchers in selecting the most suitable term for a given context, enhancing information retrieval and precision. Let's consider the example of the Medical Subject Headings (MeSH) thesaurus used in biomedical literature. It encompasses a vast range of medical terms, their synonyms, and hierarchical relationships, enabling researchers to navigate through complex medical terminology effectively. If a researcher is looking for articles on "heart disease," the thesaurus will provide related terms like "cardiovascular disease" or "coronary artery disease," ensuring a more comprehensive search (Brilakis, 2016) (Figure 10.4).

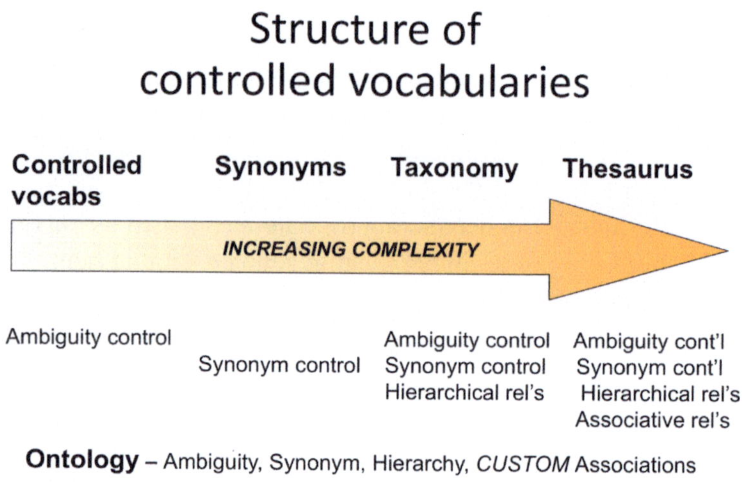

Figure 10.4. *Controlled vocabularies structure.*

Source: Zaharee, (2013); Scientific figure on ResearchGate. Available from: https://www.researchgate.net/figure/Structure-of-controlled-vocabularies-Redmond-Neal-Alice-2006–5-Reprinted-with_fig1_261545918.

The integration of these classification systems as knowledge organization systems offers an effective methodology for creating semantic data in academic libraries. By establishing relationships between terms and applying consistent and standardized methodologies, these systems enhance the organization and retrieval of information. They enable users to navigate through extensive collections more efficiently and discover relevant resources. Let's consider the example of a user searching for information on climate change. In a taxonomy-based system, they can navigate through related subjects like "environmental science," "meteorology," and "policy studies." This facilitates interdisciplinary research by allowing users to explore various aspects of climate change, ultimately fostering a deeper understanding of the topic.

Controlled vocabularies, thesauri, and taxonomies serve as valuable solutions for knowledge organization systems in academic libraries. By employing these methodologies for creating semantic data, libraries can overcome challenges related to information retrieval, indexing consistency, and user guidance. The integration of classification systems as knowledge organization systems provides a structured approach to organizing information, improving the overall user experience, and supporting research efforts. With consistent and standardized methodologies, academic libraries can effectively manage their collections, enhance information access, and foster interdisciplinary connections (Tischendorf, 2015).

10.2.1.2. Integration of Classification Systems

The integration of classification systems in semantic data creation offers significant advantages and solutions to the challenges faced by academic libraries. By adopting classification systems as part of their knowledge organization systems, libraries can effectively manage and organize vast amounts of information, improve information retrieval, and enhance the overall user experience. Let's further explore these benefits using specific examples from literature.

One of the challenges in academic libraries is ensuring consistent indexing and retrieval of information. By integrating classification systems, such as controlled vocabularies, libraries can establish standardized sets of terms that indexers must adhere to. This consistency in indexing improves the accuracy and precision of search results, allowing users to find relevant resources more efficiently. For example, the Library of Congress Subject Headings (LCSH) is a widely used controlled vocabulary in academic libraries. It provides standardized terms for indexing resources across various disciplines. When a researcher is looking for resources on "urban planning," the integration of LCSH ensures that all relevant resources are consistently indexed under this term, regardless of variations like "city planning" or "urban design."

Thesauri, as more structured versions of controlled vocabularies, offer additional benefits in semantic data creation. They provide synonyms, alternative expressions, and detailed relationships between terms, enabling indexers and literature searchers to select the most suitable term for a given context. This enhances information retrieval by capturing different expressions and nuances. In the field of psychology, the American Psychological Association's Thesaurus of Psychological Index Terms is an important resource. It includes a wide range of psychological terms and their relationships, facilitating precise indexing and retrieval. If a researcher is searching for articles on "depression," the thesaurus provides related terms like "mood disorders" or "affective disorders," ensuring a comprehensive search that encompasses various aspects of the topic (Brilakis, 2016). Another challenge in academic libraries is the organization and navigation of interdisciplinary resources. Classification systems, particularly taxonomies, play a crucial role in categorizing information and facilitating interdisciplinary connections. By employing hierarchical structures, taxonomies enable users to browse resources by subject area or interdisciplinary intersections. An example of taxonomy-based classification is the MeSH used in biomedical literature. It categorizes resources into various levels of specificity, allowing users to explore related subjects and sub-disciplines. For instance, a researcher interested in the intersection of genetics and neurology can navigate through broader categories like "genetics" and "neurosciences" and identify resources that bridge the two disciplines.

The integration of classification systems in semantic data creation also supports the discovery of resources beyond the exact search terms. By utilizing hierarchical and associative relationships, these systems enable users to navigate related subjects and discover relevant resources that they may not have considered initially. This serendipitous discovery enhances research efforts and fosters interdisciplinary connections. In the field of literature, the Library of Congress Classification system provides a hierarchical structure that allows users to explore resources beyond a specific author or work. For example, a user interested in the works of William Shakespeare can navigate through broader categories like "English literature" and "drama," discovering resources related to Shakespearean studies and literary criticism (Tischendorf, 2015).

The integration of classification systems in semantic data creation offers valuable solutions to the challenges faced by academic libraries. By establishing standardized and structured approaches to organizing information, libraries can ensure consistent indexing and retrieval, enhance interdisciplinary connections, and facilitate serendipitous discovery. The examples from literature, such as the LCSH, Thesaurus of Psychological Index Terms, MeSH, and Library of Congress Classification, demonstrate the practical applications and benefits of integrating classification systems in knowledge organization systems within academic libraries."

Furthermore, in addition to the integration of classification systems, academic libraries are increasingly adopting a linked data approach as a method for the creation of semantic data. Linked data involves connecting and interlinking data across different sources using standardized web protocols and technologies. This approach allows libraries to go beyond the traditional boundaries of their own collections and connect their resources to external datasets, expanding the potential for information discovery and integration. By linking their data to broader knowledge graphs and ontologies, libraries can enrich their semantic data and provide users with more comprehensive and interconnected information. For example, by linking their catalog records to external resources like DBpedia or Wikidata, libraries can provide users with contextual information about authors, related works, and historical events, enabling deeper exploration and understanding of the subject matter. The linked data approach enhances the semantic richness of academic libraries' collections and fosters a more interconnected and collaborative scholarly environment (Brilakis, 2016).

10.2.2. Linked Data Approach

In the ever-evolving digital age, academic libraries face the challenge of adapting their traditional practices to keep pace with the changing landscape of information dissemination. While libraries have traditionally focused on making their collections available to patrons, the paradigms and formats used for managing and sharing bibliographic records have become outdated. Approaches like MARC 21 and UNIMARC were developed before the widespread use of the internet, and they do not fully leverage the potential of modern technology for information discovery and exploration.

To address these limitations and ensure the exposure of research materials in a connected world, academic libraries need to embrace a Linked Data approach. Linked Data is a fundamental component of the Semantic Web, which enables interconnected and comprehensible handling of data across web locations. By utilizing unique identifiers (URIs) and establishing relationships between resources, Linked Data allows for easy identification, exposure, and exploration of information without losing context or relevant connections. While Linked Data has been widely adopted on the web, its implementation within library resources has been limited, resulting in a disconnect between libraries and the broader Semantic Web (Figure 10.5).

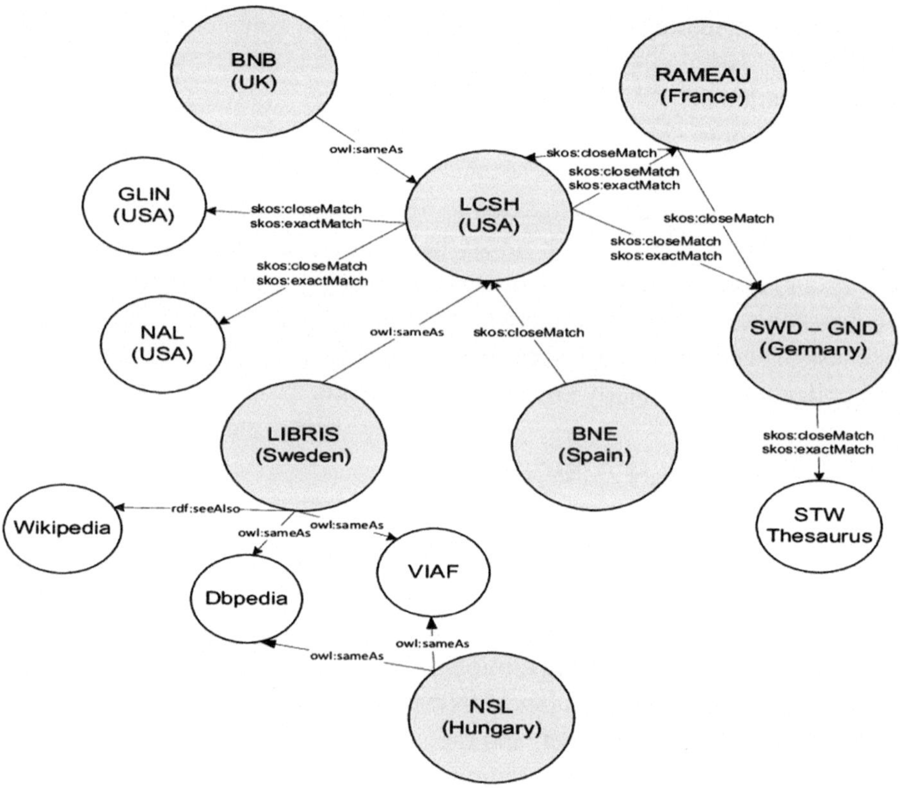

Figure 10.5. *Linked data approach (URIs and libraries).*

Source: Papadakis, Kyprianos, & Stefanidakis, (2015); Scientific figure on ResearchGate. Available from: https://www.researchgate.net/figure/Interlinking-between-libraries-in-the-lod---cloud_fig1_277897626.

The adoption of Linked Data in academic libraries brings numerous benefits. One of the key advantages is the significant enhancement of discoverability and interoperability. Patrons can access a vast array of resources for research and learning through a single, comprehensive search, rather than being limited to specific phrases, keywords, or Boolean modifiers. Linked Data also enables sophisticated querying, empowering patrons to find information with greater accuracy and context, enriched with related resources from external systems.

By implementing Linked Data, libraries can improve cataloging efficiency and increase the exposure of their collections. Linked Data provides a common language for communication with separate systems, facilitating seamless interoperability and empowering external applications to utilize the library's Linked Data resources. Moreover, Linked Data brings back the joy of serendipity by offering patrons a multitude of related resources, akin to physically exploring the library stacks but with resources always relevant to their research topic (Brilakis, 2016).

Recognizing the importance of Linked Data, leading library solutions provider Ex Libris is actively incorporating it into its ecosystem. Their applications support enriched library records with URIs and facilitate connections through linked open vocabularies, thereby enhancing discoverability and organic search engine optimization (SEO). Ex Libris ensures a smooth transition for libraries by supporting existing bibliographic records in traditional formats alongside new Linked Data records.

The implementation of Linked Data relies on key technologies such as RDF and Web Ontology Language (OWL). RDF provides a standardized data model for representing resources and their relationships, while OWL allows for the definition of ontologies and reasoning about relationships between concepts. With RDF and OWL, libraries can create semantic data that captures rich and meaningful information about resources and their interconnections.

An essential step in leveraging the power of Linked Data is the implementation of SPARQL queries. SPARQL is a query language used to retrieve and manipulate data stored as RDF triples. It enables librarians and patrons to perform advanced searches and retrieve specific information from Linked Data repositories. For instance, a librarian could use SPARQL queries to find all history books by authors influenced by Dutch publications or retrieve comprehensive information about an author, including their other works, similar authors, and related subjects (Tischendorf, 2015).

Recognizing that the transition to a Linked Data approach may require support and guidance, Ex Libris provides its customers with assistance in understanding and navigating this transformation. They offer technical services for library cataloging and advanced end-user guidance, helping libraries unlock the full potential of Linked Data.

Adopting a Linked Data approach, utilizing RDF and OWL, and implementing SPARQL queries are transformative steps for academic libraries. They enhance cataloging accuracy, enrich data display, improve interoperability, increase exposure, and restore the joy of serendipitous discovery. By embracing Linked Data, academic libraries can position themselves at the forefront of the evolving information landscape and better serve the research and learning needs of their patrons.

10.2.2.1. Utilizing RDF and OWL

Utilizing RDF and OWL in academic libraries offers numerous advantages in the creation and management of semantic data. These technologies play a critical role in representing resources, defining relationships, and reasoning about concepts, thereby enhancing cataloging accuracy, improving data interoperability, and enabling more effective information retrieval.

One key advantage of RDF is its ability to provide a standardized data model for representing resources and their relationships. By using RDF, academic libraries can capture and express rich and meaningful information about their resources in a structured and machine-readable format. This allows for more precise and consistent cataloging, as well as greater flexibility in accommodating different types of materials and their associated metadata.

For example, consider a library that wants to describe a scholarly article. With RDF, the library can create a resource description that includes information such as the article's title, author, abstract, publication date, and relevant subject categories. Additionally, RDF allows the library to establish relationships between the article and other related resources, such as the journal in which it was published, the authors' affiliations, or even references to other articles cited within the text. This interconnectedness enables researchers to navigate and explore the literature more effectively, as they can easily follow links between articles, authors, and other relevant resources (Brilakis, 2016).

OWL, on the other hand, plays a crucial role in defining ontologies and reasoning about relationships between concepts. An ontology represents a formal specification of the concepts and relationships within a specific domain. By utilizing OWL, academic libraries can create ontologies that capture the semantics of their collections, facilitating more sophisticated searches and inferencing capabilities.

For instance, let's consider a library's ontology for the field of biology. The ontology may define concepts such as "organisms," "species," "genus," and "phylum," along with their hierarchical relationships. It can also define properties such as "habitat," "diet," or "reproduction method" to describe specific characteristics of organisms. With the ontology in place, researchers can utilize the semantic data encoded in RDF to perform advanced queries that take advantage of the defined relationships and properties. They can search for all species within a particular genus that inhabit a specific habitat or find all articles related to the interaction between two species with similar dietary preferences. The ability to reason over the data using OWL allows for more nuanced and context-aware exploration of the library's resources. Furthermore, the utilization and implementation of RDF and OWL in academic libraries are critical for achieving effective data interoperability. RDF provides a common data model that can be easily understood and processed by various systems and applications. This enables seamless integration and communication between different library systems, as well as with external systems that consume or provide linked data.

For example, consider a researcher who wants to explore the relationship between literature and history in a specific time period. By implementing RDF and OWL, academic libraries can create a semantic bridge between their resources and external knowledge graphs or datasets, such as DBpedia or Wikidata. This allows researchers to leverage the interconnectedness of Linked Data to access a broader range of information and gain insights that go beyond the library's own collections. They can retrieve information about historical events, influential figures, or literary movements and connect them to the relevant resources within the library's holdings. The utilization of RDF and OWL enables libraries to participate in the wider Semantic Web ecosystem and unlock the potential of interlinked knowledge.

Moreover, RDF and OWL facilitate the creation of semantic data that retains its meaning and context even when accessed and used by external applications. This is particularly important in the context of digital scholarship and research, where data integration and analysis across diverse sources are crucial.

For example, consider a research project that aims to analyze the relationship between social media data and scholarly publications. By utilizing RDF to represent both the social media data and the library's bibliographic records, researchers can integrate these disparate datasets and perform sophisticated analyzes. They can correlate social media discussions with specific articles, identify patterns of scholarly influence based on social media interactions, or uncover trends in research topics based on the popularity of related hashtags. The utilization of RDF and OWL ensures that the semantics of the data are preserved, allowing for more accurate and reliable analysis across different sources (Tischendorf, 2015).

Overall, the utilization and implementation of RDF and OWL in academic libraries offer significant advantages. RDF's standardized data model enables precise representation of resources and relationships, leading to improved cataloging accuracy and flexibility. OWL's ability to define ontologies and reason about concepts enhances information retrieval and supports more sophisticated queries. Additionally, RDF and OWL facilitate data interoperability, enabling seamless integration with external systems and participation in the wider Linked Data ecosystem. By adopting these methodologies for the creation of semantic data, academic libraries can unlock the full potential of their collections, enhance research capabilities, and foster collaboration in the digital age (Brilakis, 2016).

10.2.2.2. Implementing SPARQL Queries

The implementation of SPARQL queries in academic libraries as a methodology for creating semantic data presents a powerful solution to address the challenges they face in organizing and managing their collections. By leveraging SPARQL queries, libraries can unlock the full potential of Linked Data, enabling advanced search capabilities, enhanced discoverability, and comprehensive exploration of their resources. In this evaluation, we will delve into the benefits and criticality of utilizing and implementing SPARQL queries in academic libraries, supported by specific examples from the literature.

One of the primary advantages of SPARQL queries is their ability to enable advanced search functionalities within Linked Data repositories. Academic libraries often house vast collections of diverse resources, including books, articles, multimedia materials, and more. Traditional keyword-based search approaches often fall short in providing precise results and fail to capture the semantic relationships between resources. SPARQL queries, on the other hand, empower librarians and patrons to perform complex queries that delve deeper into the semantic connections embedded in the data.

For example, imagine a patron in an academic library seeking information about the influence of French literature on American authors in the 20th century. With traditional keyword searches, they may struggle to find comprehensive and accurate results due to the variations in terminology and lack of semantic understanding. However, by utilizing SPARQL queries, the librarian can construct a query that retrieves books written by American authors in the 20th century influenced by French literature. The query can include criteria such as specific authors, time periods, and literary genres. By executing this SPARQL query, the librarian can present the patron with a curated list of resources that precisely match their research interests, saving them valuable time and effort.

Furthermore, the implementation of SPARQL queries facilitates the creation of semantic data within academic libraries. Semantic data goes beyond traditional bibliographic records by capturing rich and meaningful information about resources and their interconnections. By defining relationships and mapping concepts using ontologies, libraries can create a knowledge graph that enhances the understanding and contextualization of their collections (Tischendorf, 2015).

For instance, consider an academic library that wants to enrich its catalog by creating semantic connections between authors, their works, and relevant subjects. By utilizing SPARQL queries, librarians can retrieve data from various external sources and map it to their local repository, creating a comprehensive network of semantic relationships. They can link authors to their other works, identify similar authors based on shared characteristics, and associate resources with related subjects. This semantic data can then be used to power sophisticated search interfaces and recommendation systems, allowing patrons to explore resources based on interconnected concepts and relationships.

The criticality of implementing SPARQL queries lies in their ability to bridge the gap between traditional bibliographic records and the Semantic Web. Academic libraries, with their vast collections, are repositories of knowledge that can greatly contribute to the wider Linked Data ecosystem. However, the lack of semantic representation and interconnections hinders their integration into the broader information landscape.

By leveraging SPARQL queries, academic libraries can transform their existing records into semantically rich entities, making them accessible and interoperable with external systems. For example, through SPARQL queries, libraries can establish links to external Linked Data resources, such as DBpedia (a semantic version of Wikipedia), and enrich their records with contextual information. This allows patrons to explore resources within the library's collection while seamlessly navigating through related information available on the web.

Additionally, the utilization of SPARQL queries in academic libraries aligns with the broader trend of embracing Linked Open Data (LOD) principles. LOD encourages the publication and interlinking of structured data on the web, enabling the discovery and utilization of resources across different domains. By adopting SPARQL queries, academic libraries contribute to the LOD cloud by exposing their collections as Linked Data, thereby increasing their visibility and potential for discovery by external users and systems (Brilakis, 2016). The implementation of SPARQL queries in academic libraries as a methodology for creating semantic data is crucial in overcoming the challenges they face in managing and organizing their collections. SPARQL queries empower libraries to offer advanced search functionalities, enhance discoverability, and create a semantic understanding of their resources. By leveraging SPARQL queries, academic libraries can bridge the gap between traditional bibliographic records and the Semantic Web, contributing to the wider Linked Data ecosystem and providing patrons with enriched exploration and discovery experiences. Therefore, it is important to evaluate Semantic Web Technologies as methodologies for creating Semantic data.

10.2.3. Semantic Web Technologies

The use of semantic web technologies, including ontology development and semantic markup and annotation, can provide a valuable methodology for creating semantic data and addressing various challenges faced by academic libraries. These technologies enable the representation and organization of knowledge in a machine-readable format, allowing for better integration, discovery, and utilization of library resources.

10.2.3.1. Ontology Development

Semantic Web technologies, specifically ontology development, can indeed be a valuable methodology for the creation of semantic data to address various challenges faced by academic libraries. By representing knowledge in a structured and machine-readable format, ontology development enables efficient organization, retrieval, and integration of library resources, ultimately enhancing the user experience and facilitating research activities (Tischendorf, 2015).

One of the primary problems academic libraries encounter is the heterogeneity and complexity of their collections. Ontologies provide a standardized framework for modeling and representing domain knowledge, allowing libraries to create a common vocabulary and conceptual structure for their resources. For example, the National Library of Medicine developed the MeSH ontology, which categorizes biomedical information and facilitates precise indexing and retrieval of relevant literature. By using MeSH terms, academic libraries can improve the discoverability of research articles and support interdisciplinary exploration.

Another challenge for academic libraries is the need to integrate data from various sources and formats. Ontologies provide a means to harmonize disparate data by establishing relationships and connections between different concepts. The Virtual International Authority File (VIAF), developed by the Library of Congress, is an ontology that links authority data from libraries worldwide. It enables the consolidation of bibliographic records, author identities, and subject headings, promoting interoperability and enhancing the accuracy of information retrieval across libraries.

Semantic data and ontology development also contribute to the development of advanced library services. For example, the Library Linked Data project at the British Library aims to expose library data as LOD, enabling users to discover connections between different resources. By leveraging ontologies and Semantic Web technologies, academic libraries can create personalized recommendation systems, collaborative filtering algorithms, and intelligent search interfaces, tailoring their services to individual user needs and enhancing the overall research experience.

Furthermore, ontology development facilitates knowledge organization and semantic reasoning, enabling libraries to provide context-rich metadata and support sophisticated queries. The LCSH ontology, for instance, enables semantic relationships between concepts, allowing users to navigate hierarchical relationships, perform faceted searches, and discover related resources. This enhances the precision and recall of search results, leading to more efficient information retrieval and better user satisfaction.

While ontology development offers numerous benefits for academic libraries, it is important to acknowledge the challenges associated with its implementation. Creating and maintaining ontologies require domain expertise, time, and effort. Collaboration among librarians, subject experts, and information scientists is crucial to ensure the accuracy, consistency, and usability of ontologies. Additionally, the scalability of ontologies and their alignment with evolving standards and best practices should be considered to ensure long-term sustainability (Brilakis, 2016).

Ontology development, as a methodology for creating semantic data, presents a promising solution to the problems faced by academic libraries. By enabling standardized knowledge representation, data integration, advanced services, and enhanced information retrieval, ontologies contribute to a more efficient and user-centric library experience. As demonstrated by examples such as MeSH, VIAF, and LCSH, ontology development should be based on semantic markup and annotation to empower academic libraries overcome challenges related to heterogeneity, data integration, and knowledge organization, ultimately supporting research and knowledge discovery in academic communities (Tischendorf, 2015).

10.2.3.2. Semantic Markup and Annotation

Semantic markup and annotation methodology of semantic data creation can play a significant role in addressing various challenges faced by academic libraries. By leveraging these techniques, libraries can enhance the accessibility, discoverability, and interoperability of their resources, ultimately improving the overall user experience and facilitating knowledge discovery. In this response, we will explore the benefits of semantic markup and annotation methodology in academic libraries and provide examples from the literature to support our arguments.

Semantic markup involves adding structured data to the content, allowing machines to understand the meaning and context of the information. This methodology enables libraries to create rich metadata that enhances resource description, facilitates efficient search, and enables automated reasoning. By using standardized semantic vocabularies such as RDF and OWL, libraries can create a semantic layer that enriches the representation and retrieval of information.

One of the primary advantages of semantic markup is improved discoverability. By encoding bibliographic records and resource descriptions with semantic metadata, academic libraries can enable more precise and targeted search capabilities. For example, the Library of Congress Linked Data Service (LC Linked Data) provides access to structured data about resources, including books, journals, and digital collections. By applying semantic markup, libraries can enhance the discoverability of their resources, connecting related works and providing meaningful associations based on subject, author, genre, or other criteria.

Furthermore, semantic annotation methodology complements semantic markup by allowing users to contribute their own annotations to library resources. This methodology enables users to enrich the existing metadata and provide additional context, insights, and interpretations. For instance, the HathiTrust Research Center has implemented the "Annotated Books Online" project, where users can annotate digitized books with semantic tags and comments. These annotations can be used to enhance resource discovery, support collaborative research, and facilitate knowledge sharing within academic communities.

Semantic markup and annotation also facilitate interoperability among diverse library systems and repositories. By using standardized semantic vocabularies, libraries can integrate their resources with other information systems and platforms. This interoperability enables cross-domain discovery, linking library resources with external datasets, and creating new knowledge networks. For example, the Europeana project brings together data from libraries, museums, and archives across Europe using semantic technologies, allowing users to explore and access a vast array of cultural heritage resources through a single interface (Tischendorf, 2015).

Moreover, semantic markup and annotation methodology enable advanced analytics and data mining techniques on library collections. By structuring the data in a machine-readable format, libraries can leverage computational methods to analyze and extract meaningful insights from their resources. This analysis can help identify patterns, trends, and correlations within the collection, supporting research, preservation, and curation efforts. For instance, the Stanford Libraries have utilized semantic annotation and text mining techniques to analyze digitized manuscripts, uncovering hidden connections, and facilitating scholarly investigations (Brilakis, 2016).

The adoption of semantic markup and annotation methodology in academic libraries can address several challenges by improving resource discoverability, enhancing interoperability, and enabling advanced analytics. By leveraging structured data and standardized semantic vocabularies, libraries can create a semantic layer that enriches the representation and retrieval of information. Through initiatives such as Linked Data, Annotated Books Online, and Europeana, academic libraries can harness the power of semantic technologies to improve the user experience and facilitate knowledge discovery. The integration of these methodologies can revolutionize the way academic libraries operate and contribute to the advancement of scholarly research.

In conclusion, the implementation of semantic data methodologies offers promising solutions to the challenges faced by academic libraries. By addressing the challenges in semantic data creation, libraries can improve the organization and accessibility of their resources. Best practices include developing strategies to ensure data quality and consistency, training staff members to enhance their expertise in semantic technologies, and establishing processes for the ongoing maintenance and updates of semantic data. These practices contribute to the creation of a robust and efficient information ecosystem within libraries.

One of the key challenges in semantic data creation lies in addressing the complex nature of academic resources. Academic libraries deal with a vast array of materials, including scholarly articles, books, research datasets, and multimedia content. Creating meaningful relationships between these resources requires careful consideration of the domain-specific knowledge and context. However, by employing best practices such as ontology development and entity recognition, libraries can overcome this challenge and establish a rich semantic network that connects related resources.

Data quality and consistency are paramount in semantic data methodologies. Libraries must ensure that the data they create and utilize is accurate, reliable, and up-to-date. This involves establishing quality control measures, validating data against authoritative sources, and implementing data governance frameworks. By maintaining high standards of data quality and consistency, libraries can enhance the trustworthiness and reliability of their semantic data, ultimately benefiting researchers, students, and other library users (Brilakis, 2016).

Another critical aspect of implementing semantic data methodologies is staff training and expertise. Libraries need knowledgeable professionals who understand the intricacies of semantic technologies and can effectively apply them in the library context. Providing training programs and fostering a culture of continuous learning are essential to equip library staff with the necessary skills and knowledge. By investing in staff training and expertise, libraries can leverage the full potential of semantic data methodologies and provide valuable services to their users (Tischendorf, 2015).

Maintenance and updates of semantic data pose ongoing challenges for academic libraries. As new resources are added or existing ones are modified, libraries need mechanisms to ensure the accuracy and relevance of their semantic data. Regularly reviewing and updating ontologies, monitoring data sources for changes, and implementing version control processes are crucial for maintaining the integrity and currency of semantic data. By committing to the continuous maintenance and updates of semantic data, libraries can adapt to evolving research needs and provide seamless access to the latest information. Overall, the implementation of semantic data methodologies in academic libraries offers significant benefits for resource organization and accessibility. By addressing challenges in semantic data creation, ensuring data quality and consistency, investing in staff training and expertise, and establishing processes for maintenance and updates, libraries can harness the power of semantic technologies to create a robust information ecosystem. Through these best practices, libraries can better support researchers, students, and other users in their information discovery and knowledge acquisition endeavors, contributing to the advancement of academic scholarship (Brilakis, 2016).

Bibliography

1. Adler, B. T., De Alfaro, L., Mola-Velasco, S. M., Rosso, P., & West, A. G., (2011). *Wikipedia Vandalism Detection: Combining Natural Language, Metadata, and Reputation Features*, *3*(2), 31–40.
2. Alemneh, D., (2009). Metadata quality assessment: A phased approach to ensuring long-term access to digital resources. *Proceedings of the American Society for Information Science and Technology*, *46*, 1–8.
3. Alemneh, D., Hastings, S., & Hartman, C., (2002). *A Metadata Approach to Preservation of Digital Resources: The University of North Texas Libraries' Experience*. Faculty Publications.
4. Algur, S., & Bhat, P., (2014). Metadata construction model for web videos: A domain specific approach. *International Journal of Engineering and Computer.*
5. Alshammari, H., Lee, J., & Bajwa, H., (2016). H2hadoop: Improving Hadoop performance using the metadata of related jobs. *IEEE Transactions on Cloud Computing*, *6*(4), 1031–1040.
6. Arp, R., Smith, B., & Spear, A. D., (2015). *Building Ontologies with Basic Formal Ontology*. MIT Press.
7. Belsky, M., Sacks, R., & Brilakis, I., (2016). Semantic enrichment for building information modeling. *Computer-Aided Civil and Infrastructure Engineering*, *31*(4), 261–274.
8. Bisel, R. S., (2010). A communicative ontology of organization? A description, history, and critique of CCO theories for organization science. *Management Communication Quarterly*, *24*(1), 124–131.

9. Bouarab-Dahmani, F., & Hammid, N., (2015). Metadata modeling disciplines for e-learning by doing systems. *International Journal of Metadata, Semantics and Ontologies, 10*(4), 261–280.
10. Bunge, M., (2012). *Treatise on Basic Philosophy: Ontology II: A World of Systems* (Vol. 4). Springer Science & Business Media.
11. Castilho, L., & Lopes, H., (2009). *An Ontology-Based System for Knowledge Management and Learning in Neuropediatric Physiotherapy.3*(2), 23–30.
12. Chen, H., Du, J., Hsing-Yi, S., Liu, X., Jiang, G., & Tao, C., (2018). Representation of time-relevant common data elements in the cancer data standards repository: Statistical evaluation of an ontological approach. *JMIR Medical Informatics*.
13. Cooke, A., (2014). History and evolution of metadata standards for the FTI community. In: *Proceedings etc2014: European Telemetry and Test Conference* (p. 46). BoD–Books on Demand.
14. D'Aquin, M., & Noy, N. F., (2012). Where to publish and find ontologies? A survey of ontology libraries. *Journal of Web Semantics, 11*, 96–111.
15. Daniel, F., Casati, F., Palpanas, T., Chayka, O., & Cappiello, C., (2008). Enabling better decisions through quality-aware reports in business intelligence applications. *Proceedings of the 2008 International Conference on Information Quality; ICIQ 2008*, 310–324.
16. Dermeval, D., Vilela, J., Bittencourt, I. I., Castro, J., Isotani, S., Brito, P., & Silva, A., (2016). Applications of ontologies in requirements engineering: A systematic review of the literature. *Requirements Engineering, 21*, 405–437.
17. Ding, L., Xiao, G., Calvanese, D., & Meng, L., (2020). A framework uniting ontology-based geodata Integration and Geovisual analytics. *ISPRS International Journal of Geo-information, 9*(8), 474.
18. Dolenc, K., Pesek, I., & Abersek, B., (2013). Modular and branched structure of individualized intelligent e-learning materials for science and technology subject course. *Problems of Education in the 21st Century*. 57. Discontinuous.
19. Falquet, G., Métral, C., Teller, J., Tweed, C., Roussey, C., Pinet, F., & Corcho, O., (2011). An introduction to ontologies and ontology engineering. *Ontologies in Urban Development Projects* (pp. 9–38).
20. Farinelli, F., (2017). *Improving Semantic Interoperability in the Obstetric and Neonatal Domain Through an Approach Based on Ontological Realism*. 4(2), 25–34.
21. Fensel, D., Harmelen, F., Horrocks, I., Mcguinness, D., & Patel-

Schneider, P., (2001). OIL: An ontology infrastructure for the semantic web. *Intelligent Systems, 16*, 38–45. IEEE.

22. Freitas, F., Stuckenschmidt, H., & Noy, N., (2005). Ontology issues and applications guest editors' introduction. *Journal of the Brazilian Computer Society*.
23. Froeschl, K. A., (2013). *Metadata Management in Statistical Information Processing: A Unified Framework for Metadata-Based Processing of Statistical Data Aggregates*. Springer.
24. Furht, B., (2008). Multimedia adaptation decision-taking. *Encyclopedia of Multimedia*. Springer, Boston, MA. https://doi.org/10.1007/978–0-387–78414–4_45.
25. Geels, F. W., (2010). Ontologies, socio-technical transitions (to sustainability), and the multi-level perspective. *Research Policy, 39*(4), 495–510.
26. Greenberg, J., (2017). Big metadata, smart metadata, and metadata capital: Toward greater synergy between data science and metadata. *Journal of Data and Information Science*, *2*(3), 19.
27. Greenberg, J., (2017). Metadata and digital information [ELIS classic]. In: *Encyclopedia of Library and Information Sciences* (pp. 3058–3071). CRC Press.
28. Grevenhof, P., Wagner, J., Rahman, A., Naessens, J., & Evans, R., (2023). *Bringing the Data Warehouse of Standardized Medical Costs to the Web, 5*(3), 110–132.
29. Guerra, E., Souza, J., & Fernandes, C., (2009). *A Pattern Language for Metadata-Based Frameworks*. *4*(2), 45–50.
30. Harris, O. J., & Robb, J., (2012). Multiple ontologies and the problem of the body in history. *American Anthropologist, 114*(4), 668–679.
31. Henderson-Sellers, B., (2011). Bridging metamodels and ontologies in software engineering. *Journal of Systems and Software, 84*(2), 301–313.
32. Hua, Y., Zhu, Y., Jiang, H., Feng, D., & Tian, L., (2010). Supporting scalable and adaptive metadata management in ultra large-scale file systems. *IEEE Transactions on Parallel and Distributed Systems, 22*(4), 580–593.
33. Huber, M., Mithöfer, K., Schär, P., Harvey, F., & Mukasa, O., (2008). *Universal Land Registry to Support Independent Economic Development in Tanzania*. *2*(3), 37–44.
34. Humphries, G. R., & Huettmann, F., (2018). Machine learning in wildlife biology: Algorithms, data issues and availability, workflows, citizen

science, code sharing, metadata and a brief historical perspective. *Machine Learning for Ecology and Sustainable Natural Resource Management*, 3–26.

35. Ibba, S., & Pani, F., (2016). *Digital Libraries: The Challenge of Integrating Instagram with a Taxonomy for Content Management*.
36. Ingavélez-Guerra, P., Otón-Tortosa, S., Hilera-González, J., et al., (2023). The use of accessibility metadata in e-learning environments: A systematic literature review. *Univ. Access. Inf. Soc., 22*, 445–461.
37. Kaewkiriya, T., & Utakrit, N., (2012). *Research Paper: A Model of an e-Learning Management System Based on Cloud Computing and Web Service (FIG 9.2).*
38. Kleinberg, E., (2017). *Haunting History: For a Deconstructive Approach to the Past*. Stanford University Press.
39. Kleshchev, A., & Shalfeeva, E., (2008). Defining structural properties of ontologies. *Journal of Computer and Systems Sciences International.*
40. Kubler, S., Robert, J., Neumaier, S., Umbrich, J., & Le Traon, Y., (2018). Comparison of metadata quality in open data portals using the analytic hierarchy process. *Government Information Quarterly*, *35*(1), 13–29.
41. Lausch, A., Schmidt, A., & Tischendorf, L., (2015). Data mining and linked open data–New perspectives for data analysis in environmental research. *Ecological Modeling*, *295*, 5–17.
42. Li, X., Dong, B., Xiao, L., Ruan, L., & Liu, D., (2012). CEFLS: A cost-effective file lookup service in a distributed metadata file system. In: *2012 12th IEEE/ACM International Symposium on Cluster, Cloud and Grid Computing (CCGRID 2012)* (pp. 25–32). IEEE.
43. Lim, S., & Li Liew, C., (2011). Metadata quality and interoperability of GLAM digital images. In: *ASLIB Proceedings* (Vol. 63, No. 5, pp. 484–498). Emerald Group Publishing Limited.
44. Lou, J., & Zhang, Y., (2020). Semantic change analysis of Korean verbs based on massive culture corpus data. *Personal and Ubiquitous Computing.*
45. Maietti, F., Di Giulio, R., Piaia, E., Medici, M., & Ferrari, F., (2018). Enhancing heritage fruition through 3D semantic modelling and digital tools: The INCEPTION project. In: *IOP Conference Series: Materials Science and Engineering* (Vol. 364, No. 1, p. 012089). IOP Publishing.
46. Marra, A., Antonelli, P., Dell'Anna, L., & Pozzi, C., (2015). A network analysis using metadata to investigate innovation in clean-tech–implications for energy policy. *Energy Policy*, *86*, 17–26.

47. May, M. C., Kiefer, L., Kuhnle, A., & Lanza, G., (2022). Ontology-based production simulation with ontology sim. *Applied Sciences*, *12*(3), 1608.

48. Mayernik, M. S., (2011). *Metadata Realities for Cyberinfrastructure: Data Authors as Metadata Creators*. University of California, Los Angeles.

49. Méndez, E., & Hooland, S. V., (2014). Metadata typology and metadata uses. In: *Handbook of Metadata, Semantics and Ontologies* (pp. 9–39).

50. Miller, S. J., (2022). *Metadata for Digital Collections*. American Library Association.

51. Minadakis, N., Faulwetter, S., Doerr, M., Arvanitidis, C., & Keklikoglou, K., (2015). *First Steps Towards the Development of an Integrated Metadata Management System for Biodiversity-Related Micro-CT Datasets*. *4*(3), 125–131.

52. Mondorf, A., & Herborn, T., (2008). *Ontology-Based Process Mediation in the European Project BRITE*. *2*(2), 21–30.

53. Noh, Y., (2015). Imagining library 4.0: Creating a model for future libraries. *The Journal of Academic Librarianship*, *41*(6), 786–797.

54. Pal, S., Pramanik, P. K. D., Majumdar, T., & Choudhury, P., (2019). A semi-automatic metadata extraction model and method for video-based e-learning contents. *Education and Information Technologies*, *24*, 3243–3268.

55. Papadakis, I., Kyprianos, K., & Stefanidakis, M., (2015). *Linked Data URIs and Libraries: The Story so Far*. D-Lib Magazine.

56. Peel, L., Larremore, D. B., & Clauset, A., (2017). The ground truth about metadata and community detection in networks. *Science Advances*, *3*(5), e1602548.

57. Poli, R., Healy, M., & Kameas, A., (2010). *Theory and Applications of Ontology: Computer Applications*. Springer Netherlands.

58. Pomerantz, J., (2015). *Metadata*. MIT Press.

59. Pundt, H., (2023). *From Idea toward Ontology*. *5*(3), 115–123.

60. Quarati, A., & Raffaghelli, J. E., (2022). Do researchers use open research data? Exploring the relationships between usage trends and metadata quality across scientific disciplines from the Figshare case. *Journal of Information Science*, *48*(4), 423–448.

61. Quarati, A., (2021). Open government data: Usage trends and metadata quality. *Journal of Information Science*, 01655515211027775.

62. Rajaram, G., Karnatak, H., Venkataraman, S., Varma, M., & Krithivasan, K., (2018). *A Novel Computational Knowledge-Base Framework for Visualization and Quantification of Geospatial Metadata in Spatial Data*

Infrastructures. GeoInformatica.

63. Rego, H., Moreira, T., Morales, E., & Garcia, F., (2010). Metadata and knowledge management driven web-based learning information system towards web/e-learning 3.0. *International Journal of Emerging Technologies in Learning (iJET)*, *5*(2), 36–44.
64. Riley, J., (2017). *Understanding Metadata* (Vol. 23, pp. 7–10). Washington DC, United States: National Information Standards Organization. http://www.niso.org/publications/press/UnderstandingMetadata.pdf (accessed on 16 June 2023).
65. Rousseau, D., Billingham, J., & Calvo-Amodio, J., (2018). Systemic semantics: A systems approach to building ontologies and concept maps. *Systems, 6*(3), 32.
66. Roy, P., & Arora, D., (2011). Social semantic digital library: The future. *DESIDOC Journal of Library & Information Technology*.
67. Rui, L., & Maode, D., (2012). A research on e-learning resources construction based on semantic web. *Physics Procedia*, *25*, 1715–1719.
68. Salatino, A. A., Osborne, F., Birukou, A., & Motta, E., (2019). Improving editorial workflow and metadata quality at springer nature. In: *The Semantic Web–ISWC 2019: 18th International Semantic Web Conference, Auckland, New Zealand, October 26–30, 2019, Proceedings, Part II* (Vol. 18, pp. 507–525). Springer International Publishing.
69. Sawadogo, P., & Darmont, J., (2021). On data lake architectures and metadata management. *Journal of Intelligent Information Systems*, *56*, 97–120.
70. Schelter, S., Boese, J. H., Kirschnick, J., Klein, T., & Seufert, S., (2017). *Automatically Tracking Metadata and Provenance of Machine Learning Experiments*. *4*(3), 32–44.
71. Shreeves, S., Knutson, E., Stvilia, B., Palmer, C., Twidale, M., & Cole, T., (2010). *Is 'Quality' Metadata 'Shareable' Metadata? The Implications of Local Metadata Practices for Federated Collections*.
72. Smith, B., (2012). Ontology. In: *The Furniture of the World* (pp. 47–68). Brill.
73. Solomou, G., Pierrakeas, C., & Kameas, A., (2015). Characterization of educational resources in e-learning systems using an educational metadata profile. *Journal of Educational Technology & Society*, *18*(4), 246–260.
74. Staab, S., & Studer, R., (2010). *Handbook on Ontologies*. Springer Science & Business Media.
75. Stein, B. E., Burr, D., Constantinidis, C., Laurienti, P. J., Alex, M. M.,

Perrault, Jr. T. J., & Lewkowicz, D. J., (2010). Semantic confusion regarding the development of multisensory integration: A practical solution. *European Journal of Neuroscience*, *31*(10), 1713–1720.

76. Sternfeld, J., (2011). Archival theory and digital historiography: Selection, search, and metadata as archival processes for assessing historical contextualization. *The American Archivist*, *74*(2), 544–575.
77. Stvilia, B., Jörgensen, C., & Wu, S., (2012). Establishing the value of socially-created metadata to image indexing. *Library & Information Science Research*, *34*(2), 99–109.
78. Vanderperren, W., Suvee, D., Verheecke, B., Cibrán, M., & Jonckers, V., (2005). *Adaptive Programming in JAsCo.5*(2), 53–58.
79. Vanzin, M., Becker, K., & Ruiz, D., (2005). *Ontology-Based Filtering Mechanisms for Web Usage Patterns Retrieval*.
80. Wagner, M., & Henzen, C., (2022). Quality assurance for spatial research data. *ISPRS International Journal of Geo-Information, 11*(6), 334.
81. Wang, X., Chen, J., & Li, X., (2018). Research on metadata management system of linkage service of scientific data and scientific literature. *MATEC Web of Conferences*.
82. Yordanova, K., & Stefanov, K., (2006). *Selection and Use of Domain Ontologies in Learning Networks for Lifelong Competence Development*. *4*(3), 57–65.
83. Zaharee, M., (2013). Building controlled vocabularies for metadata harmonization. *Bulletin of the American Society for Information Science and Technology*.
84. Zavalina, O., (2013). Complementarity in subject metadata in large-scale digital libraries: A comparative analysis. *Cataloging & Classification Quarterly, 52*, 77–89.
85. Zechinelli, M., José, L., & Vargas-Solar, G., & Cuevas-Vicenttín, V., (2006). *ANDROMEDA: Astronomical Data Mediation for Virtual Observatories*. 5(4), 120–126.
86. Zhang, J., & Mauney, D., (2013). When archival description meets digital object metadata: A typological study of digital archival representation. *The American Archivist*, *76*(1), 174–195.
87. Zhao, B., Fang, L., Zhang, H., Ge, C., Meng, W., Liu, L., & Su, C., (2019). *Y-DWMS: A Digital Watermark Management System Based on Smart Contracts*. *4*(2), 103–109.

INDEX

E

Q

R

S